Against Depression

Against Depression

PETER D. KRAMER

Viking

VIKING
Published by the Penguin Group
Penguin Group (USA) Inc., 375 Hudson Street,
New York, New York 10014, U.S.A.
Penguin Group (Canada), 10 Alcorn Avenue,
Toronto, Ontario, Canada M4V 3B2
(a division of Pearson Penguin Canada Inc.)
Penguin Books Ltd, 80 Strand, London WC2R 0RL, England
Penguin Ireland, 25 St. Stephen's Green, Dublin 2, Ireland
(a division of Penguin Books Ltd)
Penguin Books Australia Ltd, 250 Camberwell Road, Camberwell,
Victoria 3124, Australia (a division of Pearson Australia Group Pty Ltd)
Penguin Books India Pvt Ltd, 11 Community Centre, Panchsheel Park,
New Delhi–110 017, India
Penguin Group (NZ), Cnr Airborne and Rosedale Roads, Albany,
Auckland 1310, New Zealand (a division of Pearson New Zealand Ltd)
Penguin Books (South Africa) (Pty) Ltd, 24 Sturdee Avenue,
Rosebank, Johannesburg 2196, South Africa

Penguin Books Ltd, Registered Offices:
80 Strand, London WC2R 0RL, England

First published in 2005 by Viking Penguin,
a member of Penguin Group (USA) Inc.

1   3   5   7   9   10   8   6   4   2

Copyright © Peter D. Kramer, 2005
All rights reserved

ISBN: 0–670–034053

LIBRARY OF CONGRESS CATALOGING-IN-PUBLICATION DATA AVAILABLE

This book is printed on acid-free paper. ∞

Printed in the United States of America
Set in Adobe Garamond
Designed by BTDNYC

For Grossmutti,

the Omas and the Opas,

and Eric and Lore

Contents

Prologue

I HOPE THAT THIS BOOK will prove helpful in ways that are concrete and immediate. I mean, helpful to people who have decisions to make about depression—whether and how vigorously to treat it, in themselves or in someone they love. Certain chapters can be put to that sort of use. Sometimes I tell stories from my practice, in order to say how depression looks to a doctor who tries to lessen the harm it does. I discuss recent research and biological treatments, practical and visionary, to bring into focus a new picture of depression, as it is emerging in contemporary science.

But I think it only fair to say up front that this book is less about what to do, here and now, than about meaning. How do we understand depression? How shall we address it? On these issues, I take a decided stand. I have written a polemic, an insistent argument for the proposition that depression is a disease, one we would do well to oppose wholeheartedly.

You may think that we have no need of such an argument. Increasingly, our governments, state and federal, require that depression be accorded full status as a disease, for purposes of insurance coverage and disability determination. Public health groups wage campaigns against depression. There can be no controversy over a belief we already own.

But I think we do not own it, not in the sense that we own the belief that cancer is a disease, not automatically and intimately, as a habit of mind. There is a perspective on depression that I call *what it is to us*, by which I mean, among other things, what we seem to be saying when we reveal our thoughts unthinkingly. We may find ourselves claiming that an episode of depression is *justified*, in a way that we would not call a bout of asthma justified, even when the cause is clear. We associate depression with a heroic artistic stance, one we think humankind might be worse off without. We admire traits that can accompany depression, such as alienation, without asking in each case whether they constitute aspects of an illness. That we often seem to value depression is part of what leads me to believe that, in terms of what it is to us, depression is not disease altogether. Of few other diseases can it be said that to reframe their significance is to confront what we should and do care about as we try to live good lives.

It is in the nature of polemics that they arouse objections. Reading, we protest: but, but, but. . . . Occasionally, here, I pause to debate opposing views. More often, I remain fixed in the effort to convey an individual perspective, *what it is to me*, as a person who has had many encounters with depression in those I care about, both in my role as a psychiatrist and in my private life. Now and again, my polemic has the form of memoir. Sometimes, I lapse into science fiction, imagining a society that has conquered depression.

Throughout, my interest in meaning—what are we to make of depression?—has shaped my choice of subject matter. For example, I say less about psychotherapy than about medication. I hope that it is clear from my case vignettes, and from the research findings I do mention, that psychotherapy retains an important role in the treatment of depression. But while most recent studies of psychotherapy have been reassuring—they confirm what was already well established, that different types of therapy work—to my reading, they have not been evocative. They contribute only marginally to the new scientific understanding of depression, the perspective I call *what it is*.

Equally, I have held back on discussing certain innovative bodily interventions. These include stimulation of the brain, through magnets or electric currents. The novel treatments may prove useful; but so far the research they have inspired has not affected our views about the disease.

In general, one criterion has guided my selection of research findings: does the material alter fundamental beliefs about depression? Studies reported in the last ten or twelve years have transformed the prevailing theories of mood and mood disorders—and thereby widened the distance between *what it is* and *what it is to us*. That gap, between science and values, is my topic.

About word choice: For the most part, I honor the distinction between *disease*, a pathological condition of an organism, and *illness*, the poor health that results from disease. But I am not overly scrupulous about this distinction, a tendency that I think is excusable in the case of what we call a mental illness, where we mean a disease that affects the mind. Also, for variety, I sometimes write *mood disorder* where I mean *depression*. In psychiatry, *mood disorder* can refer to a broad range of conditions, including anxiety states as well as manic depression and its variants, the bipolar affective disorders. In this book, the phrase *mood disorder* almost always means *depression*; the few exceptions should be clear in context.

Speaking of which: depression, in this book, refers to what psychiatrists call unipolar major depression, the condition characterized by extended episodes of low mood, apathy, diminished energy, poor sleep and appetite, suicidality, loss of the capacity to experience pleasure, feelings of worthlessness, and similar symptoms. I discuss bipolar affective disorder only in passing, in a consideration of heroic melancholy and creative genius. There is just too much to think about as regards depression, narrowly taken. As I put down my pen, I am in despair about how much I have left out.

Even more than has been true in my writing other books, I have composed this one in the course of conversations with colleagues. Ken Kendler tolerated regular telephone consultations for the many months in which I was assembling my thoughts about new scientific studies of depression. The following scholars and phsyicians were generous with comments, information, theories, drafts of unpublished manuscripts, or the sharing of preliminary research results: Bruce Charlton, Dennis Charney, Paula Clayton, Ronald Duman, Carl Elliott, Anna Fels, Philip A. Fisher, Alice Flaherty, Alexander Glassman, Alan Gruenberg, David Gullette, Leston Havens, David Healy, Stephan Heckers, René Hen, Steven Horst, Ronald Kessler, Donald Klein, Brian Knutson, K. Ranga Rama Krishnan, Lisa Monteggia, Charles Nemeroff, Dennis Novack, Harold Pincus, Paul Plotsky, Grazyna Rajkowska, Johan Schioldann, Yvette Sheline, Michael Stein, Craig Stockmeier, and E. Fuller Torrey. I have been aggressive in shaping disparate scientific studies into a coherent story about what depression is. Any mistakes I have made are my own.

Chuck Verrill, my literary agent, shepherded this book from its inception in the days following the 9/11 attacks, when all publishing efforts seemed uncertain. Pam Dorman, the executive editor at Viking Penguin, maintained her faith in the book at every stage. Beena Kamlani's editorial contribution cannot be overstated. She encouraged and confronted me, in her kindly manner, at every juncture and at every level of composition.

Against Depression is the fifth book that my wife, Rachel Schwartz, has seen me through. Only she (and sometimes I) can appreciate how much tolerance, grace, and patience have been required.

My parents, my grandparents, and my surviving great-grandmother came to this country as émigrés from Hitler's Germany, just before and during World War II. In their lives and in their persons, they demonstrated—and in my parents' case, continue to demonstrate—that resilience can coexist with a full measure of emotional complexity and depth. With love, with gratitude, with admiration, I dedicate this book to them.

What It Is
to Us

One

❖

The Final Memoir

S HORTLY AFTER THE PUBLICATION OF *Listening to Prozac*, twelve years ago, I became immersed in depression. Not my own. I was in my forties and contented enough in the slog through midlife. But mood disorder surrounded me, in my contacts with patients and readers. Messages from parents with depressed children and husbands with depressed wives filled my telephone answering machine; letters dense with personal history crammed the mail slot. In their volume, in their particularity, these contacts were sobering, overwhelming, disorienting. Less intimate overtures came my way. Reporters and talk-show wranglers approached me about the significance of drug company initiatives, antidepressant-related lawsuits, and mental health legislation. Colleagues invited me to join colloquia on particular therapies. Advocates of partisan views of mood disorder e-mailed me with propaganda, asking me to sign on.

Immersion has a passive sound to it. I experienced my relationship to depression in that way, being swamped by a tide. I would have denied that I had brought this condition on myself. Yes, in my book I had discussed depression—but only en route to raising issues that stood at some distance from the treatment of mental illness.

Listening to Prozac grew out of a claim that certain of my patients had made: *On this medication, I am myself at last.* These men and women had taken an antidepressant and experienced a dramatic response. Their episode of depression ended—and they reported another change as well. Temperamentally cautious and pessimistic, even before their first encounter with depression, these patients moved, on medication, toward assertiveness and optimism. This self-assured state, so they believed, represented their identity, themselves as they were meant to be.

I had used this report—*myself at last*—as a jumping-off point for speculation. What if future, similar medications had the potential to modify temperament in people who had never experienced mood disorder? There were reasons to believe that even current antidepressants might sometimes alter personality traits, making the hesitant decisive. Given access to such drugs, how should doctors prescribe? The inquiry moved from medical ethics to social criticism: What does our culture demand of us, in the way of assertiveness? Assessing my patients' attitude toward antidepressants required, I thought, attention to grand, perennial questions. How do we identify true self? Does the path matter, in the journey to contentment?

It was the medications' extra effects—on personality, rather than frank disease—that provoked this line of thought. After all, for centuries, doctors have treated depressed patients, using medication and psychological strategies. When those efforts succeed, restoring health, we are grateful. The ethical dilemmas that interested me lay elsewhere. Strange though it may sound, I never imagined that I had written a book about depression.

But authors cannot predict or control the fate of their books, any more than parents can determine the direction of their children's lives. *Listening to Prozac* emerged into an era of marked interest in depression. Everything about it had the power to fascinate: diagnosis, treatment, health care politics, gender issues, intimate experience. When *Listening to Prozac* found readers, it became *the* best-selling book about depression. In stores, it was shelved beside how-to manuals on recovering from mood disorder or living with those afflicted by it. I had never intended for my book to be *useful*. But readers wrote to say that *Listening to Prozac* had guided them to one or another resolution of their depression—through taking medication or steering clear.

As with a book, so with its author: where his readers locate him is where he finds himself. The book's career made me an authority on depression.

One unnerving development was my exposure to memoirs of mood disorder. The bedside table groaned under the weight of typescripts and bound galleys. There were accounts by sexually depleted depressives, promiscuous depressives, urban single mothers, small-town family men, femmes fatales, gay lotharios, celebrities, journalists, ministers, and psychologists. The collection represented an outpouring of autopathography such as no prior generation had known. I was asked to endorse these books, to review them, to vet them for publishing houses, to assess their worth in the midst of a bidding war.

A psychiatrist is pleased—overjoyed—to see a mental illness shed some of its stigma. But as a reader, I became ever less enthralled. Despite the superficial variety, the memoirs of depression struck me as distressingly uniform. Their constant theme, their justification, was confirmation of the new reality, that depression is a disease like any other. The authors' self-exposure was an act of witness, converting former private shame into current openness about an unexceptional and unexceptionable handicap. This much was welcome—a testimonial for the public health view of depression, often accompanied by advice to readers to seek evaluation and, if needed, treatment. But then more often than not, in these memoirs, hints of pride showed through, as if affliction with depression might after all be more enriching than, say, a painful and discouraging encounter with kidney failure. Expressions of value would emerge: *Depression gave me my soul.* The spiritual gift was not the insight that might arise in the face of any adversity. Despite their insistence on its ordinariness, the memoirs made depression seem ennobling.

I had admired the first handful of these books, not least for their courage. But the tenth confession is not so brave as the first. Soon I reached my limit. Awash in memoir, I told myself that I should complete the set. The memoir to end all memoirs. The final autopathography. A personal account of depression by someone who has never (this would be my claim) actually suffered the ailment.

If this project moved beyond the level of private joke, it was because depression had, in fact, perturbed me, as disease and suffering always perturb those who grapple with them. In my case, the point of confusion was this issue of romance—the glamour of depression. For the practicing psychiatrist, depression is grim enough.

It is true that among the major mental disorders, depression can have a deceptive lightness, especially in the early stages. Depending on the prevailing symptoms, the depressive may be able to laugh, support others, act responsibly. Depressed patients participate actively, even compulsively, in their own treatment. And depression, especially a first episode in a young adult, is likely to respond to almost any intervention: psychotherapy, medication, the passage of time. In my medical school days, if an inpatient psychiatry ward had spun out of control, a cagey chief would hold off on admissions until a good-prognosis depressive was referred. The hope was that the new arrival's recovery would restore morale, for staff and patients alike.

But the depression I dealt with in my practice had settled in to stay. The unrelenting darkness was a function of the length of my tenure here. I have seen patients in Providence, Rhode Island, for over twenty years. In a small practice, failure accumulates. As I wrote more, I let my clinical hours dwindle. The result was that patients who were not yet better filled many slots, along with those returning to treatment. And the popularity of *Listening to Prozac* meant that the loudest knocks on the office door were from families with a depressed member who had faltered elsewhere. Circumstance made me a specialist in unresponsive mood disorder. I worked amid chronic despair.

Many psychiatric practices have this quality as they mature. Light depression is depression in young adults; those patients were the ones ward chiefs favored. Suicide is always a risk; we worry over it and guard against it. Still, most patients in their twenties and early thirties do well. Often, a trigger for the acute episode is apparent, so there is something to discuss—the "precipitating event" and its relationship to prior disappointments. Psychotherapy plays a central role in treatment. The doctor feels of use. But as the patient ages, bouts of depression recur with greater frequency. Later episodes can appear spontaneously, without apparent reason. They last longer, respond more poorly to any intervention, remit (when they do) more briefly. Certain functions may remain continuously impaired—concentration, confidence, the sense of self-worth.

Even with first episodes, there will be patients who respond poorly or incompletely. These hard-to-treat depressives linger in a practice. I will refer them for outside opinions. I will consider new and experimental interventions. Often, nothing works—or else, relapse follows hard upon recovery. These patients struggle. I knew them when—or just after, when life's promise was still evident.

For the psychiatrist, then, depression becomes an intimate. It is poor company. Depression destroys families. It ruins careers. It ages patients prematurely. It attacks their memories and their general health. For us— for me—the truth that depression is a disease is unqualified. Depression is debilitating, progressive and relentless in its downhill course, as tough and worthy an opponent as any a doctor might choose to combat.

In an important respect, my clinical practice stood at a distance from the testimony of the memoirs: I had never treated a seriously afflicted patient who, on recovery, said anything favorable about depression. Yes, in the grip of mood disorder, a patient may allude to a sense of superiority. The resilient are missing something; they do not get it. This belief brings comfort in a time of suffering. But the idealization rarely outlasts the depression. When she feels better, the patient will question her own prior thought process. What was that about? She mistook illness for insight. She had been, quite literally, making a virtue of necessity. In retrospect, depression has no saving grace.

Outside the consulting room, the tendency to attach value to depression is common enough. Depression can appear to embody an aesthetic or moral or even political stance. There is a left-wing viewpoint, in which depression represents moral distance from the culture, asthenic self-abnegation, minimalism in contrast to mercantilism. There is a right-wing perspective on depression as well—the notion that one should "tough out" the suffering, without resort to "easy" remedies like psychotherapeutic support or medication. From either angle, left or right, there is virtue in experiencing illness rather than seeking prompt and thorough treatment. At least, it seemed to me that I heard, in passing, claims of these sorts, claims that would sound peculiar in relation to any other disease.

They outraged me. I discovered in myself a protectiveness toward the depressed, a wish for clarity on their behalf. I would have said that I had intended, on setting up my office, to conduct a broad psychiatric practice, extending to anxiety disorders, attention deficits, minor mental retardation, schizophrenia, marital discord, you name it. But if psychotherapy teaches anything, it is that, more than we are at first inclined to acknowledge, we are responsible for our circumstances. Chance plays its part, but we collaborate. As a child, I had been exposed to transient, low-level depression in relatives. I may have set out, in wandering fashion, to protect those I loved. This passion might be evident—I could imagine as much—in my writing. Perhaps my readers had placed me where I belonged.

As I focused on the discrepancies in value that attach to depression, I began to enjoy my situation more. Around me swirled an eddy of arguments and assumptions about depression. I was in an odd current, full of flotsam and jetsam. I began to save scraps that seemed evocative. I found myself trying to fashion a mental sculpture, a multidimensional collage, from shards that had floated into reach.

Perhaps one stray piece can serve as an example of the fragments I collected. I had finished my talk and was back in the audience at a regional conference on mood disorder. A psychoanalyst was next to present. He described his treatment of a middle-aged patient who had come for help with depression that had arisen out of the blue. The main features were leaden paralysis, obsessive self-doubt, and low self-regard. The analyst had the impression that for the whole of his life, the patient had been self-centered, blandly confident, and lacking in insight. So the doctor allowed the episode to continue. He hoped that the loss of confidence in particular would motivate the patient to engage in a psychotherapy that would make inroads against the narcissism.

I might once have considered this presentation unremarkable—an example of a psychoanalyst "optimizing" a patient's level of discomfort in the service of a process of self-exploration. But now—with my own patients' mood disorders so clearly in mind—I was seething. Is there another disease with which a doctor would make this choice? If a patient had cancer or diabetes and seemed psychologically the better for it—humbled, taken down a notch—still, we would treat the condition vigorously. Nor would a comparable argument, to let the syndrome be, arise in a discussion of other mental illnesses, such as anorexia or paranoia.

I found myself thinking about the particulars of depression in this patient, the one who turned to the psychoanalyst for help. What do we make of its unexplained appearance at midlife in a previously confident man? Perhaps the mood disorder resulted from a specific medical condition, outside the brain. Anemia can cause depression. If it did here, would the analyst tolerate a blood disorder, to provide the benefit of low self-worth? If the patient recovered spontaneously, might the doctor recommend therapeutic bloodletting? The thought was an angry one, I knew, but I was familiar enough with the brutality of depression to feel riled by the pride the speaker took in his choice, to let the patient flounder.

Causation aside—anemia or no anemia—the decision to leave depression untreated raises any number of ethical and practical concerns: Who will take responsibility for the harm depression does to the patient's marriage or career? Who will guarantee against suicide—since self-injury is always a risk when mood disorder drags on? And isn't it simply bad faith, when a person asks for help with an illness, to remain silent about potential treatments? The moral jeopardy (for the doctor) is only magnified when the hoped-for collateral benefit—alleviating a personality defect—concerns a problem that the patient might not acknowledge.

I took my disgust as a sign that I fully accepted depression as disease. How not, given the recent accumulation of evidence? Scientists were demonstrating that depression is associated with specific abnormalities in brain anatomy. Depression was being implicated as a risk factor for stroke and heart disease. And depression is its own risk factor; the longer you are depressed now, the more liable you are to chronic and recurring mood disorder, with its harm to brain and blood vessels and the rest. Surely depression had earned its status as disease in this particular sense: doctors ought not be content to let it persist.

Interacting with colleagues, submitting to interviews, treating patients, I became increasingly aware of a gap between two aspects of depression: *what it is*, insofar as we can put together recent research findings, and *what it is to us*, depression as we approach it informally. Our habits of mind lag. They have roots in traditions that take depression, or its distant cousin melancholy, as a sign of heightened awareness, social disaffection, moral insight, and creative genius.

I grew up in that tradition. In my college years, traits that resemble (and sometimes just are) symptoms of mood disorder were in vogue, alienation especially. I read widely in the literature that takes a journey through the slough of despond to be a prerequisite for full humanity. I saw bravery in the melancholic postures of my classmates, anhedonic, self-destructive young men and women who wore their depression with panache. Even now, in my years of close contact with depression, I was not immune to being charmed—except that when I caught myself in this attitude, it seemed utterly mistaken.

When I spoke in public, I began to challenge audiences about our double-mindedness. I used a test question: We say that depression is a disease. Does that mean that we want to eradicate it as we have eradicated smallpox, so that no human being need ever suffer depression again?

In posing this challenge, I tried to make it clear that mere sadness was not at issue. Take major depression, however you define it. Are you content to be rid of that condition?

It did not matter whether I was addressing physicians or pharmacology researchers or relatives of patients gravely affected by mental illness—all proponents of the "medical model of depression." Invariably, the response was hedged. Just what do we mean by depression? What level of severity? Are we speaking about changing human nature?

I took those protective worries as expressions of what depression is to us. Asked whether we are content to eradicate arthritis, no one says, well, the end-stage deformation, yes, but let's hang on to tennis elbow, housemaid's knee, and the early stages of rheumatoid disease. Multiple sclerosis, high blood pressure, acne, schizophrenia, psoriasis, bulimia, malaria—there is no other disease we consider preserving. But eradicating depression calls out the caveats.

To oppose depression too directly or completely is to be coarse and reductionistic—to miss the inherent tragedy of the human condition. And here it is not only the minor variants—the psychiatric equivalents of tennis elbow—that bear protecting. Asked about eliminating depression, an audience member may answer with reference to a novel that ends in suicide. Or it may be an artist who is held forth, a self-destructive poet. To be depressed—even quite gravely—is to be in touch with what matters most in life, its finitude and brevity, its absurdity and arbitrariness. To be depressed is to adopt the posture of rebel and social critic. Depression is to our culture what tuberculosis was eighty or a hundred years ago: an illness that signifies refinement. Major depression can be characterized as more than illness, or less—a disease with spiritual overtones, or a necessary phase of a quest whose medical aspects are incidental.

I retained sympathy with these claims, but in decreasing degree. It took only a year or two of immersion for me to discover that I had moved a fair distance toward philistinism.

Two

❖

Return

OFTEN, DEPRESSION ABATES by imperceptible degrees. But occasionally change is sudden—darkness into light. Medical practice contains its share of drama. A coma patient wakens. A stroke victim, mute since the event, speaks. Oncologists may witness the spontaneous remission of a seemingly terminal cancer. But for the doctor, little rivals this particular return to life, depression's end—especially if the episode has been a long one.

The psychiatrist's relationship to the patient is intimate. If psychotherapy plays a role in the treatment, the two will have sat across from each other, week after week, perhaps for years. By virtue of the disorder, the patient may have been guilt-ridden and scrupulous, disclosing all. The inquiry reveals emotion and its origins, immediate and distant. The doctor may have traced the patient's inner life more minutely than his own—the coloration will be subtler, the dark corners more closely examined. And then the day arrives.

I was walking from your office to my car, and just like that, the depression ended. In an instant, the sense of living in the world returned. I sat in the driver's seat and let sensations fill me. A passerby rapped on the window and asked if I was all right. I said: "At long last."

Or, *I got out of bed, and I realized it was not with me. At breakfast, I told myself, this can't be. Breakfast! When last have I been able to stomach food in the morning? I poured myself a bowl of the kids' cereal.*

Or, *I buzzed Bill's office, to tell him. He was annoyed at the interruption. In the past, I have tried to humor him, to define myself as healthy when I knew I was not. How could I convince him that this time was different? "Bill," I said, "I'm coming by. It can't wait for lunch. I want you to see me now."*

Memory of these moments sustain us, in the bleak hours. If we can keep this patient alive, if she can cling to the structures that support her, the happy day may come.

Lifting is a verb patients use. They speak of depression rising, like a fog. *My mind was clouded*, they say. Then they comment on an insidious quality depression has: it dulls awareness of its own force. Depression damages the ability to assess the self. *I did not appreciate how distorted my thinking was.*

Equally, the report may be in the passive voice, of a burden having been lifted. A weight off the back, a load off the mind. Again, a past distortion of awareness is apparent. *Until it was removed, I had no notion how heavy it was.*

For me as well, the gravity of depression is evident in the lightness, the unburdening that I feel when someone I am treating recovers.

Imagination is a weak instrument. Restored, the patient will be more vital and less predictable than the person I had been awaiting during the months of depletion. It's like the difference between thinking of a friend and spending time with him. If he is quick and clever, on his return, those traits will be more marked than you had remembered them to be. And he has other dimensions. You forgot that calm look he gives you, the one that throws you back on your own resources.

The contrast between a patient depressed and a patient recovered is the contrast between absence and presence. The depressed lack roundedness. Their interests are narrow, their repertoire of behaviors is limited, their account of their own past life has become repetitive and stale. Rarely do the depressed surprise. Willpower is missing, and spontaneity. Depression is the opposite of freedom.

When depression lifts or is lifted, the person who emerges will appear shockingly strong, full, human. There are shadings and dimensions. It is not a case of "better than well" but of "back to myself." She has returned.

If I am a reductionist, these dramatic and welcome recoveries from depression are a reason. They are utterly convincing. To see the patient healthy is to understand how gravely impaired she was these many months.

Lately, in the era of aggressive psychopharmacology, the sharp transformation has become more common. *Last week, the medication kicked in.* The particular recovery I have in mind took place fifteen years ago, before my immersion, before Prozac, not long into my tenure as a private practitioner here in town. These abrupt transitions were rarer then. Each was burned into memory—but this one for an additional reason.

Margaret was a patient whose depression was visible in the body. In the waiting room, she would sit slouched on the furthermost chair, staring at the floor, ignoring my entrance, moving only when I spoke. As her appointment approached, I would be braced for an hour of fatigue, pain, and frustration.

And then one Tuesday, there she was, nearby, upright, eyes open, smiling warmly. There is no mistaking the glorious truth, in these instances. The affliction is gone. Entering the consulting room, Margaret pinched herself, the universal sign of being here against all expectation.

With Margaret, the role of medication was unclear. She was taking antidepressants only because she had seemed yet worse without them; it had been months since I had adjusted her dose. Months, too, that the psychotherapy had meandered. Though it took place in the midst of treatment, the change was something like spontaneous.

How extraordinary to have Margaret before me. Her voice was brassy where it had been wavering. Her vivacity, the pace of her speech, the alertness of her mind—every aspect of her demeanor and behavior contained a lesson about the power of depression to distort identity. For all that I had opposed the depression, actively, I had underestimated its effects. This error is common. Even family members come to forget what the depressive was once like, or to disbelieve memory.

Margaret's restoration took place over the course of an evening. She walked me through it:

> I was sitting at dinner with Gregory. He was talking office politics. My mind drifted to my own work. I thought of the moves that one of my colleagues has been making against me. I've mentioned her, Callie, the head of planning. It turns out that Callie's been scheming to absorb my staff. I was at the kitchen table, nodding at the right spots while Greg went on. I found that I had conceived a plan to derail Callie, and what is more, I knew I would carry it off. Which made me realize that I cared. I took a bite of the vegetable. It was awful. When had I stopped paying attention to cooking?
>
> Does that place the moment? Between my preparing the eggplant dish—poorly—and my thinking about Callie an hour later? There I was across from Gregory, half listening, and I saw that results mattered—the job, the meal, what would happen with the two of us.
>
> I said to Gregory, "I'm better."
>
> How could he know what I meant?
>
> I kept repeating, "No, look. I'm back."

Margaret filled me in on her new life, for that is what she called it. She spoke of her appreciation for this man who had stuck with her. She was amused at his flaws, the ones that only weeks ago drove her to despair.

She said, "I've been working on the consultation project—marking up the interim reports. I can't believe I let my staff get so far off track. And that Callie—how did I give her the chance to walk all over me? I'm at work on my plot, to ease her out. I'm such a sly fox."

Margaret had described herself as hard-nosed. But I had never seen her exercise her powers. As Margaret had insisted all along, she had not been herself—in the particular sense that we ascribe to ill health. She had been laid low.

That was how the session started, with my seeing Margaret, well, for the first time. Later in the same hour, she pulled the rug out from under me. To understand that brief confrontation requires some context.

Margaret had first approached me two years before. Intent on making a good impression, she had arrived prepared to present her life history in compact fashion. She gave an opening summary. She had notes. She would have done well at a business meeting, except that she could not sustain her composure. Within minutes, Margaret was in tears. She had come so far. How was it that the depression had returned?

Margaret was then in her late forties, five years into a successful second marriage. She was close again to her twenty-three-year-old daughter, Kate, from whom she had been estranged. Margaret's work life was back on track. She should have taken satisfaction in it. But nothing seemed to matter.

This episode of depression was Margaret's second or third, depending on how you assess her early adult years. Is the tendency inborn? Margaret asked. Margaret's father had been alcoholic, and Kate went through a patch of alcohol abuse.

Margaret described a negative fairy-tale childhood—Cinderella or Snow White. She had one brother, a cheerful bruiser whom her mother, the strong figure in the family, had favored at every turn. As a girl, Margaret had been steady and meticulous; the flamboyant mother faulted Margaret for her self-control, her pedestrian mind. Margaret's father had been loving, if spineless. He died while she was in college. About then, Margaret began to falter.

Margaret became not so much sad as passive. She stopped protecting herself from possessive men. The abuse she allowed was verbal, the treatment she had gotten from her mother.

This pattern is one that our culture produces with regularity. Controlling men are drawn to vulnerable women. Many sorts of fragility suffice: low self-worth, drug abuse, social anxiety. But depression is a prime offender. As the history emerged, I came to suspect that Margaret had been depressed in her early twenties. Certainly, she had had trouble defending herself.

She moved forward, to graduation and then to public health school, all in a sort of daze. A young professor, ten years her senior, reached down to rescue and wed her.

The marriage seemed just right for Margaret. Career, daughter, time with friends. The unpleasantness of the college years had been erased. The husband knew how to navigate life—to protect Margaret from her mother, to engineer Margaret's leap from academia to private sector work at a health insurance company. With the help of the marriage, Margaret enjoyed the pleasures of adulthood. The very qualities her mother had mocked—straightforwardness, attention to detail—served Margaret well.

And then Margaret's life went off the rails again. The husband's affairs came to light. For years, he had been carrying on with students. Now he had gotten a young woman pregnant. He wanted to move in with her. He listed Margaret's shortcomings. Her tastes were prosaic. She was uninvolved in the life of the mind. She was not a playful partner. Margaret recognized these complaints as boilerplate—what a man says to justify running off with a young student. But because they echoed the mother's taunts in Margaret's childhood, the accusations shook her confidence. Was she lacking? And what of her having chosen this man? Could she trust her judgment ever again?

When the abyss opened, Margaret turned to a male friend for comfort. The husband put Margaret out the door, using her brief affair as justification. And then Margaret's mind stopped functioning. She could not make choices. She did not eat or sleep. She began puncturing her wrists, using knitting needles. That impulse, toward self-destruction, led to overwhelming guilt. She was a mother with an adolescent child.

This first (or second) episode, in Margaret's thirties, lasted twenty months, full force, and then lingered for another two years. Margaret went through the motions. She rented an apartment and set it up for visits from her daughter. At work, Margaret thought she was holding up her end, but co-workers found her distracted. Always a slight woman, she became alarmingly thin. The daughter stayed away, more disgusted by her mother's single brief affair than her father's many protracted ones. Before Margaret could mobilize herself, the husband had moved off with Kate, to the university where his pregnant graduate student had found a job. At her own work, Margaret was effectively demoted. It became clear that much of her social life had turned on an intact marriage and her husband's university status.

Nothing touched Margaret's mood disorder. Antidepressants gave only side effects. The medications had been administered in spotty fashion, by psychiatrists who favored psychotherapy but then threw up their hands in the face of this unengaged depressive. Where therapy helped, for Margaret, was in creating a clear awareness that the flaws she ascribed to family members were not imagined but real, constant, and damaging to her development. The mother had been cruel, the father weak, the brother heedless. The husband was every bit as self-centered and treacherous as Margaret remembered him to be. The therapy threw into question Margaret's automatic assumption that the disappointments and rejections she encountered arose from her own essential worthlessness. Yet, like the medication, these insights seemed to have had little effect on the duration of the illness.

In its own good time, the depression waned. Recovered, Margaret relied all the more on caution. It is said that depressives are especially perceptive. Some are. But Margaret was a poor judge of character, and she knew as much. She misinterpreted or ignored social cues. Her own emotional responses were broad, rather than nuanced. She did not fit any standard feminine ideal—she liked fiddling with data, and with organizational charts. Boyfriends found it a challenge to "make a woman of her" by eliciting her vulnerabilities. Because she was prone to prolonged decompensation, Margaret could not afford to make further mistakes that put her at risk of disappointment or betrayal. She became cautious with men.

Gradually, Margaret reassembled the elements of her life: the career, the relationship with the daughter, surviving friendships. The workplace had served Margaret especially well. Certain colleagues had tried to protect Margaret during her years of compromised functioning. She came to rely on these women more generally, shifting the center of her social life away from the university community.

A friend introduced Margaret to Gregory, a civil engineer with his own business and his own story of betrayal in marriage. For a while, the relationship was tentative, centered on group activities. In time, Margaret decided that Gregory was trustworthy. The wedding was an important symbolic event, attesting to the possibility of new starts.

By her own account, since her recovery Margaret had led a contented life, built around work, motherhood, marriage, and friendships. The new episode of depression came on for no apparent reason.

In her sessions with me, Margaret had been slow to reveal the extent of her symptoms. She was puncturing her wrists again, without knowing why. She was not eating or sleeping. Life was uniformly flat, except for the fluctuation in her feelings of pain.

Margaret and I talked weekly. We worked with medications, the few that were available back then. Research shows that psychotherapy and medication help to ameliorate depression and that the two in combination work better than either alone. Margaret's response to treatment was modest and sometimes paradoxical. Psychotherapy gave Margaret a feeling of security; in this new state, she felt freer to obey her impulses and attack her forearms with knitting needles. I raised doses, added adjunctive medicines, to no effect—until one day, a particular combination worked, in this sense: Margaret lost the compulsion to injure herself.

Substantial elements of the depression remained. For Margaret, her apathy was a form of torture. Her enthusiasm had defined who she was.

Margaret had little self-protective impulse. She would as soon have died as lived on—although she did fear being "found out" in her depression. She struggled to produce a semblance of normal affect for Gregory and for her staff at work. She wanted her daughter to feel loved; but for Margaret, in the midst of the prolonged depressive episode, many of the components of love—the upwelling of feeling, the hopes for the future—were hard to access.

• •

Treated with medication and psychotherapy, even second and third episodes of depression should moderate within weeks. When depression lasts, psychiatrists worry. We have seen too much; we know how corrosive mood disorders can become, how capable of obliterating the self.

My first clinical encounters with depression involved frightening afflictions. I did my training in the 1970s. Psychiatric instruction in both medical school and residency began on the inpatient ward. If patients were hospitalized more liberally back then, still, ward populations were dominated by the gravely debilitated. Medications were used sparingly. Illnesses ran their course.

In its late stages especially, depression had a typical look. Blank stare, downcast eyes, knitted brow. Head supported by a hand, or face masked by one. This expression is one that artists have depicted for centuries, what doctors call the *facies* of the illness. Depression also has a *habitus*—the body slumped and inert, muscles flaccid. I saw the face and posture of depression repeatedly in my training—not only on the psychiatric ward but also in the general hospital and in the outpatient clinic. End-stage depression was common.

The face and the posture are products of the *career* of depression. Reviewing the chart of the depleted inpatients, you would see notations that stretched back over decades. Accounts of recurrent hospitalizations and incomplete recoveries. And then, hidden in the back of the folder, perhaps, notes from the initial interview at an outpatient clinic. They would contain a description of someone resembling a "good prognosis" patient of the sort who might be admitted to bring hope to an embittered ward—or assigned to a beginning student for treatment in psychotherapy.

Tortured immobility was a destination for the depressed, a *terminus ad quem*. A few would commit suicide. Many would get better. Some would trade depression for the nonspecific "neurosis" that in those years was the most common psychiatric diagnosis. But a number were headed toward this bleak fate. Working with the sickest patients first gave every student a picture of the arc of depression. Even for the young, responsive depressives, it can end here.

• •

Today, we encounter the face of depression less often. If I believe that treatment works—and here I do not mean any one treatment in particular, but the psychiatric enterprise, everything we throw at depression— it is in part because the end stage of depression is rarer. Now what we see, down the road, is a subtler picture: aimlessness, diminished functioning, spotty memory and poor concentration, dense apathy, tears and a pervasive sense of suffering. The symptoms tend to wax and wane. The depressive may find a good hour or two in the day, and enough energy to fake it for a while. That is the progress we have made—from the horrific to the terrible.

Still, this patient could be the one we lose for good and all. And so when depressive symptoms settle in to stay, doctors exercise a tendency Freud warned against, therapeutic zeal. With Margaret, the less the medication helped, the more intent I was on making a difference with psychotherapy. But it was hard to find the path.

Margaret complained of listlessness. Did the symptom bear interpretation? Many depressed patients are listless, and they come with diverse histories. Listlessness is part of the syndrome. Yes, Margaret was listless today, in the face of a particular challenge, but she was listless many days, without apparent reason. Rarely was I optimistic that interpreting this lethargy now—its origin, its quality—would move us ahead.

Often I tried to provide what any injured person needs: hope, steadfastness, support. I might choose simply to turn down the volume, to tiptoe past apparent meaning. Margaret would complain of her inability to feel what a mother should feel toward her daughter. Sometimes, I would refer to the hurt Margaret had felt when Kate chose to go with the ex-husband. But often I would favor a response from within the medical model: Yes, I would say, that's a symptom of depression. In the midst of an episode, it is hard to muster warm feelings or the energy to convey them. That's the illness, I would say. I have seen patients recover from worse.

I stood alongside Margaret, in solidarity with her and in opposition to her ailment. Rather than interpret self-accusations, I would make the case for setting them aside: *It does seem that way, when you're depressed.* My goal was to put distance between Margaret and her negative certainties.

Depression skews the proportions of good and bad recalled in self and others. The *I* has always been needy and useless; *they* have always been justified in their rejection of the damaged, sinful, demanding self. It would have been folly to take every one of Margaret's outcries at face value—except as expressions of her current state. Besides, Margaret had done some of the heavy lifting of a traditional psychotherapy during her earlier bout of depression. Now, her self-explorations were repetitive and mechanical.

Our sessions functioned as a repository for pain. Because Margaret brought it here, she could face the rest of the week. My role was to help Margaret to hold on to her job and her marriage. To help her sustain the relationship with Kate. To keep Margaret bound to life.

My training had been in depth therapies, the ones that attend to unconscious conflict. And here, depression sets traps for the psychotherapist. The depressed appear to be ideal candidates for treatment. The depressed are impaired in their ability to sustain feeling. Many have experienced early trauma and later violations of trust. In the midst of an episode, the depressed have ready access to a library of negative memory. They are caught between choices, as if torn emotionally, mired in uncertainty.

I knew that in her good years Margaret had been less introspective and more action-oriented than the troubled figure before me now. But how could I sit with Margaret and not explore the obvious questions— whether she was paralyzed by ambivalence about the people and roles that defined her life?

Had Margaret's attachment to Gregory been weakened by mistrust of men in general? When she gave her daughter encouragement, did the effort arouse difficult memories from Margaret's own early years with the critical mother? Surely Margaret's enthusiasm for her career was alloyed by recollections of its origins in the awful years on campus and the failed first marriage.

For much of the last century, depression was understood to arise from a particular type of inner struggle. When love is intertwined with hatred so shameful it cannot be acknowledged, the result is a sapping of energy and an inhibition of action. We dislike or fear or disdain our husband, daughter, mother, and career, though we tell ourselves that we should love them merely. This unresolved ambivalence gives rise to guilt, self-hatred, and finally depression. Therapists had moved some distance from that set of beliefs. All the same, it was hard not to view depression as Margaret's secret, forceful critique of her circumstances— marriage, motherhood, career, the whole investment in a "fulfilling" modern life, every element of which had already revealed its shortcomings to her in prior years.

Empathy is a tool of psychotherapy. Mirroring the patient's mood state with great exactness can be stabilizing, soothing, reassuring. But which emotions shall we mirror?

In therapy, I found myself filling in for Margaret. She might report that Kate had received a promotion at work. You must be proud, I would say.

In truth, Margaret was all but untouched. Proud, yes, if one counted a thin version of pride, achieved with difficulty. This aspect of depression is one of its most painful: alienation from feelings that accord with one's values, the inability to treasure the things one *should* hold dear. It was when I mistook this difficulty that Margaret was most likely to rebuke me. That I of all people would attribute pride to her! When what I was treating was an absence of feeling.

And then I might say—how hard, to be unable to care!

That sort of empathy could throw Margaret into a tailspin. Was she an uncaring mother? In her depressed state, Margaret was so prone to self-accusation that she was open to accepting any hypothesis, as long as it put her in the wrong. Psychotherapy depends on the patient's being able to correct the therapist: *No, it's not that way.* Margaret would correct me only if I complimented her.

• •

But she corrected me now. We were at the end of the session in which Margaret had announced her recovery. Was I expecting thanks, for having pulled her through? Margaret's priority was to set the record straight.

She looked me in the eye and said, "I'm annoyed with you, for pushing me so hard. You wanted too much from me—at work, or with Gregory. You deal with depression every day. Didn't you know how much each effort cost me?"

These are the two images that stick in memory: Seeing Margaret recovered. And then, as I sit self-satisfied before her—having her face me head-on and bring me to attention. I had done it wrong, the project of psychotherapy.

Margaret's complaint was not entirely fair. Because I worried about her career and marriage, I had made behavioral demands. I had encouraged her to persevere at work, even though the job had lost all meaning for her. I like to see patients sustain the semblance of normal life. Sometimes it pays to ask for miracles.

But then she added a second charge: *In here, too.*

I understood the complaint and agreed with it. I had pushed Margaret too hard emotionally. Not often. In a handful of sessions over the course of two years, I had stretched to make connections—asked Margaret if *that* was the way it was. She had said, yes, exactly, it's just that way—even upped the ante. But the dark mixed feelings, about Gregory and Kate especially—those were illness. Ordinarily—in health—Margaret was an enthusiast. If Margaret had appeared ambivalent about her husband or daughter, that was because she had been suffering apathy and pessimism. When you simply cannot experience warmth or attachment, then past disappointments and humiliations will play a disproportionate role in your mental landscape.

As our session wound down, I recalled another patient, a man whose guilty ruminations disappeared when his depression ended. *I'm burning my diary,* he told me. *I was like a torture victim confessing to fantastic crimes he never committed.* The intrusion of that memory helped me understand the source of Margaret's resentment. She wanted to know why, in our discussions, I had granted an impostor—the depression—such standing. I had been negotiating with an occupying government, of Margaret's mind, while the legitimate ruler was in exile.

Often, the therapist's task is straightforward. Imagine a troubled man who is hostile toward women, in ways that interfere with his own happiness. Secretly, let us suppose, he fears women, because he considers himself needy and inadequate, and therefore vulnerable—and so he has constructed this defense, contempt. His hunger for attachment gives rise, paradoxically and against his own interest, to aggression. Here, the therapist must select the emotion that requires acknowledgment, so that in time the whole picture will come into focus. The therapist might say, "You despise women," or "You fear them," or "You adore them," and in each instance, the therapist would be right. Those emotions attach to the man; however contradictory, they are his, all of them.

Margaret's claim was that her case was mostly not of this sort. The emotions—those we had discussed during the months she was depressed—were externally imposed, by the onset and then the persistence of an illness. My empathy had been misplaced, my interpretations ill-founded. The guilt—that was not Margaret, nor the indifference either.

Past disappointments might have injured Margaret and made her vulnerable to recurrences of depression, including this seemingly spontaneous one. Arguably, before her prior course of psychotherapy, memories of past harm exercised whatever troubling effect undigested experiences impose on the mind. But those same memories did not, in any meaningful sense, cause or sustain the disabilities Margaret bore during this latest episode, the one that arrived out of the blue.

Margaret never had substantial misgivings about motherhood, career, or her current marriage. A disease had robbed her of feelings that were properly hers and imposed alternative ones. Margaret was the one who experienced those depressive feelings and reported them in psychotherapy; but they did not arise from, or had only weak roots in, the psychology that was hers in health.

Later, reading a Philip Roth novel, I came across a passage in which a political progressive recalls his mistaken thoughtfulness about the behavior of a mindlessly vicious right-wing politician: "In the name of reason, you search for some higher motive, you look for some deeper meaning—it was still my wont in those days to be reasonable about the unreasonable and to look for complexity in simple things." In time, I felt that way about my approach to Margaret's depression. I had attributed too much meaning to an arbitrary opponent.

In the following weeks, I came to know Margaret, healthy. She was a steady, reliable, highly competent woman. She was even-tempered and frank—not an ounce of neuroticism in her. There was an ease in Margaret's loves, for her daughter and for Gregory. Her work excited her; what others would have called dull, she found absorbing.

I have referred to a roundedness that can seem to be absent in the depressed. Elements of a self are missing. As onlookers, we may be tempted to fill them in, using our imagination to supply intentions, wishes, or beliefs, in order to provide a coherence that is lacking. In the process, we may create false drama; the depressive runs a similar risk, of ascribing to herself motivations (especially guilt-inducing ones) that *must* be present, to explain feelings or their absence.

Recovered, Margaret was an altogether less complex person than she had appeared in the midst of her depression—which was all to the good, in her view and my own. She was straightforward and vibrant, straightforward and whole. The rounded, the immediately present person was a largely untroubled one.

Margaret felt no guilt—that change alone would have been remarkable. Where her emotions were contradictory, she forgave herself, leaning on the truisms of the day. *Do I sometimes hate my daughter? Look, it's a generation of ingrates. Who doesn't hate these kids sometimes?* The negative feelings were not one pole of a paralyzing ambivalence. They were passing breezes. Margaret adored her daughter, simply, directly. Margaret's emotional structure was less convoluted than any psychological theory of depression would have predicted.

She was sunny, frank, jocular. She called 'em as she saw 'em. She could stand to be tough. She was untroubled, not a ruminator.

If Margaret was inclined to move on, I was not. For me, the shaky psychotherapy contained a moral, that depression was yet more pathological than I had made it out to be. One collects these lessons—long before my scrap and shard project, I was gathering patient stories, as every doctor does. Those uplifting, most welcome recoveries, when I was lucky enough to witness them, seemed often to reinforce the point: depression is more distorting than we imagine, more self-estranging, more other.

Superficially, depression sometimes resembles passion, strong emotion that stands in opposition to the corrupt world. This impression can arise from the solidity of the symptoms; depression looks like a sit-down strike. Or it can arise from depressives' tendency to act impulsively. Who would puncture her arms but a woman of passion? In truth, the puncturing is an attempt to feel anything at all. Depression is passion's absence.

Simply to name emotions—*you feel such guilt*—is to lend them legitimacy. With Margaret, in employing the most basic elements of therapy—empathy, tentative interpretation, the search for meaning—I had in effect sided with the illness and against the person Margaret was in health. The feelings I had underscored for Margaret were foreign to her. She experienced them, she reported them, but there is a sense in which they were not hers.

I don't mean to exaggerate my doubts over Margaret's treatment. The episode of depression we worked on together ended more quickly, and with less destruction in its wake, than the one that preceded it. I was open to the possibility that I had done Margaret some good. I am pointing to one of many experiences that convinced me, cumulatively, on an intimate basis, that depression is best understood as disease, for good and all.

One wants to take care to avoid negotiating with impostors. Seeing Margaret in the weeks after her recovery reminded me how much I do, in fact, appreciate self-confidence and contentment. It was wonderful to hear of her slashing her way through the thickets of the business world.

Many depressed patients, between episodes, remain moody and introspective. Margaret had no such tendency. Her personality style left the period of depression sharply demarcated. If a bout of depression arises without evident causation, if the mind-set it produces is distinct from the patient's usual attitudes, if the episode ends cleanly—that sequence contains some of what we mean when we say that depression is pathology. In a discussion about eradicating depression, anyone inclined to favor that project would include cases like Margaret's.

But think about Margaret's prior encounter with mood disorder, following her discovery of her first husband's treachery. That episode was prolonged and disruptive, but its causes were entirely obvious. Does the episode's being *understandable* influence our attitude toward it? And what about the college years? Margaret's difficulties then fit into any number of available categories: mourning, immaturity, adolescent adjustment. That episode, if it was one, would cause trouble, in the eradication discussion; but in retrospect, we may feel compelled to count it as illness. And with good reason on additional grounds: even early, mild depression can be distorting of memory and identity. Even first episodes can spawn impostors—that is, traits that are foreign to the self.

Disease is a concept that we understand through usage. Epilepsy is a disease—not each seizure, but the underlying condition, the tendency to experience convulsions, and the sweep of recurrences. Similarly for asthma. If the fifth, serious bout is asthma, then so was the first, mild one. This model holds especially strongly for depression, which is progressive. Each episode confers a greater liability to the next; each is a risk factor for a lifetime of chronic and recurrent mood disorder. By this logic, late and clear-cut episodes cast a shadow backward, inviting us to treat every episode vigorously, to halt illness in its tracks.

As new research evidence emerged about the harm depression does, I became ever more wedded to the notion that depression is disease altogether, across a wide range of presentations. But alternative views of depression, the ones I have called romantic, are so ordinary a part of our assumptions that they can persist even in the face of decades of work with patients. In my years of immersion—traveling, addressing different audiences—I discovered that outside the office, my own understanding of depression remained muddled.

Three

❖

What If

FOR TEN YEARS OR LONGER, my weekday routine had been constant: write mornings, see patients afternoons. With the publication of *Listening to Prozac*, new elements were added: travel and public appearances.

One question followed me from lecture to lecture, from talk show to talk show, bookstore to bookstore. Because the question was so automatic, so predictable, it took me months to appreciate how peculiar it was.

At a book signing, I might give a short introduction to this or that aspect of *Listening to Prozac*, discussing workplace pressures to remain upbeat, say, and the ethics of using medications in response. What I spoke about seemed not to matter. As soon as I had finished, a member of the audience would signal politely, but with insistence. A wave of a half-cocked hand. Over here.

Yes, the "events manager" would say. In smaller stores, it would be an owner who called on attendees. The moderator might know the questioner's name. This regular, this reader, this eager and unself-conscious man would receive the nod. With discouraging reliability, he would ask: "What if Prozac had been available in van Gogh's time?"

Speaking to a small group, I wanted to *represent* my book, by enacting the doubt and speculation I put into my writing. I worked to tailor my response to each suggestion from the audience, taking into account the way in which it had been posed. In this instance, what was called for—reassurance, or an attempt to disrupt assumptions?

The *what if* question left me cold. I heard it regularly, especially once *The New Yorker* weighed in. In late 1993, the magazine ran a vertical strip of three drawings under the heading "If they had Prozac in the nineteenth century." In the top cell, broad looped squiggles showed a contented Karl Marx. Below were Friedrich Nietzsche and Edgar Allan Poe. Each spoke in a cheerful caption. Poe made nice to a raven. Nietzsche expressed contentment with ordinary people. Marx was sure capitalism could work out its kinks. Marx must be a marginal case—people don't think of him as a depressive. But in the wake of the cartoon, Poe and Nietzsche began to show up in the tortured artist slot, in rotation with van Gogh.

What varied little were the questioners. They were hearty men, trying to win standing with the audience about them, as if we were all complicit in a good joke. And of course, the question contained a simple absurd image, of catapulting a famous man from depth to bland superficiality. But the questioners seemed, if I heard them right, to be claiming broader territory—to be posing a conundrum about identity, or aesthetics, or medical ethics. One central concern was the art or philosophy we might have lost—the insight about the human condition.

In the bookstore, I would smile at the questioner's cleverness. If van Gogh was the genius chosen, I might speak about the treatment he did receive. His doctors had tried to stabilize his condition with the drugs at their disposal, probably high-dose digitalis as a mainstay, and with companionship and the calming influence of a rural sanatorium. To the extent that the interventions succeeded, we may owe a late painting or two to nineteenth-century medicine. If doctors had been able to moderate the illness more effectively—who knows? Are we asking about van Gogh works we value but might have lost—or about canvases he never had the chance to paint? Do we wish he had received less treatment, suffered deeper depression younger? And so forth.

More often, I found myself referring to the debate, in this country in the 1940s, over art and neurosis. Is it true that suffering is a prerequisite for genius?

My response was perfunctory. I resented the joking distraction from issues I had raised. I did not treat the *what if* question as I did others. I did not attend to it, puzzle over it, take it to heart.

And then, one day I did. The setting was a professional meeting in Copenhagen, in 1995.

At home, as the Prozac book's popularity grew, my standing among my colleagues fell—or so I feared. With a few thousand copies sold, a man is all right. With hundreds of thousands of sales, it is another matter. I was a popularizer, an opportunist who had made his way on the backs of others, the real researchers. Again, this apprehension was a matter of hypersensitivity, of mild paranoia—although when a book succeeds, there are always belated "debunking" reviews, to feed an author's insecurity. Speaking invitations poured in, and still I thought I heard snickering from the back row.

But in Scandinavia! There I was a prophet with honor, like Jerry Lewis in France. The Finns were among the first to translate *Listening to Prozac*. Now it was being translated into Swedish, with an introduction by the most eminent biological psychiatrist in northern Europe, Marie Åsgard. The technical editors were devoted young researchers who had recommended the book widely to colleagues. The Swedes had persuaded the Scandinavian Society for Psychopharmacology to invite me as the keynote speaker at their annual meeting.

My hosts had proposed the topic "Myths and Realities" about antidepressants. I fiddled with the idea. Could the distinction hold up, myth *versus* reality? We were in the land of the Norse gods. We knew that myth, like science, attempts to transform observation into theory, within a broader context of knowledge and belief. Might we concede that when it builds new models, science spins its own myths, meant to serve for a while? Fruitful research in pharmacology has grown out of paradigms known at the time to be a bit wrong—paradigms elaborated in the face of contradicting evidence. The idea that depression results from a deficit in neurotransmitters, like serotonin, was one such hypothesis, flawed but productive. In this sense, the new antidepressants, Prozac and the others that affect the way the brain handles serotonin, are the product of myth. And so on.

The core of the talk would concern an orthodoxy I considered mythical, the one that said antidepressants treat only depression. I wanted to review evidence that the drugs might influence personality traits in people with no mental illness at all.

I spent a pleasant afternoon in Copenhagen on my own. The morning of my presentation arrived. I was treated to a generous Danish breakfast. The table talk buoyed me up. I was in serious company, laboratory and clinical researchers. The practicing doctors had seen effects similar to the ones I had described in my book, dramatic responses to medication. They had predicted those very results on the basis of theory. I felt myself on solid ground, the honored guest.

I was ushered to the podium and introduced. I launched into my talk. The audience was attentive, applause polite. Time had been set aside for discussion. A hearty fellow stood up to ask the first question. He had a smile that was familiar to me, from other audiences. His question was: "So, Dr. Kramer, what would have happened if Kierkegaard had taken Prozac?"

Why do we hope for something different? We travel, we seek new company. Here at last we will be taken as we take ourselves.

The truth is the truth therapists tell patients. You can fly across the ocean, but if you are a figure of fun here, you may as well bring your clown makeup there.

Or rather, some topics necessarily inspire fun, and this is one: the notion that assertiveness might come in a capsule. It did not matter who introduced my book or how I tailored my remarks. The question would be the same.

Of course, in Copenhagen the suffering artist would be Søren Kierkegaard. Who else? He is the most famous Dane, give or take Hans

Christian Andersen. Certainly Kierkegaard is the Dane best known for his melancholy, if you understand Hamlet to be fiction. Danes know Kierkegaard the way we know Mark Twain or Henry Thoreau—perhaps more intimately. I was once told that when Danish children are sullen, parents will scold them, "Don't be such a Søren!"

Kierkegaard is part of what had brought me to Copenhagen, what had made the invitation appealing. I read Kierkegaard when I was young. My college roommate and I plowed through *Either/Or* together, after my roommate's mother died. She had lived with Hodgkin's disease for almost the whole of her son's life and had never told him, for fear of blighting his childhood. That was like something out of Kierkegaard—self-sacrifice so radical as to be disturbing.

My roommate and I approached Kierkegaard as fiction—tales of alienation, with a place on the bookshelf alongside the J. D. Salinger stories. Kierkegaard's early writing is laced with meditations on failed romance. A young man adores a girl, he earns her love, he comes to feel unworthy. He decides to ruin his own reputation—to play the cad, as the noblest way of letting her down. Back when I was in the habit of adoring women of whom I felt unworthy, I identified with Kierkegaard. Nostalgia made the writing precious to me still.

On the flight to Denmark, I had browsed in a paperback version of Kierkegaard's diaries. How grim they are. Kierkegaard describes self-loathing, pessimism, dread, isolation, guilt, and anomie. He writes of wanting to shoot himself. Kierkegaard complains of a "primitive melancholy . . . a huge dowry of distress." He writes, "My whole past life was in any case so altogether cloaked in the darkest melancholy, and in the most profoundly brooding of misery's fogs, that it is no wonder I was as I was." And then: "How terrible to have to buy each day, each hour—and the price varies so!" And again: "The sad thing with me is that the crumb of joy and reassurance I slowly distil in the painstakingly dyspeptic process of my thought-life I use up straightaway in just one despairing step." I don't mean that I had these quotations by heart three days later; but on the plane, I had read the passages and wondered at my early sense of identification with the author. What tendencies in my own psychological makeup had Kierkegaard addressed?

On my arrival in Copenhagen, I had taken a walk to the Kierkegaard statue, in the garden of the Danish Royal Library. For good measure, I sought out Kierkegaard's grave in the old central churchyard. The walks gave time and occasion to take the measure of the man. So when I heard *Kierkegaard* in the usual question, I was aware of a particular person. What if effective treatment had been available to *this man*, the one who pays a terrible price for each day and each hour?

That was how, standing before a group of friendly faces in a standard hotel conference room, I caught a glimmer of the problem with the *what if* challenge: The question had nothing to do with my talk and not much to do with my book. I had asked my listeners to consider medication's effects on people who meet no criteria for any illness. How did that presentation suggest Kierkegaard? The same applied to van Gogh, Nietzsche, and Poe. With those figures, what is at issue is suicide, paranoia, or alcoholism—the huge dowry of distress.

Addressing my European colleagues, I found myself cutting short the stump speech, about the neurotic artist. I restarted at a slower pace, considering the ubiquity of the *what if* question. We pose it automatically— but why? Do we have qualms about treating or preventing depression? It is fine to debate "cosmetic psychopharmacology"—my term for the effort to sculpt normal personality with medication. But for as long as psychiatry has been a profession, its aim has been to conquer mental illness. The *what if* question, the Kierkegaard question, expresses unease with the psychiatric enterprise, with the life projects of Scandinavian psychopharmacologists.

The ideas were undeveloped. Effectively, I was starting a conversation with myself. For months, I had been running up against the van Gogh question. Why had it not struck me as unusual? What was depression to me, if I could hear the *what if* question dozens of times before finding it strange?

There (which is to say nowhere) the matter might have stood but for a change in the weather. A colleague had invited me for a stay at a family castle in Jutland, Denmark's more rural peninsula. But a storm grounded the ferry, so we settled instead for the usual automobile tour of Zealand, a well-traveled loop of castles and museums.

On the way back to Copenhagen, we stopped at the Isak Dinesen homestead. Dinesen, the master short story writer and diarist, is another Danish icon—all the more since the appearance of the film version of *Out of Africa*, based on her accounts of her early married life. I had read Dinesen's work, too, in my teens. I had been taken with the ominous fables. To my family, driven from Nazi Germany, the Old World had two simultaneous meanings, high culture and cruelty. The Dinesen stories captured both.

Here we were now, my pharmacologist host and I, walking the grounds of Rungstedlund, Dinesen's farm on the North Sea. The estate—a museum now—sits across the roadway from the strait that separates Denmark from Sweden. The main bungalow is furnished as it was during Dinesen's residence, which is to say in spartan fashion, the few objects, some exotic, all perfect, a reflection of her prose style.

My colleague and I were discussing Dinesen's ailments, her recurrent stomach pain and leg weakness. I assumed, as Dinesen had in her lifetime, that the symptoms were late effects of the syphilis she contracted in the first year of her marriage to the feckless Baron Bror Blixen. "What," I asked my host, "if penicillin had been around in Dinesen's day?"

My question was by way of teasing—making light of any annoyance I had betrayed at the conference. The joke (if there was one) was that there was and could be no Dinesen question. Of course, if penicillin had been available in 1915, doctors would have prescribed it. No one would withhold an antibiotic from a wife innocently infected by her husband. Indeed, no one withholds antibiotics from anyone infected in any manner. No moral dilemma attaches to their use. Any questions are technical ones, related to the development of resistance. The fear is not that antibiotics will be too effective but that they might become ineffectual. Antibiotics' purpose, to lessen the burden of disease caused by bacteria, is unexceptionable.

It is possible to wonder whether Dinesen would have written differently if she had suffered less. Syphilis has shaped our cultural heritage.

Gauguin painted his greatest canvases when he was dying of syphilis, in pain and acutely aware of his mortality. The diagnosis has occasionally been disputed, but for over a hundred years experts have asserted that much of Nietzsche's work was composed while he suffered a mental illness, one caused by the form of syphilis that damages the brain. Still, we have no moral or aesthetic ambivalence about penicillin. We have lived with penicillin for half a century, and no one considers the world of art or ideas to be shallower, at least not for that reason.

Infectious disease *can* be idealized. I have mentioned the romance that once attached to tuberculosis. Susan Sontag traced the form of that fantasy in her famous essay *Illness as Metaphor*. TB was a disease of recklessness, longing, sensuality, serenity, decadence, sensitivity, glamour, resignation, instinct, and instinctual renunciation, that is to say, of passion or passion repressed, but in any case a disease of emotionally enhanced or refined creatures. (In the extreme, depression and tuberculosis are indistinguishable, in their affective, metaphorical significance. When George Sand noted of Frédéric Chopin that "his sensibility is too finely wrought, too exquisite, too perfect to survive for long," she might have been writing of his depressive traits; as it happens, it was an episode of active tuberculosis—Chopin had been coughing blood—that led to the comment.) Sontag quotes a passage in Thomas Mann's *The Magic Mountain* where a character holds that "disease is only love transformed."

The cachet attaching to consumption diminished as science clarified the cause of the illness, and as treatment became first possible and then routine. Still, as Sontag points out, there was a lag; scientific explanation did not trump metaphor in any quick or simple manner. When the fashion finally changed, it did so with a vengeance. Tuberculosis became repulsive before it became unremarkable, one pneumonia among many. By and large, we take syphilis this way, merely as infection. Certainly we are neutral about residual manifestations, treated syphilis that shows itself as leg or stomach pain. If syphilis has moral or metaphorical overtones, they are not outsize—at the least, they are in remission. That is why there is no Dinesen question.

A simple version of this perspective informed the discussion in the walk with my colleague on the grounds of Rungstedlund. He was, it turned out, something of an expert on Dinesen and her medical condition. His belief was that the nature of Dinesen's affliction is obscure. Dinesen's father committed suicide when she was ten. (Legend has it that *he* had syphilis and did not want to pass it on to his wife.) In her adult life, Dinesen's medications included antipsychotic medication, stimulants, and sedatives—Thorazine, amphetamines, and barbiturates—in addition to narcotics. Each drug may be explainable in the context of managing chronic pain; still, the collection of psychotherapeutic agents is impressive. Effectively, it includes every class of psychopharmaceutical available in the 1940s and '50s. After the initial episode of syphilis, Dinesen's spinal fluid showed no sign of the illness. Gastric crises are not typical of the residual stages of syphilis. Throughout her life, Dinesen had appeared anorexic.

Dinesen may have suffered not from any sequel of infection but from heavy metal poisoning—she treated her syphilis with arsenic and mercury. Or (here was a turning point in the discussion) she may have been hypochondriacal and depressed. If this assumption were commonplace, it would put Dinesen in the same category as Kierkegaard—the depressed creative genius. And then lecture-goers would ask, "What if Prozac had been available in Dinesen's day?" There would be a Dinesen question after all.

This contrast—no question in the face of infectious disease, but a routine question in the face of mood disorder—implies a special status for depression. Why? If both illnesses cause the sort of suffering that can alter worldviews or shape art, why do we react to the depression and syphilis differently?

After the trip to Denmark, I began to put the *what if* challenge to use, as a probe for eliciting material I might add to my collection of beliefs about what depression is to us. Slowing my response, I would ask the van Gogh questioner what he had in mind.

Most audience members took van Gogh to have been very ill—but with an ailment that carries something extra, its own special vision. In a story, Poe refers to "an utter depression of soul" as "the hideous dropping off of the veil." The questioners maintained that nineteenth-century belief, that depression reveals essence, to those brave enough to face it. Their *what if* rested on a concern that amelioration of depression might cloud a person's moral clarity or dampen a divine spark. Depression is more than an illness—it has a sacred aspect.

For some questioners, *what if* referred to a general lifting of the genius's mood, setting aside or taking it as coincidence that the person chosen—Poe or Kierkegaard—was actually ill. One might say, Some coincidence! In *Listening to Prozac*, I had worried over the use of medication in healthy people, to alter personality traits like shyness. Now, these concerns were extended to cover antidepressants' *intended* recipients, those suffering from mental illness, like Nietzsche and van Gogh. The questioners seemed to understand mood disorder as a heavy dose of the artistic temperament, so that the symptoms of depression are merely personality traits and *any* application of antidepressants is finally cosmetic. Here, depression is less than an illness.

One confounding concern has to do with depression as a source of creativity. Much later, further into my years of immersion, I tried to tackle this issue—whether in truth there is a basis for linking depression and artistic accomplishment. But early on, when I began to pay attention to the van Gogh question, I was focused on the issue of depression's special status. Why is depression different, less than fully worthy of decisive treatment? Is a link to art enough to alter the way we think about a syndrome—to move it from straightforward disease to disease-in-a-manner-of-speaking?

Consider epilepsy, the set of disorders characterized by seizures, sometimes alternating with a variety of mental auras and intense experiences of emotion. Chronically, between attacks, patients with a subtype of epilepsy can be afflicted with hypergraphia, the tendency to write compulsively, and at length. They may also display a characteristic personality style, one that includes intense enthusiasms, often religious fervor, and an alternation between aggression and emotional clinginess.

Dostoevsky, Flaubert, Tennyson, Swinburne, Byron, de Maupassant, Molière, Pascal, and even Petrarch and Dante have been named as

presumptively epileptic in one or another medical treatise. Edgar Allan
Poe makes the list. An epileptologist updated the case recently in the
American Medical Association's *Archives of Neurology*; but the theory
that Poe was epileptic dates to the 1870s.

And in his lifetime, van Gogh was understood to suffer epilepsy. Two
doctors made the diagnosis in the 1880s; that was the illness for which
digitalis would have been prescribed. Van Gogh's diaries and his physicians' notes contain descriptions of seizures that include both auras and
drop attacks, in which van Gogh lost consciousness and fell. Neurologists today have speculated that van Gogh had the type of epilepsy that
produces hypergraphia. His correspondence fills seventeen hundred
printed pages, and he died young.

Epilepsy is another sacred affliction, or was once. And there are
medications—anticonvulsants—used to prevent or manage epilepsy.
But you might give a dozen talks about quirky uses of anticonvulsants
and not hear a single joking question about an artist. The vividness of
the pathology and the consequent solidity of epilepsy's status as a disease cast their shadows over attempts at humor. To withhold treatment
would be cruel. In the context of seizure disorders, a van Gogh or Poe
question, if asked, might point to the ironies of medical practice—how
necessary interventions have unknowable consequences. But the question would not be funny. To put the matter differently: we would be
happy to eradicate epilepsy.

It was my experience on the road that led me to formulate the eradication question. It seemed to me that *what if* revealed a common worry
about the capacity to treat or prevent depression with great thorough-
ness. In the question, "Prozac" stands as an imaginary substance that
reliably averts or reverses mood disorder and associated traits. This
prospect causes unease, even as we work toward it.

So long as the imagined substance, the universally effective antidepressant, is outside our grasp, *what if* remains science fiction. *What if a
cure had been available in the nineteenth century?* means *What if one
were available tomorrow?* How would it affect our art, our literature,
our philosophy, our image of the fulfilled life? Equally, *what if* is about

the here and now. The question asks what we value in depression and what, in terms of depression-related traits, we value in ourselves.

For me, the *what if* question led directly to another: What would it be like for depression to go through the transformation experienced by tuberculosis? Depression might be on the verge of that metamorphosis, from romanticized affliction into ordinary disease. Hard-to-ignore evidence was accumulating, about the bodily harm depression causes, and about the brain pathology that underlies its symptoms. Increasingly, the prevailing scientific myth—*what it is*—had it that depression is neither more nor less than illness, but illness merely. I added a project to my scrap and shard work: to imagine how our beliefs, our art, our sense of self might change as the medical view became a cultural commonplace. But I had no illusion that the moment was at hand. My work with patients reminded me, daily, that we retain a confused—partial, anachronistic—understanding of depression.

Four

❖

Ambivalence

IN THE POST-DENMARK DAYS, I treated a molecular biologist, Emily, who was prone to quite serious breakdowns. Afflicted, she would pace the room, crying, wringing her hands, regretting decisions, doubting her talents and achievements, fearing death and wishing for it. Emily responded readily to medication and psychotherapy—truthfully, medication seemed the critical factor. But she was leery of antidepressants and so cut back once she felt stable.

Emily and I discussed the wisdom of this decision. Research suggests that staying on the dose that got you well is the best strategy for preventing relapse. On the other side of the balance is the unknown risk of chronic medication use; many doctors do have patients taper medicines after a time, even when recurrent depression is at issue. But then, that consideration applies only to patients who are decidedly better. Residual symptoms predict relapse. And here is where Emily and I disagreed, over how well she was doing.

Emily impressed me as unconfident and emotionally fragile, in ways she had not been in young adulthood. She continued to experience the type of insomnia that ordinarily preceded, and then accompanied, her mood disorder, a bolt-upright wakening at four A.M. To my way of thinking, the depressive episode had not ended cleanly, or else Emily had slipped some, after tapering the drug. Emily was in the midst of a progressive, debilitating illness. The sleep disorder and self-doubt were symptoms. In ignoring them, she was endangering her well-being.

If a change in the medication was out of the question, might we resume more frequent psychotherapy? We had cut back to twice a month. Emily thought the schedule was fine as it was. Perhaps here I was not fully convincing; as I say, medication had seemed critical to her recovery.

I did not waver in my belief that more vigorous treatment might benefit Emily. How to understand her choice? Often, I thought I heard her saying what bookstore audiences said—that to her, depression was more and less than an illness.

Information was never at issue. Emily conducted research into the biochemistry of mood disorder. She was, if anything, an extreme proponent of the theory that vulnerability to depression is encoded early, through genetics or the biological accidents that shape the fetal brain. The irony—a scientist afflicted with the very ailment she studies—was not due to coincidence, or perhaps there was no irony. At the start of her career, Emily had chosen to investigate a disorder that runs in her family.

But I thought I heard hints that in everyday terms, Emily did not understand her depression as a disease. In her sessions with me, Emily would regularly express wonder at other people's ability to bear misfortune. Her next-door neighbor, a diabetic, was losing his eyesight. "How he can stand it?" Emily might say. "To go through life like that!" Emily's exclamations were heartfelt and generous, but they made sense only in a limited way. The especially nearsighted man would turn out to be constitutionally cheerful, someone more capable than Emily of enjoying each day. Hers was the more disabling, the more painful handicap. Despite her conviction that liability to depression is a matter of brain biology, Emily never made that comparison—because she never grouped her depression with her neighbor's diabetes.

Instead, she defended the legitimacy of sadness: given how tough life tends to be, a legally blind man's equanimity is inexplicable. To lack psychological fragility is to live with emotional limitations. Emily simultaneously pitied the visually handicapped man, admired him (as a phenomenon of nature, the resilient animal), and doubted his completeness as a human being.

In her outcries, Emily also seemed to be saying something about herself: "I am weak. Others bear real burdens, and they don't whine." She made that sort of self-accusation often. She saw conditions like near-blindness as afflictions imposed from without, while her depression struck her simply an aspect of who she was, a contemptible person with a limited tolerance for setbacks—and the setbacks were not the depression, but particular disappointments that overwhelmed her when she was depressed.

Depression provided Emily with a perspective, a fixed tragic view of the human condition. The neighbor's good humor was striking but illogical, as if he did not appreciate a truth about his own existence. Life is cruel, unfair, arbitrary—hard enough without extra handicaps. Emily suspected that optimists were missing the point. Her husband was in this category, a welcome support, dear and lovable, but a bit superficial. Even insomnia became a virtue in this context; the husband was a slugabed beside her. How could he ignore life's horrors? Emily suspected me of being in the same camp, the affective lightweights, emotionally obtuse. She granted her pessimism special standing, as an element of taste and wisdom. She was a little superior on this point, her gravity. This superiority helped her bear her affliction.

For Emily, depression was less than an illness—a mere character flaw, not so worthy of compassion as diabetes. And it was more than an illness—a character strength, without which a person might be morally, intellectually, or emotionally stunted. Of course, depression was also illness after all. Emily treated it as such in her work, and sometimes in our discussions of her family heritage and her need for medication.

The manner of Emily's entertaining these contradictory beliefs was itself problematic. In its commonest form, depression is a disorder of emotional assessment of experience. Of a disappointment, the depressed person will say, "I know it should not feel catastrophic, but it does." In depression, a person understands matters one way and feels them another, or sustains multiple understandings, of which the darkest are the most compelling. To condemn yourself for your hopelessness and your husband for his optimism is to be profoundly stuck.

In the course of treatment, Emily offered moral or aesthetic judgments about issues that I, and in other contexts she, would have taken as medical. Sometimes Emily considered herself weak, where weak means too sensitive. Sometimes, or at the same time, she considered others dense and insensitive. The matching of trait and valuation varied, so that a given tendency might be now admired, now denigrated. In varying degrees, symptoms of depression—despair, irritability—would color and intensify these assessments. What was constant was Emily's inclination to take her vulnerability, and others' armor, to be virtues or shortcomings.

With Emily, I did not have the luxury of smiling benignly at double-mindedness. When Emily expressed superiority, through her attunement to the tragic, I wanted to show the other side of the coin: Was she clinging to her depression, because by now it was what she knew best? When she shook her head over the difficulties others faced, I asked whether she could reserve some pity and admiration for herself, in light of her own burden. I wanted Emily on my side, which I took to be her own side, the side that longed for a return to a fuller range of affect— both joy and the nuanced sadness that, in depression, are displaced by emptiness. I wanted to diminish Emily's ambivalence over the intimate *what if* question: What if I were free, radically free, of depression?

Treating Emily, I found my own perspective at stake. Single-minded opposition to depression did not always feel comfortable. I had been trained in psychoanalytic psychotherapy, where the preferred doctorly stance is neutrality. The mature analyst sits equidistant from competing aspects of the patient's makeup, respecting insecurity as much as self-sufficiency, numbness as much as hope or desire.

Neutrality is partly a technique. By declining to assume a directive role (against which the patient might only rebel), the therapist permits the patient to own both sides of her ambivalence. The patient who has heretofore insisted on her despair may be moved to acknowledge the part of the self that still hopes for recovery.

But neutrality, if not feigned, is also an inner state—one that an embrace of the medical model forces the therapist to abandon. If doctors are content for a patient to make her own choice about treatment, still they do not stand equidistant between cancer and freedom from cancer—nor between mood disorder and emotional flexibility. Partisanship is a necessary outcome of the decision to take depression seriously as a disease. Increasingly, as evidence about the harmful effects of residual symptoms accumulates in the research literature, it is the notion of giving the devil his due—"respecting symptoms," as authentic aspects of the self—that seems strange.

Encounters with patients like Margaret—who accused me of negotiating with an alien power—made me chary of putting too much weight on attitudes and preferences that arose in the shadow of depression. By the time I met Emily, I had treated any number of depressed patients who linked their identity to their sense of emptiness in an uncaring world—but who later, when their depression remitted, were pleased to claim a share of joyfulness.

There is an attitude I call *faute de mieux*; when we cannot alter a misfortune, we may attribute value to it, for lack of anything better to do. Doctors were in this position when we had few tools to fight depression. We found merit in postures that have some appeal: world-weariness, emotional ambivalence, and social alienation. Most depressive symptoms can be construed as virtues—in Emily's view, even insomnia, when contrasted with the untroubled sleep of the dull-witted. This assessment should always have been suspect: why should disordered or constrained mood be preferred to a flexible response to circumstance? As the harm depression does becomes more evident, and as the disease becomes more treatable, this attribution of worth becomes less necessary, and less tenable.

Van Gogh and Kierkegaard will never be before us, but Emily was in my office—with her belief that depression reflected who she was, an inadequate person or a superior one. Hearing these claims, I was faced with a question parallel to the one that dogged me on two continents:

What follows from the availability of reasonably effective treatments here and now?

I was not convinced that Emily's symptoms represented authentic self or special grace. I continued to recommend treatment, while discussing its risks and shortcomings. That seemed to me a moral posture, to stand forthrightly against the persistence of disability, suffering, and harm.

In time, Emily pulled out of her nosedive. She sounded more competent in every sphere, and less prone to catastrophizing. I told her so.

I should, she said.

Some weeks prior, she had noticed that she was less sharp mentally, with her students and in the laboratory. Festering depression had started to impair her concentration and clarity of thought. She had resumed taking the medication at full dose.

"Don't look so pleased," she snapped, as if it had been a matter of competition between us, of winning and losing. It had been hard, she said, to acknowledge how relentless depression was in her case.

No, no, I said, and yes, yes, of course. I think it is fair to say that I had felt immense relief before I knew the cause of the improvement, relief at seeing my patient recover. I hoped that this time Emily would experience a complete remission. If she did, I doubted that she would miss any aspect of her depression. She might well, I imagined, come to pity her former self as she had pitied her neighbor.

For my own part, I saw little cause for ambivalence. I understand, as every doctor must, that the human lot is difficult, that misfortune strikes the innocent. But ever more it seemed to me that truths of this sort argue in favor of treating disease, where we can, in favor of relieving suffering and restoring resilience.

Five

❖

Altogether

IT WAS SCIENTIFIC PROGRESS that had made this issue, the status of depression, increasingly urgent. The late 1990s and the early years of this century were extraordinary in the history of psychiatry. Every month seemed to bring a new research result, one capable of reshaping our understanding of mood disorder. Certain findings seemed especially relevant to the question that concerned me, depression's meaning. Which is to say that of the shards that caught my eye, results from the laboratory were among the most brilliant.

I have been a little naughty or pushy, I know, in calling this knowledge, the type that arises from controlled observation and experimentation, *what it is*. To link science to identity is, in the language of social theory, to privilege one viewpoint—to place technical research before introspection, popular wisdom, or literary tradition.

But don't we, routinely, accord science that priority? It is hard to envisage a philosophical consideration of tuberculosis that ignores its status as an infectious disease. The acid-fast bacillus, communication through cough and droplet, devastation to lungs, response or resistance to antibacterial agents, disability and early death—no good-faith attempt to assess tuberculosis will deny or ignore those realities, whatever tuberculosis's past standing. We do privilege science. The rap against depression, or against psychiatry, has been that it fails to earn the privilege.

If anything, it is mainstream psychiatry's critics who have insisted on the primacy of the physical. The most insistent demand for concrete evidence has come from Thomas Szasz and his followers. Szasz is the psychiatrist known for his assertion, first made in 1960, that mental illness is a myth—this, with a less kindly view than my own of the function myth serves. Szasz claimed that mental illness cannot be a disease. That term, he wrote, implies defined pathology localized in an organ, in this case, the brain.

In the trivial sense, Szasz was making a statement about classification. Szasz wanted the concept *mental illness* to disappear. Faced with demonstrable anatomical pathology, Szasz would remove the modifier *mental*. Many of the dramatic mood and thought disorders observed in the nineteenth century turned out to be late forms of syphilis, at the stage when the disease attacks the nervous system. Szasz called neurosyphilis a brain disease. By definition (Szasz's), if you cannot point to pathology in depression, the syndrome is not an illness; if you can, it is not a mental illness.

In a more substantial vein, Szasz's denial of mental illness was a prediction. He asserted that science would never show disorders of thought or emotion to be characterized by anatomical pathology. He wrote that "a person's *belief*—whether this be a belief in Christianity, in Communism, or in the *idea* that his internal organs are 'rotting' and that his body is, in fact, already 'dead'—cannot be explained by a defect or disease of the nervous system."

Even at midcentury, Szasz was on shaky ground. It was known that paranoia can, in fact, signal a brain tumor. And it soon became common medical knowledge that the onset of epilepsy can turn a previously dispassionate person hyperreligious, even between seizures. Dostoevsky is the most-cited model of the epileptic mystic. The reverse of what Szasz wrote was true: from the start, there were senses in which beliefs and ideas of the sort he named could be explained by neurological abnormalities.

In his early papers, Szasz had put forth a second reason that depression could not be an illness: its diagnosis relies solely on patient report. But with the wider use of psychotherapeutic medications, psychiatry had come to recognize a form of depression that has the pattern of a dementing illness. The condition is often called pseudodementia, but the impairment of mind is quite real. The deficit resembles the one caused by parkinsonism in its late stages, with problems in motivation, memory, concentration, word finding, and reasoning. This dementia occurs in patients who have suffered past mood disorders, and it responds to antidepressants. Patients with dementing depression can lose intellectual function quite independent of any complaint of sadness; often the diagnosis is made "empirically," when a neurologist thinks to prescribe an antidepressant in the course of a treatment for cognitive deterioration.

As evidence accumulated about biological aspects of a variety of mental disorders, Szasz made refinements in the grounds of his objection. By the 1990s, a particular taunt emerged as a Szaszian refrain: depression does not appear in pathology textbooks.

During my interval of immersion, I participated in a television debate in which Szasz stood on the opposing side. The topic was "Is Depression a Disease?" Szasz said, "As you know, depression is not listed in textbooks of pathology. Maybe when it's listed in textbooks of pathology I might be willing to concede . . . that it's like neurosyphilis or epilepsy."

There is (I would argue) an inadvertent concession in Szasz's late positions. Saying "show me the pathology" implies that but for the final piece of evidence, depression qualifies as a disease.

And of course, it does. Over the years, when the profession answered Szasz, it had pointed to the other criteria. Depression causes profound pain and impairment. It is syndromal—characterized by a reliable cluster of disabilities, such as sadness, appetite and sleep abnormalities, and problems with memory and concentration. Depression progresses, in the fashion of disease. With recurrence, depression's symptoms become more diverse and less responsive to treatment. Depressives die young. Depression runs in families. Depression is found in every culture. Throughout most of Western history, scientists, doctors, and sufferers have considered depression to be an illness. This list covers criteria sociologists generally enumerate when they explain how our culture defines disease: severity of disability, effect on mortality, coherent form, predictable course, and historical acceptance. Evidence of this sort ought to suffice.

It does, but not entirely. When psychiatrists argued that *of course* depression is a disease—because it is syndromal, progressive, universal, and so forth—part of what lent the claim cogency was a further implication: when ailments meet those criteria, a physical substrate exists and will, in time, be found. In effect, mainstream psychiatrists, too, were awaiting evidence of "biological markers" for depression, independent of patient report. What distinguished the mainstream doctors' position from Szasz's was an assessment of probabilities—of the likelihood that research would demonstrate characteristic brain pathology in depression.

By the final decades of the last century, every research dollar in psychiatry was going to studies that accepted the "medical model." The field was operating fully on the assumption that depression is a disease sustained by physiological anomalies and producing further damage of its own. Still, in terms of a final level of confidence, in terms of putting an irksome distortion to rest, it was an embarrassment that evidence of frank brain pathology remained elusive.

And then it came, with the advent of subtler investigative tools. If anything, the evidence arrived all too forcefully. The biological markers of depression corresponded to psychiatrists' worst expectations. Depression appeared to cause anatomical abnormalities in the brain—damage that might itself predispose to further depression, and further harm.

In May 1999, the prestigious journal *Biological Psychiatry* published a "priority communication" timed to coincide with the annual meeting of the American Psychiatric Association. Grazyna Rajkowska, an anatomist who had studied neurodegenerative disorders, like Alzheimer's and Huntington's diseases, had turned her attention to depression, an ailment that had afflicted her own family. The prevailing theory of depression had emphasized variation in the availability of messenger molecules (such as serotonin and norepinephrine) that the brain uses for communication between cells—the popular "chemical imbalance." Rajkowska suspected that the pathology in depression extended to changes in brain anatomy, and she found them.

Rajkowska was examining brain tissue from depressed patients who had died suddenly—not of old age, but of suicide, homicide, car accidents, and natural causes, such as heart attacks. She had obtained her material through a unique arrangement with cooperative coroner's offices that managed to preserve brains within a few hours of a victim's death. Though Rajkowska was working in Mississippi, the first tissue samples came from Cleveland, Ohio, where Craig Stockmeier, her colleague and future husband, had established an autopsy "bank" of brains for research purposes. In time, Rajkowska and Stockmeier trained a worker in the Cuyahoga County Coroner's Office to obtain permission quickly from family members and to remove and preserve just the small portion of brain relevant to Rajkowska's work.

Rajkowska examined the samples with tedious, labor-intensive techniques. She cut the brain in narrow slices, applied stains taken up by differing cell types, and then counted cells in representative subsections of different layers of the brain. The data from these counts was then fed into a computer, which (this mapping was a crucial technological advance) re-created a three-dimensional image of the cellular architecture of the brain region. The coding and counting process was then repeated independently by a second investigator. Neither researcher knew the diagnosis of the subject whose brain she was scrutinizing.

For the study that appeared in *Biological Psychiatry*, Rajkowska examined tissue samples from a dozen depressives and an equal number of controls. One of the depressed subjects had been afflicted for a few months; one, for half a century. The subjects' ages at death ranged from thirty to eighty-six. Two subjects had never taken antidepressant medication. The subjects' diagnoses had been confirmed through research that included reviews of medical records and interviews with treating clinicians and family members. What these people had in common was a substantial degree of depression in the absence of drug abuse, head trauma, or (nonpsychiatric) neurological illness.

For reasons related to her training, Rajkowska was an expert on the prefrontal cortex, the part of the brain that sits just behind the forehead. Rajkowska had been born in Poland and taken her advanced degrees in Leningrad and Warsaw. There, students of Pavlov still ran the laboratories. Research in the Soviet bloc was done on dogs, a species peculiar, among lower mammals, for having (as do humans) large prefrontal cortices. The prefrontal cortex is a late-developing part of the brain concerned with moral sensibility, planning, and other capacities essential to social functioning. (It is tiny in the cat.) Eagerness—the anticipation of pleasure—requires an intact prefrontal cortex.

Although Rajkowska's early work had concerned progressive neurological disorders, the prefrontal cortex was equally of interest in depression. Studies had shown decreased blood flow and decreased energy utilization in the prefrontal cortex of patients in the midst of depressive episodes, with the diminution correlated to the severity of the illness. Normal subjects, when they think sad thoughts, are found on brain scans to have diminished prefrontal blood flow.

Under the microscope, the prefrontal cortex of depressives looked normal. But the computer-aided mapping gave a different picture, one that had remained hidden from earlier investigative tools. The cells in regions of the cortex were weakened, disorganized, disconnected. What Rajkowska's maps revealed was not normal variation, one way of being a human rather than another. The changes looked like brain damage—anatomical pathology.

Huntington's disease and Alzheimer's create gross disturbances in the prefrontal cortex—marked losses of neurons in every layer. The change in depression was less dramatic. Still, Rajkowska identified decreases in cortical thickness, cell size, and cell density within brain tissue. The abnormalities were more specific, more local than the losses in gross neurodegenerative disorders. Some cell layers were spared, others markedly affected. And mood disorder had its own signature.

The nerve cells responsible for mood, thought, motion, and the diverse functions of the body—the neurons—do not live in isolation. They are supported by cells called glia (the word comes from the Greek for glue), which provide external structure, digest debris and toxins, and generally help mediate between neurons and environment they live in. In the neurodegenerative disorders, glia multiply, in a failed effort to save neurons. Depression was characterized by a relative absence—a deficit—of glia.

The changes Rajkowska found occurred in the relevant parts of the prefrontal cortex. One of these, the orbitofrontal cortex (it sits just above and behind the sockets, or orbits, of the eye) had been shown, in nearly simultaneous research, to be implicated in a type of depression in the elderly that is caused by small strokes. The affected areas were also ones in which cells communicate via norepinephrine and serotonin, messenger chemicals involved in mood regulation. And the affected cells within those areas were ones that help modulate that communication.

It was unlikely that the changes represented nonspecific effects of stress. Schizophrenic patients, who face high levels of stress, have much more restricted glial loss, and in different brain regions.

The differences Rajkowska found were not simply in group averages. The results did cluster nicely. But the brains of some depressed individuals showed extreme deficits, so that by counting cells in relevant tissue slices, a pathologist could say with confidence that the samples had not come from a normal control subject. And with just the right sample under the microscope—a slice markedly depleted of glia—an expert could, after all, make a firm diagnosis of depression by eyeballing the anatomical disruption.

Rajkowska had found measurable changes in the composition of the brain in depressives. She concluded her report with a bold statement of her achievement. Hers was the first evidence, in depression, of abnormalities of form at the level of the cell. These findings, she said, suggest that depression is a brain disease characterized by distinct cellular pathology.

Rajkowska had identified a pattern of brain abnormality bearing a resemblance to the neurodegenerative diseases but particular to mood disorder. The relationship of the nerve cell disruption to the syndrome—the experience—of depression was unclear, but there were hints that it might be reasonably direct. The disordered architecture occurred in a relevant part of the brain—a cortex tied, by brain scan evidence, to both feelings of sadness and episodes of depression. And although Rajkowska's study was too small to allow for a firm conclusion on this issue, trends in the data suggested that the degree of pathology reflected the duration of disease—the longer a patient was depressed, the worse the condition of the prefrontal cortex.

In this research, depression appeared to be tied to a failed protective mechanism, the absence of glial cells. That result made the findings especially evocative. Rajkowska was observing under the microscope what psychiatrists encounter in the consulting room. Depression looked strikingly like a disease of vulnerability. If the unprotected nerve cells came under attack, from any of the many stressors that can affect the brain, those neurons would lack the capacity to resist that insult or to initiate repair.

The shapes of the disordered cells in the Rajkowska study seemed to indicate a losing battle in progress. Some glia had atrophied. Others were large and misshapen, as if engaged in an unsuccessful attempt at compensation. These distorted cells had oversized nuclei, a change that might indicate attempts by one cell to manufacture the proteins ordinarily made by many. But why had the glia not proliferated in number, as they do in Huntington's disease? In the depressed brain, there might be problems in two directions. The capacities to resist attacks and to rebound from damage might both be impaired.

Depression was probably not, strictly speaking, a neurodegenerative disorder. That label is reserved for diseases in which a narrowly defined insult results in progressive damage, one sort of enzyme or immune cell or nutritional deficiency relentlessly causing atrophy or death of neu-rons. Here, the degeneration might be set off by any of a number of fac-tors: infection, blood vessel disease, environmental toxins, hormonal imbalances, oxygen deprivation, exposure to free radicals—whatever just does injure brain cells, including the toxic processes set off by stress. In the computer maps and under the microscope, depression ap-peared to be a disorder of neuroprotection or, to coin another clumsy word, neuroresilience. Depression looked like a lack of armor in a hos-tile world. A second insufficiency might also be at issue, in the re-sources needed for recovery, once an attack has done its damage.

In *Listening to Prozac*, I reviewed the monoamine theory of depression—the hypothesis I likened to myth, in my lecture in Copen-hagen. The monoamine theory has it that depression results from an ef-fective deficit in certain chemicals, such as norepinephrine and serotonin, which carry messages between cells. Serotonin is sometimes ascribed an indirect role. It may not be that a deficit in serotonin causes depression, but serotonin is protective. When serotonergic brain path-ways are healthy, a good deal else can go wrong, and still mood will be unaffected. Deplete serotonin, and depression is unmasked. This possi-bility is called the permissive theory: "low serotonin" does not cause mood disorder; but it permits injuries that do. One researcher quoted in *Listening to Prozac* said:

> Maybe serotonin is the police. The police aren't in one place—they're not in the police station. They are a presence everywhere. They are cruising the city—they are right here. Their potential presence makes you feel secure. It allows you to do many things that also make you feel secure. If you don't have enough police, all sorts of things can happen. You may have riots. The absence of police does not cause riots. But if you do have a riot, and you don't have police, there is nothing to stop the riot from spreading.

Glial cells are also police. Their absence permits harm. The Raj-kowska evidence suggested an analogue, or an extension, of a theory already in place. Perhaps harm to glia and to serotonin pathways are related. The two defects are different facets of a single problem—inadequate protection, no police.

The Rajkowska findings were almost too neat. At every level, from social circumstance, to psychological take on the self, to brain chemistry, to cellular anatomy, the depressive lacks support. In the brain and in daily life, the core deficits in depression are identical: vulnerability to harm, failures of resilience.

The Rajkowska study was followed hard upon, in June 1999, by a separate, equally provocative research result, one that relied on different novel technology. Yvette Sheline, a young psychiatrist with expertise in radiology, had decided to use improved computer-aided brain imaging (of living patients) to look at a problem that had so far puzzled researchers.

Various studies seemed to show that the hippocampus, a part of the brain that handles emotionally charged memories, is sometimes smaller in patients who have suffered depression. If the phenomenon was real, its cause was unclear. It was possible that people with small hippocampi (from the the Latin for seahorse, the name refers to the structure's curved shape in cross section) were prone to depression. Alternatively, blood vessel disease and stroke, which in old age lead to a subtype of depression, might be the culprit. Or it might be that depression caused cell atrophy or even cell death in the brain. The particular team doing the study, at Washington University in St. Louis, was reasonably certain that the hippocampus shrank with age; one goal of the study was to establish age-based norms for hippocampal size.

The Sheline study was carefully designed. The researchers looked at twenty-four women who had suffered depression and twenty-four women of the same age and educational level who had not. None of the women was actively depressed, nor had any been depressed in the prior four months. The women's ages covered the adult spectrum, from twenty-three to eighty-six. All of the women were healthy; none had conditions even indirectly associated with blood vessel disease, such as high blood pressure. This sample was, in fact, highly select: women who had nothing wrong with them except (in the test group) a prior history of depression.

The two groups had no difference in brain size. But high-resolution magnetic imaging showed that the depressed women had lower hippocampal volumes, and corresponding differences in the size of another part of the brain associated with emotion, the amygdala. Contrary to the experimenters' expectations, in these extremely healthy women, there was no relationship between age and hippocampal size. Only one set of correlations held up: the more days a woman had been depressed, the smaller the volume of her hippocampus and amygdala. And the smaller the hippocampus, the worse the verbal memory—despite the fact that the women with past depressive episodes looked normal on other tests of intellectual functioning.

The assessment of the women's history of depression had been conducted with care. The researchers had supplemented a conventional life-charting method, based on the patients' reports, with collateral interviews with the subjects' relatives and treating psychiatrists. The depressed women's experience covered a broad range—from one episode to eighteen. But on average, their burden of illness had been substantial—five episodes of depression, consuming a total of two or three years of life. Duration is an important measure, because the diagnosis of depression is most reliable in those with long-standing illness.

So: the hippocampus did not shrink with age. It got smaller with depression. That was the article's title: "Depression Duration but Not Age Predicts Hippocampal Volume Loss in Medically Healthy Women with Recurrent Major Depression." In terms of hippocampal size, a seventy-year-old woman who had suffered three years of depression spread over the prior forty years looked like a thirty-year-old woman who had been depressed for three years in her early twenties. The damage done by depression in early adulthood looked like the damage from recent depression in old age. The harm to the hippocampus was not transient but persisted when the depression was in remission. The deterioration was substantial, accounting for an 8 to 10 percent loss in hippocampal volume. (Subsequent similar studies found greater loss, in the range of

20 percent.) And this change in brain anatomy was not an incidental finding; it affected intellectual functioning, and in the predicted way.

This result caught doctors' attention. It suggested that depression was eroding their patients' brains. The study gave urgency to preventing episodes, or shortening them. Every day counts. There is no writing off depression as a normal variant or a stage people go through, not if each day causes further permanent loss in hippocampal volume and verbal memory. The Sheline study was compelling, in terms of its rigor and the simple nature of the harm demonstrated, to brain integrity and mental function.

The research attracted particular attention because of the region of the brain involved, the hippocampus. Seven months before Sheline published her study, hippocampal research had produced one of the most exciting results in the history of neuroscience, evidence of new cell formation in the adult brain.

A few paragraphs back, I slipped in references to repair and resilience. Those concepts are crucial to current theories of depression. But the notion that thoroughgoing renewal is possible in the adult brain gained currency only recently.

In 1993, I had written: "There may be mechanisms of repair in these neural systems, ways to learn or relearn resilience. Then again, there is no good biochemical model of repair, only of prevention of injury and of compensation." In 1998, Fred Gage of the Salk Institute (along with Swedish colleagues) capped years of research by showing that in the adult brain, change and repair take place constantly. Gage's article begins, "Loss of neurons is thought to be irreversible in the adult human brain, because dying neurons cannot be replaced." Its conclusion opens with this proud sentence: "Our study demonstrates that cell genesis occurs in human brains and that the human brain retains the potential for self-renewal throughout life."

Gage used a clever technology to demonstrate the formation of new neurons. Cancer doctors occasionally employ a chemical marker, bromodeoxyuridine, or BrdU, to check for tumor proliferation. BrdU is valuable because it is taken up specifically into new, growing cells.

Gage reasoned that BrdU might equally serve to reveal cell production in the nervous system. He looked at tissue from the brains of cancer patients in their sixties who had, in the course of their usual medical care, been tested with BrdU and died shortly after. Sure enough, on autopsy, the brains of these patients revealed BrdU-containing neurons, and in the very region thought most likely to display new cell growth, the hippocampus.

That it took until 1998 to demonstrate brain neurogenesis in human adults testifies to the technical difficulty of the research. In the 1960s, the phenomenon had been found in mice and, more impressively, in guinea pigs, a species born with a relatively mature nervous system. But studies in primates proved frustrating. As recently as 1985, a thoughtful researcher had argued that neurogenesis might be impossible in humans and monkeys, because it would interfere with memory and learning. Thirteen years later, new neuron growth was demonstrated in marmosets, and then in humans.

Subsequently, primate research found neurogenesis in other brain regions, notably the prefrontal cortex. The new cells can take differing forms—they can become neurons, or they can become glia. These findings raised the possibility that part of what Rajkowska had seen in her autopsies of depressives was a failed reparative response—inadequate neurogenesis.

But it was the Sheline results that were especially disturbing in light of Gage's demonstration of neurogenesis. It was known, from the animal studies that preceded Gage's work in humans, that stress inhibits new cell formation in the hippocampus, while a secure and stimulating social environment enhances growth. In other words, the very factors that set off or protect from episodes of depression set off or protect from problems with cellular renewal.

None of the Sheline subjects was acutely depressed. The hippocampal damage was the residue of illness, volume loss for which the brain had failed to compensate. If the hippocampus is a site where repair is especially likely, then a recently depressed patient might be expected to have a smaller hippocampus than a patient who suffered a similar episode years back, at a young age, with time for cell growth intervening. But for depressives, the self-renewal that Gage wrote about seemed to be lacking. The chain of logic was admittedly a long one, but it was possible that depression might entail a failure of resilience at the level of the cell or the cellular environment. Like Rajkowska's results, Sheline's suggested two problems in depression: vulnerability to harm and impaired healing.

Sheline's and Rajkowska's work had been previewed in the mid-1990s in announcements of the outcome of pilot studies. The final papers were eagerly awaited—at least, I looked forward to them. I remember elbowing my way into the meeting at which Rajkowska presented her data. I interviewed both women repeatedly.

For me, these research results *embodied*—that word seems right—clinical experience. It wasn't simply a matter of depression being associated with differences in the brain; I think any reasonable person would have conceded in advance that depression must have some physical representation. It was that the changes were resonant, poetic, metaphorical, full of apparent narrative content, evocatively connected to what doctors see in their daily work. Depression in the brain looks eerily like depression in the person. It is fragility, brittleness, lack of resilience, a failure to heal. Depression is chronic and progressive, with each episode—perhaps each day!—leaving damage in its wake. Depression is not normal variation; it is pathology—and risk of further harm.

I don't mean that these two papers are conclusive. Like the research pointing to serotonin and norepinephrine as critical factors in mood disorder, the evidence for harm to the hippocampus and prefrontal cortex coexists with contradictory findings. But Sheline's and Rajkowska's work sits in an extensive literature that confirms the clinical perspective. Any plausible definition of disease that would include cancer, heart attacks, strokes, epilepsy, and diabetes must also embrace depression.

The anatomical account of depression has changed the way doctors view their patients. The depressed person sits before us. She speaks, wretchedly, of the trivial disappointment that threw her into a living hell. Hearing of vulnerability in daily life, we imagine vulnerability at the level of the neuron. No need to look forward to the face and habit.

We can imagine glial cells retreating, and neurons withering, at this very moment.

Not long ago, the treatment of depression might proceed at a deliberate pace. One theory had it that the way out of depression was down. Since self-examination would lead patients to confront fears worse than those they had so far recognized, emerging symptoms were a sign of progress. I always found that model cruel and hubristic, in its belief that therapists could know when more suffering would lead to less. Now, we have learned that symptoms signal ongoing injury. Recovery is urgent. The time to interrupt the illness is yesterday.

For the doctor, pathology is often pictorial. Hearing of chest pain, the cardiologist sees blocked arteries. In this way, the Rajkowska and Sheline findings gave rise (for me, late in my interval of immersion) to visions—unsettling illustrations that appeared as patients told their stories of paralysis, frustration, and emptiness. The visions only strengthened my incomprehension of accounts that attribute transcendent qualities to depression. When I stumbled upon these claims—in memoirs, in conversation, in clinical practice—they were accompanied now, in my mind, by discordant images, of the shrunken hippocampus and disordered prefrontal cortex.

Six

❖

Charm

I F ANYTHING, I HAVE UNDERSTATED depression's appeal. Depression elicits warm feelings, from those who observe it. Certainly, in its mild and early forms it does. Depressive traits have their allure. So do the depressed, even in the midst of their affliction. Depression has the power to charm.

At her first appointment, Betty says, "If it's not too odd a place to begin, I want to tell you about the laundry."

The clean wash sits at the foot of her bed. It began as two mounds, whites and darks, with a dollop of delicates on the side. Now, weeks later, it is one preposterous scoop of vanilla swirl. What would it take, really, to move the laundry from floor to dresser drawer?

Betty's tone says she is embarrassed, defeated. She looks to see whether I understand how debilitating it is to fail at simple tasks.

Betty's is a considerate opening. No disheartening history of anguish. She sets about her task as a short story writer might, with homely detail, complete with appeal to the senses—shape, color, time.

Go on, I signal, and Betty does. The account turns on comic hope-lessness. The pile has a history. It began as a stash of dirty clothes on the closet floor. As it grew, Betty would buy new items rather than wash, and she could ill afford the outlay. Even so, there were often unpleasant decisions—whether to reiron a blouse tinged with body odor. These subtle humiliations are the hardest to reveal: the secret uncleanliness, the dishonesty in the seemingly crisp outfit.

Betty describes her distaste, nearly a phobia, for the basement room that houses her apartment building's washer and dryer. She makes a mime performance of it, the way she shivers at the thought of doing the wash—her frustration at her own foolishness. She smiles at the para-dox: she is too delicate to descend the stairs, but not too delicate for the stage of domestic life she calls living with the dirties.

Finally, it became too much. She stuffed the wash into her car and late at night drove it to one of those Laundromat multiplexes where the machines take credit cards. At which point life lurched into this alter-nate state, in which the cleans dominate.

Betty has often wondered whether the laundry is meant to save her from men—to prevent her from bringing them home. She invites them anyway. And then the wash signals her vulnerability. Men understand. Even fairly dense ones do. Betty's most recent episode of depression began in the wake of a failed romance.

Betty is sidling into new territory, her tolerance for mistreatment. In my office, Betty has been considerate of my sensibilities. She has en-gaged me through a seemingly solvable problem—laundry—before re-vealing real trouble.

I suspect that the story form is no coincidence. What does Betty know about me? That I am a writer and a therapist. She is addressing me in my vernacular. She guesses I do not want conclusions, that I pre-fer texture, anecdote, the tale in the teller's voice.

Betty is artful and self-aware. She laughs at herself and brings me in on the joke. She manages to set a problem here in the room, between us. In this sense: the open-with-the-laundry gambit is what it describes, an instance of postponing necessary business—I mean discussion of the more worrisome tasks that are languishing. Steps toward career (she is a sculptor), marriage, every one of Betty's goals.

Surely Betty intends for the habitual avoidance to peek through. I am meant to see that it is not only laundry that defeats her. Daily life is framed and dominated by problems at once petty and intractable. If the laundry monologue shields me from other particulars of Betty's despair, she trusts I know they will emerge. Her indirection hides a compliment and a plea. She expects me to understand more than is said.

Perhaps Betty is asking for a comparable approach in return, a delicate intervention. For her own part, she is not afraid of engaging in gentle confrontation. By way of illustrating the laundry problem, Betty points to the stacks of paper on my desk. It's a nice touch, simultaneously implying a commonality of human frailty, hers and mine, and demonstrating a comfortable willingness to challenge me, one adult to another.

I am charmed. I admire social grace. I find it comfortable—who does not?—to spend time with people who put creative energy to work in the service of considerateness. Betty is terribly likable. How, I wonder, can she have so much *social* trouble? She is subtle, generous, self-effacing. In her presence, I feel coarse and overbearing. Betty understands the intricacies of relationships better than I do, has wider tolerance for others' foibles. How lucky I am to be having this conversation.

But it is also true that when I am charmed, I think depression. In this way, I resemble those who romanticize mood disorder—the difference is the direction of the inference. Betty's skillful entry worries me. Charm wards off aggression, sometimes at the price of self-abnegation. Like insomnia or excessive guilt, charm may not always accompany depression, but the pairing is frequent enough.

Some of this relationship is indirect. Depression occurs in all sorts of people. There are gruff and grumpy depressives; there are depressives who haven't a clue, socially. In fact, gruffness and cluelessness often lead to the sort of relationship train-wrecks that trigger mood disorder. But it is also true that many depressives fit a stereotype; they are socially fastidious and emotionally attuned. Research confirms this association. Emotionality, especially fragility in the face of disappointment, is a risk factor for depression. There is probably genetic overlap as well: neuroticism and liability to depression sometimes travel together. And people who make broad social investments—who feel linked to a wide range of relatives and neighbors—may sustain losses that (in terms of their tendency to cause depression) are not compensated for by the support that the network provides in return.

But these studies refer to correlations between distinct ways of being. Empathy is not depression. There are emotionally intense people who never suffer mood disorders. Some attachments remain supportive and sustaining throughout. In the face of depression, we detect graciousness that has become compulsive, attachment characterized by dependency and desperation. We see bad judgment, indiscriminate trust.

Doctors learn to take charm with a grain of salt. Psychotherapy mimics melancholy—it is an exercise in amplification of affect and attention to social detail. That a patient relates comfortably to her therapist does not mean she is easy to live with at home or in the workplace. That she is adept here does not mean she is safe from the consequences of her ailment. Attuned patients will respond to the doctor's hope of improvement, saving their energy for the therapy hour, appearing lively and competent then. Charming patients are almost always more impaired than they appear in the office.

I worry most about compulsion. Is attentiveness to others a freely chosen posture that expresses Betty's benign intentions toward the social world? Is it a stigma of injury?

Betty's mother was depressed. It is said that the children of depressives develop exquisite awareness of the needs of others. From an early age, they must read a parent's mind, in order to avoid trouble and get themselves raised properly. They are necessarily desperate to please. If in adolescence, these children themselves become prone to depression, their requirement for acceptance and stability only increases. They become yet more socially vigilant.

In adulthood, the depressive's anxious sensitivity and compulsive generosity have their appeal, to colleagues, lovers, and relatives, who reinforce the tendencies by admiring them—and then criticizing minor shortcomings. Desperate and confused, the depressive has difficulty separating her own desires from those of others to whom she feels bound. She may develop a general difficulty in ranking priorities, call it a disorder of perspective. Depressives catastrophize the problem at hand.

It occurs to me during the first meeting with Betty that when she begins with the wash, it may be because, at the moment, that problem looms large for her. What appears to be artfulness may contain an admixture of ditziness. But then ditz and charm are not mutually exclusive. Impracticality can be attractive. It empowers others; it does not threaten. There are contexts in which a woman can indulge her ditziness, because it will be rewarded. The therapeutic encounter might be one.

If the accumulating symptoms of depression—disorganization, timidity, subservience—carry their quota of social worth, still they inflict costs. Anxiety about others, inattention to her own needs, professional failures—these recurrent stressors condemn Betty to further bouts of depression.

I do not want to reinforce social skills that might leave Betty trapped, competencies that she exercises at her own expense. I suspect that a prior therapist took the opposite tack. Betty has the sound of someone taught to tread lightly, so as not to overwhelm. I make a mental note not to respond too enthusiastically to Betty's entertaining, considerate reports. It is conventional to say that in therapy a patient should be free to express anger. I will want something more difficult. I will want Betty to be boring, oppressive, and repetitive—if dullness would communicate the experience of her daily life.

Often I imagine I know patients' stories before I hear them. Midway through the first meeting with Betty, I have an impression of what further conversation will reveal. A difficult childhood—indifferent parents, perhaps, emotionally flattened by their own anhedonia. A sense in junior high, and growing with the years, of outsider status. Inexplicable bad days. An extra dose of the anxiety ascribed to teenage girls, the inhibition that holds them back from classroom participation. But Betty will have enjoyed solid peer relationships, with the sorts of friends that accrete around a considerate girl when she is in the same school system for years. And recognition from a teacher, drawn to Betty's delicacy. An intrusive affair with that teacher? Perhaps not. The interaction may have been positive. The teacher ran the art department, appreciated Betty's need to express herself through indirection.

Betty (as I imagine her story) is enthused about college. It represents a chance to overcome her estrangement and to spend time with other artists, who see the world as she does. But the transition proves unexpectedly difficult. Betty did not realize how dependent she was on her long acquaintance with friends from home. At college, she discovers that there is something she has not grasped, about how a person knows which group is hers. She gets on with everyone but feels all the more disconnected.

There is a bad incident with a boy. She goes too far too fast, only to see him run off like a scared rabbit. She feels awkward discussing the incident, suspects the misunderstanding is her own fault. The failed relationship upsets her longer than she thinks it should. She becomes anxious at a quiz, fails it.

Work begins to prove hard, or perhaps it is the bleak winter. Caught between competing projects, she finds herself doing neither. She bites her nails to the quick. For an art assignment, she does sketches of split nails and inflamed cuticles. Once she scratches her wrist with an X-acto knife. The episode makes her feel crazy. That is her new secret, how strange she has become. Although often she feels no stranger than the next person. Adolescence is like this, isn't it? She buckles down and gets through the term. In February, a black mood immobilizes her for a week. She leaves her room only to eat.

For our purpose, characterizing depression, it does not matter whether my speculation is accurate. Betty introduces herself indirectly, allusively. My response to this projective test reveals what depression is to me, as a clinician. And what charm is. Exposure to depression has soured charm for me, at least here in the office.

Descriptions of depression tend to focus on acuity. Pain, confusion, and desperation take center stage. One of the earliest English-language memoirs of melancholy, by the poet William Cowper, begins that way. In 1763, nominated to a political sinecure for which he feels unsuited, Cowper is stricken by dread. He dashes about London, intent on suicide—by penknife, laudanum, drowning in the Thames. Each time, the hand of God saves him. Contemporary autobiography is similar. The crisis justifies the narrative.

Today, psychiatry does well with crisis. Not always—there are patients we never reach. But for the most part, once a person is in treatment, the doctor will find a way to take the edge off, to turn a sharp depression into a dull one. In my experience, depression is characterized less by acuity than duration. Depression is what settles in to stay.

I am afraid for Betty. Leaden paralysis will slow Betty's progress as an artist. She will fail to achieve milestones, or she will come to them late. If her career falters, if she needs to seek out real jobs, employers will find her a bargain, someone with more talent than her degrees indicate; they will underpay and underpromote her. She will have difficulty asserting herself on her own behalf. For Betty, work will become a source of constant strain.

Betty will be a bargain in the dating marketplace, too. Men can rescue her from one depression and, when she begins to feel at ease, throw her into another. They can dominate her, mistreat her.

Betty's handicaps will expose her to what researchers call stressful life events, and the SLEs will lead to further depressive episodes and more handicap. Acute depression will eat up more of each year. Later bouts will be complex and resistant to treatment. Safe environments will be ever harder to find.

Looming behind this downward slide is an image of the brain, ever less resilient, ever more vulnerable.

In my speculation, I have worried over the course of Betty's life without specifying what she experiences when she falters. Depression is notoriously "polymorphic" or "pleomorphic," taking different forms in different people or in the same person over time.

Many diseases announce themselves with an isolated symptom. Cancer of an internal organ can present as a skin rash. Depression's variety of form is not limited to the "presenting chief complaint." A single symptom, out of the many that constitute the syndrome, may predominate for years. In one person, the obvious feature will be self-loathing. In a second, apathy. In a third, agitation. A patient may do well in many spheres but remain hamstrung by self-doubt. Twice I have treated patients in whom crippling grief lasted years. Depression's diversity of form was apparent to the ancient Greeks. Robert Burton, in the seventeenth century, quotes earlier scholars to the effect that among melancholics "scarce is there one of a thousand that dotes alike." This, despite the fact that depression is syndromal—that its pattern of disruption can be boiled down to a short list of common symptoms.

Over the course of a few meetings, the form of Betty's difficulty becomes apparent. For Betty, it is unsorted laundry all the way down the line. The controlling feature of her depression is paralysis of action, which Betty calls "exhaustion." This exhaustion is not physical in the obvious sense. Betty can lead the way in an aerobics exercise class. Summers, she does distance swims, in the open ocean. She loves caring for her brother's young children and can hold down the fort for a long weekend.

In Betty, exhaustion refers to a mental incapacity to apply herself to the projects that matter to her own success. Her exhaustion is limited to her love life and her career. And, of course, her time alone, in her apartment. She cannot complete—often feels she cannot start—the simple tasks that contribute to a productive day. What Betty refers to as exhaustion reminds me of what once were called *anomalies of the will*. In the nineteenth century, anomalies of the will were understood to be fundamental to depression.

Over the course of a few conversations, Betty's history emerges. By my reckoning, it contains three clear bouts of depression. However much she resembles them in sensibility, by virtue of those recurrences Betty stands apart from many of the patients I wrote about in *Listening to*

Prozac. Experience three episodes of major depression, and you are all but certain to have a fourth and a fifth. If you have three episodes followed by residual symptoms, your psychiatrist is bound to focus on eradicating every trace of depression, in the hopes of forestalling a lifetime of mood disorder.

What Betty cares about is making art. She aspires to grand commissions, the monumental pieces that adorn public spaces. She has the engineering training and apprenticeship experience to attempt them. Meanwhile, she is known for small constructions, three-dimensional collages, resembling Joseph Cornell boxes.

Betty supports herself by teaching sculpture at a local college, under an ad hoc arrangement. Though her classes are popular, by her own lights she is always unprepared. Unease over her perceived shortcomings makes her put teaching tasks first. Her out-of-class hours are filled with ill-organized attempts to develop lesson plans or acquire materials. She has no time or energy for anything else. Forget mounting an exhibition. Dishes pile up in the sink. The dog is six months overdue for his vet appointment. It has been years since Betty filed an income tax return. Her academic department has invited Betty to apply for a tenure-track job, but she cannot face assembling a portfolio.

It occurs to me that Betty would make a suitable heroine for one of those film comedies premised on a woman's unself-conscious, awkward appeal. Last night—the one before the morning in which I am writing these words—I saw a slight Italian effort on video, *Pane e tulipani* (*Bread and Tulips*). The heroine, before she comes into her own, has a sweet incompetence that resembles Betty's. The stumbling belies other traits—adeptness and reliability—that succeed in the service of others and might flourish altogether in a milieu that gave adequate encouragement. That is the development in the movie, of course—blossoming.

Betty's brother has a recurring illness. Betty responds to his emergencies, and then she finds herself yet further behind. The tendency to put others first extends to her relations with men she dates, so that she shuttles from crisis to crisis. Although she often dreams of motherhood,

Betty fears she cannot afford—emotionally—to have children. One more set of claims on her attention will about do her in. The demands of relatives, students, and friends dominate her week, eclipsing the effort put into artwork. Betty's energy runs out before attention to the self begins.

Though she focuses on her exhaustion, to my way of thinking, Betty has other depressive traits. The lethatgy is compounded by perfectionism and low self-regard. She feels guilt all too readily. She focuses on the painful aspects of any situation. She requires solitude. She feels an outsider in social groups. She obsesses over trifles. These tendencies are symptoms. The standard definition of depression refers to feelings of worthlessness, excessive guilt, and indecision. More complete accounts, in textbooks, refer to social withdrawal and paralyzing ruminations. But these facets of mood disorder are so familiar to Betty that they feel like aspects of self; her focus is elsewhere, on regaining her energy.

It is true that the traits that worry me resemble admirable personality elements in a certain sort of aesthete or altruist. The low self-esteem is also selflessness. The need for distance shows itself as a willingness to let others approach her in their own time. Her alienation contains a critique of the emptiness that characterizes common forms of interaction—self-serving small talk, narcissistic flirtation, social climbing, instrumental networking, flattery of the powerful. Betty's low expectations are linked to a tearful gratitude for small victories; her pessimism borders on joy, so thankful is Betty for any success. Her finickiness makes her an exact composer of words and relationships—and, of course, three-dimensional objects. On the rare occasions when Betty exhibits her work, critics praise the consistency of the aesthetic—every nail hit square. Betty is, moreover, morally scrupulous. (We have not adopted this criterion in the United States, but certain German psychiatrists consider scrupulosity—excessive conscientiousness—to be the core feature of depression, the one that gives rise to every other symptom.) In this arena, weighing right and wrong, Betty is sure in her judgments.

This dual function—symptom as social grace—helps explain depression's charm. Other mental illnesses—panic anxiety, say, or paranoia—generally lack this feature.

Here is an anecdote from Betty's student days:

She is in the midst of a depression. She badly wants to apply for an advanced class in portrait photography with a famous visiting artist-in-residence. Betty knows her portfolio is inadequate—she has no chance of being admitted. She fears that if she tries hard and is rejected, she will be thrown into further turmoil. To protect herself, and because she knows effort is hopeless, she fills out the application in desultory fashion, leaving whole sections blank. At the interview, Betty believes the teacher is going through the motions. Betty tells him the truth, that she cannot work up enthusiasm for anything, least of all portraiture. Betty is brusque, cannot end the encounter quickly enough. She is paralyzed for the rest of that day and the whole of the next. When the acceptances are posted, she does not go to check them—but friends bring the good news that her name is atop the list. Betty joins the class. When she turns in some good work, the teacher nods his head in pride. "That's why I accepted you," he says. "I could see you had the artistic temperament."

Now (in her adult life) friends, colleagues, students, and relatives adore and admire Betty, not despite her handicaps but because of them. The very traits that paralyze her make her attractive.

Over time, depression wears poorly—it leads to divorce, it leads to unemployment, it leads to social isolation. As depressives age, they can turn very lonely. I have had patients who used shunning as a marker; when their friends avoided them, these patients knew it was time to make an appointment with me. Often, frank episodes are more than friends can bear. But certain people—not a few, by my observation—are loved or admired for their residual symptoms.

Still, it astonishes me how readily Betty's friends look past, or overlook, her depression. Not to be able to arrange small objects in a box! The level of paralysis is terrifying. Later, I will think of Betty when I treat patients with writer's block or difficulty researching a graduate school thesis. The issue is never the task. Rarely is anyone—writer, scientist, manager, line worker—set an assignment for which he lacks the skill. The issue is the ailment. Apathy, despair, confusion, perfectionism, anomaly of the will—the symptoms are as paralyzing as those of almost any illness we might name.

Unlike patients who might speak in favor of their symptoms—Emily, say—Betty does not consider herself superior. It is a matter of having no distance from her tendencies. She experiences others' demands as imperatives. She feels guilt over her paralysis, given that most people push ahead, even in the face of evident obstacles. She understands her situation to be hopeless. All the same, Betty is not set on freeing herself of depression, in all of its aspects.

After a few sessions, I understand better what disturbed me from the first about the laundry vignette. It contained a hint of ambivalence over, or blindness to, the extent of Betty's problem. In displaying her charm, in asking me to respond to it, to admire her exact considerateness and her because of it, Betty is hoping for the impossible. She wants to be rid of the exhaustion without being changed fundamentally. The scrupulosity, perfectionism, and low expectations have been with her so long that she relies on them in her dealings with the world. If only she could be liberated from this one aspect of depression, the anomaly of the will, she might be content to leave other traits and symptoms undisturbed or to remain blithely unaware of the risk they pose.

The wish to pick and choose—to alter only certain manifestations of the illness—this tendency is another aspect of depression's singularity. Heart failure, anemia, chronic pain, infections, cancer—all include or lead to low energy. Someone who despairs of a cure might say, "If only I had more energy, I could live with the pain." But that wish would be a compromise, a definition of an acceptable minimum, a bargain with fate or God. No one comes to the doctor and asks, Please take away the enervation and leave the rest. No, the assumption goes in the reverse direction: treat the ailment successfully, and the lethargy will disappear as a matter of course. But often with depression, patients may actively hope to hold fast to part of the syndrome. In effect, they say, That element is foreign, but this one is who I am.

I was, in my college years, an admirer of many of the traits I mistrust in Betty. To be more giving, sensitive, scrupulous, and generous—those would have been improvements in my own character. Certainly, I felt the charm of the artistic sensibility in others. Here is one area where extended immersion changed me. The doctorly eye sees these personality traits, the ones that serve as social graces, in a jaundiced light. Too often, they are symptoms of a progressive illness, or risk factors for or adaptations to it. Let's get you better, is my implicit suggestion to Betty, and then see how you feel about the compulsion to put others first. Betty already suffers from low self-esteem. I will not devalue traits she experiences as aspects of her makeup. But I cannot envisage a cure that leaves them untouched.

A complex ethical issue lurks in that last statement. In *Listening to Prozac*, I bemoaned the culture's demand for assertiveness; we might be hungry for a pill that makes each of us feel more like an alpha ape, a top banana. For the doctor, in the clinical moment, faced with a patient prone to recurrent mood disorder, that issue fades. It's not that I want to transform Betty into an egotist, but I have no doubt about the direction she has to move in, if she is to be safe. The goal of treatment is to spare her the illness she is prone to, with all its consequences: endangered neurons, early blood vessel disease, crises where suicide is at issue, and the rest.

In some future world, medication might resolve the ethical dilemma. We can imagine (barely) a substance that protects Betty's prefrontal glia and hippocampal neurons while leaving her scrupulous and self-effacing. Although it seems that enough of what troubles her *is* depression that to cure *that* would change her utterly.

Here and now, too, medication will play a part in Betty's treatment. It seems a matter of some urgency for her to feel less despairing, more in control, and wider awake. But set medication aside. If we were to rely on psychotherapy alone, what would count as progress? Working with Betty, I would want to examine her thought processes in slow motion. How does she go from hearing that a boyfriend is in need to dropping everything to tend to him? What past patterns inform that automatic response? Insight will count for little without behavioral change. I will take it as good news if Betty applies for tenure. I will be pleased to see her set hours aside for art and guard them ruthlessly. I might smile if she tells me what is on her mind, without quite so much attention to my preferences as an audience. How is Betty to protect herself from stressful life events, in the form of needy, domineering, or predatory men? We may well conclude that Betty can ill afford to be ditzy, timid, or emotionally operatic. Almost any intervention that addresses Betty's vulnerability to depression is likely to leave her less charming.

Treating Betty, I was willing to see those delicate qualities fade: the paralyzingly exact judgment, the compulsive caretaking, the catastrophic response to the misfortune of others. No doubt it was a matter of *furor sanandi*, the zeal to cure. But I saw certain forms of ordinarily appealing behavior as if through a distorting or correcting lens that made them grotesque. Awareness of the harm depression does had inured me to its charm.

Seven

❖

More Charm

I WAS HARDENED AGAINST CHARM, and not only in the consulting room. I carried the attitude everywhere. It colored my response to the many memoirs of depression.

I had admired the first in the series, William Styron's *Darkness Visible*. Styron's is a meditation on the ineffable. Depression, Styron writes, is "so mysteriously painful and elusive in the way it becomes known to the self—to the mediating intellect—as to verge close to being beyond description." And again, "I was feeling in my mind a sensation close to, but indescribably different from, actual pain." And, "For myself, the pain is most closely connected to drowning or suffocation—but even these images are off the mark." And once more, "To most of those who have experienced it, the horror of depression is so overwhelming as to be quite beyond expression." Styron reaches for adequate words: "dank joylessness," "murky distractedness," "anarchic connections," "a toxic and unnamable tide," "a trance of supreme discomfort," "ferocious *inwardness*," "this curious alteration of consciousness." As a writer, he is engaged (hopelessly) in a time-honored struggle: "Since antiquity—in the tortured lament of Job, in the choruses of Sophocles and Aeschylus—chroniclers of the human spirit have been wrestling with a vocabulary that might give proper expression to the desolation of melancholia." Depression lays bare writing's limitations. Words fail.

I liked Styron's insistence that depression is distinctive—so different from everyday sadness as to make attempts at description futile. But the personal histories that followed Styron's misfired for me. I would reexamine a memoir and find that the technique, the method of drawing the reader in, was simply to describe a homely mishap that turned on depressive traits. Such passages were meant to create an alliance with the reader—and evidently for others, they succeeded. For me, an observer schooled in the face and the career of depression, and now weighed down with depression in the office, the horror story began prematurely.

When the books did work, I imagined, it was because many of the characteristics associated with depression are appealing. Irascibility, pensiveness, self-consciousness, loyalty, and sentimentality—these traits become strengths for a certain sort of first-person narrator. Similarly for the symptomatic effects of a minor depressive episode—despair, confusion, agitation, apprehension, social withdrawal, global apathy. The traits seem to imply humility. They suggest existential attunement, in a world devoid of meaning.

And then there is the subset of depressives who come to grief through excessive innocence, unprotected attachment. I saw how readers might be enchanted by these authors, more than by other writers who shared news of their ailments—nephritis or Crohn's disease. Our hearts go out to the naive. I had been asking myself why, if panic disorder is as prevalent as depression, there is not a single widely read autobiography by a patient whose primary problem is panic. I thought that the difference must concern charm.

An odd example of my problem: In connection with a trip to Spain, a friend gave me *On Bullfighting*, A. L. Kennedy's account of months she spent researching the corrida. Kennedy begins by describing her brush with suicide:

I should jump now, while I can.

Because I don't want anyone looking, or there to be hurt by me when I fall. It's only me I want to kill. And I don't wish to be gawped at while I am killing. I believe I've had enough embarrassment for one life.

Fortunately, a neighbor is singing a bathetic tune. To die to schlock music would be one more humiliation, so Kennedy soldiers on, enervated, in pain, indifferent to her former vocation as a writer.

I do get it. Kennedy's effete suicidality contrasts effectively with Ernest Hemingway's macho version. The isolation, the struggle with fear, and the evident mortality of the depressive resonate with parallel traits in the matador. Death stalks us. Bullfighting and depression are both noble ways of acknowledging that reality; matadors and depressives are specially endowed. Kennedy's wry account of her narrow escape gives us to understand that she will have writerly virtues: sensitive observation, alienated perspective, attunement to absurdity, ironic self-awareness.

It would be equally true to say that I do not get it. I flip the pages searching for news about the treatment or course of illness. The more fool I. For Kennedy, depression is a marker of discernment. It has served its purpose. Sharing your death wish with the reader is an effective form of "meeting cute."

A side note, on what suicide is to the psychiatrist: My experience is limited, for which I knock on wood daily. Limited, and exceedingly painful. There is no death from illness worse for survivors than the suicide of a loved one.

I recall a patient who came to me for a few sessions, not enough to establish a clear diagnosis. Weeks later, he died in a car crash, alone on a small road. In his bloodstream were high levels of drugs, prescribed by an internist. The death was ruled accidental, but I had my doubts. I met with two family members. There was little to say. So much was unknown, and I did not want to add to their burden. The events cast a shadow on my mind for two years, steadily. Long after, I can scarcely stand to think of the victim or the survivors or my own role.

I am not certain how many suicides I have had in my practice where depression was the primary diagnosis. Perhaps one, in twenty years. I am thinking of a patient who died of overdose. With him, I am not convinced that suicide was intended, though here, the coroner said yes. Two other patients killed themselves years after they had moved away; both had other mental illnesses. These three haunt me also. I live in terror of suicide; that is another aspect of immersion.

Suicide is at issue in a particular, poignant way when we make use of antidepressants. These medications are effective tools in the prevention of suicide. Study after study has shown that when the new antidepressants, like Prozac, are introduced into a given nation, or when they become widely used in a particular region of a country, suicide rates go down, among adults and adolescents both. But antidepressants can also, infrequently, foment suicidal thoughts and impulses in people who have never been depressed before. We have known as much for years—I wrote about the phenomenon in *Listening to Prozac*. So our efforts to avert suicide may sometimes cause it; the possibility of suicide is nearby always, for psychiatrists, in their daily work.

Because of our new tools, psychiatry does a better job of preventing suicide than it did in the past. We are fairly good, as I say, at turning acute illness into chronic. But we can fail. We never forget the failures. Colleagues I have treated as patients always say the same. If they live nowhere else, the suicides live within us.

Charm had also come into focus for me, as an observer of depression, because of a peculiarity of my clinical work. My practice always includes patients struggling to repair relationships. Marriages fascinate me, and the respite from work with mental illness leavens the weekly mix.

But marital discord and mood disorder share territory in common. I had explored that overlap in a brief section of the book I wrote after the Prozac one, an account of theories of intimacy, *Should You Leave?* After its publication, I began to hear from an unexpected group of patients, a series of men with an identical concern. They all had a weakness for women who became depressed. At least, the men seemed, for reasons that were opaque to them, to attract that sort of woman and to be attracted by her.

One man had struggled for years with the problems of a recurrently depressed wife who went on to kill herself. He was a rough, raw giant of a guy, the type who looks invulnerable. But years of living with depression had shaken him, and then the suicide. What he feared most, in remarriage, was exposing his children for a second time to that ordeal. And yet, when he got serious with a woman he was dating, he would discover that she was prone to mood disorder. The woman had been through bouts in the past, or she let slip indicators of a suggestive family history. Of me, the man wanted to know, what led him to make that sort of choice?

Fifty years ago, this concern would have been deemed unremarkable. In doing the very thing he says he fears, a man acts out a repetition compulsion, a basic pattern of human behavior. Faced with such a case, the classical psychoanalyst would look for unconscious motivation. Why must the widower trip himself up in this particular way? If there is depression in his family of origin, is he compulsively "marrying his mother"? Does he secretly hate and fear women, so that he chooses vulnerable targets and then brings out the worst in them? Does his castration anxiety move him to seek out a weak partner? Is sexual perversion at issue—sadism masked as solicitude? A careful practitioner would have resisted jumping to conclusions, but these sorts of questions formed a template for an answer that might be expected to emerge over time. And it is true enough that memory, longing, and cruelty do mingle to create destructive and self-destructive patterns of behavior.

Today, we tend to ask whether seemingly problematic aspects of a patient's story are best understood as normative or adaptive. That approach compacts and isolates pathology: Let's set *these* complaints aside and focus on *those*. Perhaps we ought to address the anxiety (in this case, the worry that one chooses perversely in romance), not the behavior (the choice itself) that the patient says makes him anxious.

I was especially open to that tactic since I was in the midst of my scrap-and-shard depression project. Here were men who said they were drawn to mood disorder in others. That claim connects to issues of social value. How pathological—how perverse—is it, to find charm in depression?

Well, it may just be that vulnerability to depression is very common. If a man defines the condition broadly ("prone to mood disorder," "bouts in the past," "suggestive family history"), scores of women will meet his criteria. The men I was working with would oscillate between their core concern (*I end up with depressed women*) and this very exculpation (*we live amid depression*). They would say that to love women is to love depression—or to accept it.

I should add that this perspective is hardly limited to men who worry over their involvement with unstable women. Depressed men and women themselves make similar claims: *But everyone's depressive.* They see signs of mood disorder everywhere, in the way that some gay men, only half jokingly, find repressed homosexuality ubiquitous. This contention, universal depression, emerges in psychotherapy when my own viewpoint peeks out—a belief that most people muddle through happily enough, despite life's setbacks. A patient will challenge me: *But I don't know anyone like that—contented in marriage, fulfilled at work.* Her few insistently cheerful acquaintances the depressed patient will dismiss as freaks of nature.

Of course, with depressives, it may be a matter of having surrounded themselves with other depressives—of having created an unchallenging subculture of friends who see the world as they do. Men and women do seem to take one another's degree of melancholy into account when marrying. Compared with married people whose spouses are free of mood disorder, husbands or wives of depressives are twice as likely to be diagnosed with or treated for depression. The phenomenon has been looked at repeatedly, and most studies conclude that the similarity has to do with choice. Depressives seek out depressives.

They may say they do not. If the marriage precedes the first symptoms, the patient may protest, *But how could I have known?* The nondepressed husbands with depressed wives asked the same question.

Often we do know—or might, were we observant. Depression has its precursors. We will look at them in detail when we return to *what de-*

pression is. There will be few surprises. Moodiness, as a personality trait, is a predictor of future depression. If the men drawn to depressive women did not seem perverse—and for the most part they were strikingly free of kinks—it is in part because attraction to risk factors for illness (as distinct from attraction to illness itself) is unremarkable. The pale skin that correlates with melanoma has its appeal. Behaviors that predispose to deadly disease—smoking, excessive drinking, sexual promiscuity—are notoriously seductive, or have been in their day. Moodiness carries its allure. And of course, most moody people never suffer the career of depression.

I asked my new patients what drew them to their wives, when they were still well, and what drew the wives to them. These husbands were calm and reasonable. If anything, they might be judged overly controlled. They appreciated emotionality in a woman, and sensitivity, and discernment. They did not mind a little fussiness; they associated femininity with a need to have things just so. They preferred diffidence to open self-assertion.

As for their own social strengths, these men appealed to women who valued solidity. The men were proud to be attractive on that basis. They served as anchors for storm-tossed vessels. They chose mates on the principle that opposites attract—the more contrast, the better.

After that: a claim of ignorance and innocence. A man offers support. He does his all to make the marriage work—given the demands of business, given real-life constraints. We may believe this account or not. Perhaps these reasonable men drive their wives up the wall. But the husbands' version meets a standard of plausibility. A man could choose in that way, choose vulnerability indirectly, through experiencing a particular sort of desire, connected to a conventional vision of the feminine—intense emotionality and deference to the strong male. In a course of psychotherapy, we will consider a combination of causes for repeated social failures: the man seeks out depressive women and then drives them to grief, or merely disappoints. And here it could be a matter of sadism or a more innocuous pattern.

What is less remarkable, finally, than this story? A man is a bit mechanical emotionally. He is attracted to the dimension he lacks—to moody women, women with *depth*. These very women seek him out. And then, down the road, the good he offers, stability, no longer suffices. A woman finds him insufficiently supportive in a time of renewed stress—not fully available, by her standards. She feels isolated. She succumbs to depression—because of her husband's shortcomings, or for quite other reasons, related to genes and early bad experience and adversity that preceded the marriage. She may, like Margaret, in her years with Gregory, succumb to an "untriggered" depression, incongruous with her present circumstances.

Given these constraints, these social probabilities, perhaps the series of depressed girlfriends and wives is simply bad luck. Although, from another angle, it might be argued that something like the charm of affliction is playing its part after all—the charm, at the least, of liability to depression, the charm of moodiness and vulnerability.

The more I thought about the phenomenon with my patients, the more it struck me that to be charmed by the precursors of depression, like moodiness or obvious fragility in the face of stress, is ordinary, routine, unremarkable. Depressives are drawn to hints of depression in others; so are the sturdy and stolid. In therapy, I might make a remark to this effect, in hopes of drawing a patient out.

Often, this therapeutic approach failed—the effort to minimize my patient's anxiety by turning our focus away from depression and toward traits that are only risk factors, at some distance from frank disease. I should have known that it would, that it deserved to fail, or to succeed only partially—should have known from my experience reading autopathography, where suicidal impulses capture readers' sympathy. It is not only vulnerability that appeals, or emotional openness. As I let my patients speak, it became apparent that many were drawn to mood disorder quite directly.

Eight

❖

Eros

PROVOCATIVE THOUGH IT MAY BE, the claim *depression charms* does not go far enough. Depression partakes of the erotic.

Occasionally in my practice, I will see a woman who sustains what strikes me as an extraordinary social career. She will be plagued by depression, and in particular by a trio of symptoms: lassitude, apathy, and anhedonia. That is, she will lack the energy or inclination to throw herself into any task or look forward to any activity. She will for the most part remain passive and withdrawn—certainly not focused on dating. She will perhaps be only ordinarily attractive physically, and uninterested in tending to her appearance. And she will be like catnip to a certain sort of man, a type that must exist in abundance.

My impression is that such women's popularity arises not despite but directly from their depression. Their exhaustion bears a family resemblance to Marlene Dietrich's languorousness. I am thinking of the trait that Josef von Sternberg, the director, highlighted when he cast Dietrich as Lola Lola in *The Blue Angel*. There Dietrich sings "Falling in

Love Again," an anthem of indifference that became her signature. The enervated vamp is not to blame for her dalliances. She *just can't help it*. Alfred Hitchcock took a similar tack, in *Stage Fright*, when he had Dietrich style herself (in Cole Porter's lyric) "The Laziest Gal in Town." The women whom Dietrich portrays desire little, and they promise nothing in the way of follow-through. These characters may not suffer from depression. For that matter, they may not meet a realist's standards of psychological coherence or credibility. But they do embody a form of sensuality that incorporates and popularizes depressive traits.

Indifference can signal strength. Often that is how potential lovers see it, as a challenge to be overcome. But for the depressed, indifference arises from weakness, an inability to care about one's own fate, even an absence of self-protective instinct. Early in my psychotherapy training, I went through a phase of reading Jean Rhys novels, accounts of passive young women preyed on by the socially adept. The heroines are virtuosos of lassitude, apathy, and anhedonia. They are not victimizers but victims. As readers, we dislike the men (and sometimes, their wives) who would take advantage of a vulnerable young woman, but we find their appetites plausible.

Here it seems less a matter of romanticizing melancholy than of melancholizing romance—*defining* romance in terms of emotional deficit. Affective blandness, social withdrawal, anomie, alienation— according to the decadent aesthetic, each symptom of depression is sexually stimulating. The woman who waits impassively in the darkened room, insouciant, nonchalant, inattentive to the future, anesthetized to disaster, requiring arousal, demanding the bold gesture—which man is so wholesome that he has not pursued her once, this dramatic heroine?

In the movies, this pursuit ends in disaster. In life, it will on occasion lead to a satisfying outcome in the long term. The seeming siren may be amicable and reliable, once she enters a secure social relationship and her depressive symptoms diminish. She will lose her operatic allure but gain companionable traits that wear well over time.

Is melancholy an ideal of inter- and postwar decadence only? Or has the genre *romance* enshrined depressive traits for much longer? The image of the passionate-but-depressive woman prevailed for well over a century. The two great novels by men about women, the two that qualify for the conventional label of classic, *Anna Karenina* and *Madame Bovary*—how is it that they both end in the heroine's suicide? For Emma Bovary, we can substitute Chateaubriand's *Atala*, at the origins of the romantic novel, or Zola's *Thérèse Raquin*, at the genre's end. There is no lack of eponymous heroines ready to take their own lives. Sex and suicide, adultery and suicide, these are constant pairings in the romantic imagination.

Nor is only female attractiveness at issue. Goethe's "young Werther" and Chateaubriand's René, the former a suicide and the latter nearly so, embody a male romantic ideal. The brooding, unreachable young man, the rebel without a cause, the neglected younger brother, the sardonic outsider, careening on his spiraling downhill course—what woman can resist his dark appeal? Here sometimes what is at issue is mutual masochism, the depressive in one calling out to the depressive in the other. But even to quite stable women, depression can seem attractive. The glum and indecisive intellectual, the bitter and isolated observer of life—constellations of traits that look a good deal like depression serve even in middle age to define a certain sort of fascinating man.

Does this speculation go too far, that chronic depression informs high romance? I have observed love affairs that seem spurred on by depression—seen them from over the shoulder of the besotted lover. Men can be obsessed with depressed women, and inexplicably, as if this one urge—to feel the force of a lover's moodiness—had the power to overwhelm every sober consideration.

One example will stand for a small handful. I have had to camouflage the story even more than usual, because they can be so public, these operatic entanglements.

Harry was a successful business entrepreneur in a failed marriage. He was open to brief affairs and accustomed to pursuit by women ready, as he saw it, to latch on to a good thing. The wife was acid, bitter, unsatisfied. She did what she could to slow the divorce.

Harry had met a woman at a cocktail party. What he liked about Mariana initially was her diffidence. In contrast to the gushing, bubbly types who pursued Harry, Mariana appeared reserved and self-contained. Once approached and drawn out, Mariana proved sharp-witted, in a way that threw Harry off balance. At the same time, she remained ethereal. In midsentence, she might look past Harry, as if her inner world were more compelling than any casual conversation.

I love her smile, Harry told me more than once, as if this fact explained a good deal. Harry was not given to elaboration. I came to believe that what captivated him was his occasional power to elicit that smile, to make Mariana warm up despite herself.

The cocktail party was one of Mariana's few forays from home. She would agree to see Harry sporadically and—spurning his offers of expensive entertainments—almost only at her apartment. Her living room had a cavelike quality—dimly lit, decorated with small primitive objects each with its proper place. This was on winter nights.

For dinner, Mariana fed Harry what she had on hand, delicacies in small quantity, or she would set out treats he had brought along. She seemed scarcely to eat. She wore gauzy outfits from secondhand shops. She lived on air.

Generally the evening would end in lovemaking. Now and then, Mariana could be avid. More often, she would be all but absent, as if waiting for Harry to have his way and leave. Her passivity, her lethargy, her open apathy looked like honesty and authenticity. Sometimes, the evening would end with agitation—Mariana's quietness turning to despair when Harry neglected her in some minor regard.

Harry found himself addicted—jealous, even though he knew Mariana wandered out only on errands. He was convinced that she would leave him for someone worthier if ever she gathered the energy to socialize. This fear was never realized. The affair continued for months, throughout the whole of the end-game of the divorce. The wife was furious over it.

Harry was confused. Mariana was not the woman he wanted. He had been looking for a young companion who was simultaneously practical and showy.

When I asked Harry what kind of romantic partner he imagined he would end up with, he answered in concrete terms. An expert skier and sailor, like his friends' wives. A woman who could decorate and oversee first, second, and third homes. But Harry could not let go his attachment to a recluse. What was wrong with him?

Mariana asked for nothing. She had a few dollars, apparently, through her mother. She did Web site design, via the Internet. At first, she was pleased when Harry sent clients her way. Then she said, no, these referrals made her feel pressured. Which was just as well, since Mariana's work habits had sometimes embarrassed Harry. Mariana was skilled but unreliable.

She seemed the same way in the relationship. Mariana understood Harry. Her opinions about his business relationships proved practical. He found himself acting on her advice. She could be equally incisive about Harry's narcissism. It was hard to tell whether she favored honesty or simply (in her depression) lacked the energy, forethought, and determination a person needs to engage in pretense.

If Mariana could be perceptive and helpful, she could also shut Harry out for weeks, with scant explanation. Sometimes he would show up and find her a wreck, overwhelmed by a minor setback. In the summer, Mariana would agree to accompany Harry on drives to the country, or on business trips. But she canceled frequently or stood Harry up. She was not cruel so much as erratic, distracted.

It was a mixture of fantasies for Harry. Mariana was his alone, a sleeping beauty repeatedly wakened by his kiss. She was a maiden in distress. She was unattainable, capricious, *mobile* like the wind.

Harry understood his infatuation this far: he said Mariana represented a counterbalance to the purposive, commercial, driven world he lived in. He admired that she did what she pleased, although sometimes it seemed only that she was doing what she was able. I worried that Harry was projecting virtues onto Mariana, that he was blind to her illness.

Once the divorce was final, Harry said he wanted to end the relationship with Mariana as well, so that he could turn toward finding a happy life. But he was overcome with a sudden, terminal illness, a fulminant leukemia. The will left a substantial sum to Mariana. The ex-wife was uncomprehending and told me so. She demanded to know whether I had tried to bring Harry to his senses—to open his eyes to Mariana's wiles.

Yes and no.

I had tried to help Harry make sense of what he found confusing. We ran through the perspectives that might be applied to an infatuation or compulsion. Theories of personality—why a man is narcissistic or nurturing or open to being treated arbitrarily. And theories of relationship—fixed patterns based on early disappointments, needs arising from idiosyncrasies of self-image, attempts to atone for the failed marriage in the new affair. There was no lack of curiosity, I want to say, nor of structures to channel it.

But I *had* tried to bring Harry to his senses in quite direct fashion. She's depressed—I had said that often. I never intended that the comment should be decisive. I admire those who can love the ill, and the mentally ill in particular. (Had Mariana been my patient, I might have hoped to see the relationship succeed.) At the same time, it seemed to me that good faith required telling Harry how his account of Mariana's behaviors added up, to a psychiatrist.

I thought Mariana was in need of treatment. I thought suicide was a risk. As was progression of the disease—the emergence of more disabling symptoms and an increased ratio of bad days to good.

I said: "For her sake, see if you can persuade her to get evaluated."

And again: "If I am right, then if you stay with Mariana, you are in for predictable difficulties."

But depression was not an important category for Harry. It did not occupy much room in his universe of explanations for human behavior.

And here we would stumble onto the wife's question, about Mariana's wiles.

By his own account, Harry was drawn to Mariana because she held back, because she surprised, because she marched to her own drummer. Often, those traits signal independence. They indicate confidence in the dating game—the ability to play cards skillfully, even when the stakes are high. In this instance, I thought, the identical behaviors might signal illness.

When Martin Luther posts the theses and says he *can do no other*, we admire him because the imperative is a matter of conscience. Safer courses are open to Luther, but his faith constrains him to this one. If a man in Luther's position were so obsessed as to be robbed of freedom of action, then he, too, could *do no other*—but we might admire him less. To act from independence is one thing, from compulsion, another.

To return to the dilemma I was facing with Harry, in the course of the psychotherapy: Mariana's circumstance lies between these extremes, between free will and the determinism that ill health imposes. Whatever she does is inflected by her taste and judgment. When I say, *Don't you see that she's depressed?* I am pointing to the compelled element in her behavior. But I know what Harry's ex-wife would say, and I do not entirely disagree: Mariana deploys depressive traits well.

The assumption that troubles me, the one I want to put at issue for Harry, involves the significance of Mariana's posture. Is she a rebel against the values of consumerism, competition, and crassness? I say, Not so completely as might at first appear.

We have an imperfect notion at best of Mariana's ideals. We do not know whether if she were well, if she were free, she would despise materialism, striving, and small talk. We know that she has trouble leaving her house, trouble socializing, trouble following through at work, trouble maintaining a level of desire that would lead or amount to motivation. If our opinion of the contemporary culture is negative enough—if Harry has sufficient contempt for himself and those who love him— then we may be at risk of misreading the depressive's incapacity as principled resistance to social norms.

Certainly, I have seen people recover from depression and participate vigorously in routine social behaviors—the very (competitive, acquisitive) ones they seemed when depressed to scorn. I am not referring only to cure via medication, which we may mistrust, if we understand antidepressants as conformity-inducing. I mean spontaneous remission, or a response to bright lights, or to psychotherapy, or to magnetic stimulation of the brain. I mean any recovery from depression at all, not omitting the joyous, sudden recoveries that, as I have confessed from the start, color my view of the illness.

Can any one perspective embrace the whole truth? Perhaps (to adopt the ex-wife's viewpoint) Mariana is no less skilled a temptress if her wiles arise from, or consist of, illness.

In the case at hand, I am pointing to a worry. I suspect that Harry is misreading social cues. He takes Mariana as devil-may-care, where she may be merely erratic in her responses to his overtures. He loves Mariana in the midst of her chronic depression and because of that depression. He does not make this misreading (if it is one) in a solitary way, but as a participant in a culture in which rebelliousness, sensuality, and depressive traits mingle in a standard romantic ideal.

There is this about practice in a small city: you learn how incidents turn out. Sometimes history is conclusive. Three months after Harry's death, Mariana was hospitalized for depression. She recovered poorly— although it is fair to say that she had not been doing well in the months that Harry knew her.

We have examples aplenty of devotion to partners who develop illness. C. S. Lewis's deepening attachment to Joy Davidman as she struggled with bone cancer (the story is the subject of Lewis's memoir *A Grief Observed* and the movie *Shadowlands*) has periodically provided a popular model for romantic love. John Bayley's care for Iris Murdoch as her mind gave way to Alzheimer's disease (as recounted in his *Elegy for Iris* and elsewhere) represents a similar ideal. In each instance, it is not the illness that elicits affection or passion, but rather the injured beloved's integrity in the face of deterioration. Also, we admire Bayley and Lewis for overcoming a natural aversion to disease.

With depression, it is not always a case of resisting revulsion. Depression produces suffering without disfigurement, a combination suited to eliciting fantasies of nurturance and rescue. The symptoms and even the state of illness—Mariana in her passivity—can be attractive, and in ways that do not seem especially perverse. To a degree, this difference is simply fortunate. We want the ailing to be valued and cared for.

Still, it is striking how the social response to depression gives rise to paradox and oxymoron. Depression is alluring and pathological, admirable and destructive. In depression, we have a disease that (in terms of *what it is to us*) contains moral worth and erotic appeal.

These attributions are depression's differences, its more and its less. They cover distinctive territories. To say that depression should not be eradicated because it spawns creativity is different than to say we are drawn to the depressed sensually, without quite knowing why. But of course, the regions overlap. The depressive is self-absorbed and self-critical, a posture that mimics the brave stance (important to both art and romance) of the Socratic hero dedicated to the examined life. By long-standing convention, the male melancholic—artist, poet, adventurer, seducer—is brave and desirable. The Lady of Shallot, in poem and painting, represents a moral, aesthetic, and romantic ideal—a woman too sensitive for cruel reality, weaving beauty, loving and loverless, wasting away.

For me, Harry's infatuation with Mariana was not an isolated instance of the erotic power of depression. I was treating a collection of men in similar circumstances. Often their attraction was not to women bearing up under the strain of depression but to women submerged in mood disorder, women who were failing. To these were added the usual cases of depressed young women who (having rejected a series of supportive and caring suitors) told of finding themselves in relationships with depressed and narcissistic young men who, for their part, might have provided a similar and complementary story. In fact, because of the additive impacts of *Listening to Prozac* and *Should You Leave?* I had become, by attribution, an authority on issues of mood disorder and intimacy, and so was witnessing the attractions of depressions in every imaginable form. Puzzling out the origins of these attachments, and helping patients make fine distinctions between competing inclinations, consumed an ever greater part of the workday.

To understand my mental condition, you need to think of a layering of events. Conversations with readers, encounters with memoirs, work with patients like Emily who located their superiority in symptoms of depression—all these took place simultaneously and were accompanied, in counterpoint, by the accumulating evidence about depression's status as an insidious, progressive disease. Everywhere, I saw a chasm between *what it is* and *what it is to us*, between pathology and charm. Looking into the gap induced a sort of vertigo.

In this altered state, I began to wonder how the prevalence and intractability of this particular disease, major depression, had shaped our views of diverse, if interrelated, concepts—character, beauty, morality, the good life. Outside the consulting room—with friends over dinner, or amid strangers in a museum gallery, or alone at my writing desk—I found myself asking strange questions, ones with no obvious connection to depression, the disease, or only a slight and indirect one. Why is loss an especially sublime subject for art? Why is pessimism the proper stance for intellectuals? Why are melancholic traits profound? Most of these question I dismissed or forgot. But a few I saved, to add to my odd collection—out of a suspicion that, not for me alone, but for many people who made this transition, taking depression as *disease simply* might color any number of habits of mind.

Nine

❖

Obvious Confusion: Three Vignettes

i

FROM CHILDHOOD, I have found museums soothing and transporting. My habit, when I travel for my books, is to spend any downtime in museums.

It is 1997. *Should You Leave?* has just reached the stores, and I am off on the media circuit. You would think I had just written about antidepressants again. Interviewers ignore marriage and ask about mood disorders. My new book does contain stories that bear on the topic. But the press is confining me to territory I thought I had mostly left behind, and which I had always inhabited uneasily. I am grinding my teeth.

And so I head off to a museum, to take in an exhibition of Picasso's early work. Picasso is an artist I have loved uncritically, the major pieces and the throwaways. I am looking forward to the show.

Painting and sketches from Picasso's childhood line a corridor that turns back on itself to lead the viewer to the canvases of the late teenage years. Picasso is mimicking established artists, but he displays technical virtuosity and the genius-student's ability to make each style his own. I have the thought the curator doubtless intends, "What talent!"

Suddenly at the end of the corridor, and now opening out dramatically to the right, there they are—the paintings of the blue period. And not just any selections, the most painful ones. The curator has selected pieces arising directly from Picasso's response to the suicide of his friend, Carles Casagemas: *Head of the Dead Casagemas, Casagemas in His Coffin, The Burial of Casagemas*. My response is automatic: "How profound!"

This thought, too, is one the curator has aimed for, is it not? That intent seems to me implicit in the arrangement, the way these canvases lie in wait to surprise and overwhelm.

Here is a death head of Casagemas, and now another. Then a mother with her eyes shut, now a mother with her back to us, and here another crouching and unseeing, images of desolation and resignation. Two women sit at a bar, slouched toward each other, an empty absinthe glass between them. Conventional gestures of melancholy abound—women with shoulders slumped and heads canted, in the classic habitus. Here, a trio—barefoot man, boy, and woman—stands on a featureless beach. The figures' eyes are downcast. Too much space surrounds them. The boy appears to be touching the man for comfort; no response is apparent. "Tragedy" is the label.

What are we to find in this collection? Surely, the quality required for greatness: depth.

The response to my own work shapes my attitude in the gallery. Petulance wells up. I think, Profound how? What confers those qualities, the ones linked to greatness? What is the strength of that link?

I flip through the show's catalogue. It features an essay on Gustave Coquiot, an early-twentieth-century critic unfavorably disposed to the blue period, on the grounds that it is derivative. Picasso voices his own dismissive opinion of the blue period work: "nothing but sentiment." It is easy to see what he means; the "*Greedy Child*" spooning out her porridge bowl is a weeper if ever there was one. Turning back—looking up the corridor—it is possible to imagine how a critic might judge the earlier work to be freer and tougher, more astonishing in the way it cap-

tures character and circumstance. But the exhibition seems to stand
against disparaging judgments, Coquiot's or Picasso's or the viewer's
own. The dramatic placement of the paintings cries out "deep."

Deep how? Properly speaking, isn't profundity in graphic art a matter
of vision and representation? Of seeing the world as no one has seen it
before, or of reminding us of how we sometimes do see it?

Does the blue period amount to a technical or stylistic breakthrough?
The folding brochure that comes with the entry ticket says otherwise.
"The monochromatic use of blue was not uncommon in symbolist
painting in Spain or France, where it was associated with representa-
tions of melancholy or despair." Is it that these somber images forecast
the future of art? I recall one of Picasso's erotic sketches. He cannot
have been twenty when he made it—surely the drawing would be included here were we not puritanical. A woman's body stretches diago-
nally away from the viewer, but her face is seen from above, and the
vagina full on. I came upon the sketch years ago, in an exhibit where it
held its place in a sequence culminating in analytic cubism.

Despite its technical brilliance, despite its aesthetic prescience, despite its complexity, that early sketch elicited no gasp of "deep." The
erotic may be provocative or liberating, when it is not merely tawdry
and degrading. But in conventional terms, the erotic is not profound.

I try to conjure up the mood of that other room, with the cubism display, and of the many-perspectived sketch. Did the woman, a prostitute
I presume, embody the existential isolation implicit in the Casegamas-
inspired paintings? I recall a certain pathos. Now it occurs to me that I
may have imposed that sense of loneliness on the work. As an uptight
American, I considered a sophisticated, continental undertone of alienation to be redemptive in a work of art. But why precisely does the conjuring of inner emptiness confer depth? The erotic picture found joy in
the sensual, the dirty. Taken directly, it conveyed the response to a
woman's body that you might hear on shock-jock talk radio: "How
great is that!"

A salacious exclamation may understate the dramatic tension within
the sketch, the dialectic between the delicacy of the female form and

the rawness of intimate anatomy—between classical ideal and porno-graphic frankness, between adoration and lust. The erotic sketch was accomplished and innovative and multifaceted. It contained its own complexity of vision. But it mined aspects of the human condition absent in the blue period work—exuberance, appetite, an appreciation of the exquisite in the ordinary.

More than technique or novelty or sophistication of viewpoint, what distinguishes the blue period is its subject matter. Joy and lust and a love of what life offers are not profound. Suicide is profound. Grief is profound, and emptiness, and despair.

A confession: one of the blue period canvases has elicited an idiosyn-cratic response. I have seen and admired *Tragedy* often before, on its home turf, in the National Gallery in Washington. Today, it seems to me that the stoop-shouldered, raven-haired woman, her head tilted in the iconic posture of melancholy, bears a physical resemblance to a pa-tient I treated for ten years. It is a matter of the mutual imitation of art and life—posture, hairstyle, drape of clothing, chiseling of facial fea-tures. Or of my fevered imagination.

An internist referred Eva during my years of hospital practice. He had worked her up for a wasting disease, which turned out to be depression, or pathological grief. Eva was a Czech Jew who had trained as an athlete in her school years. In early adulthood, she emigrated, after a series of failed efforts that involved risk and humiliation. Later, she managed to get her mother and sister out as well. Three years after their arrival, both contracted cancer. They died within two months of each other.

Eva grieved, recovered, returned to work—she was a physical educa-tion teacher—and then slid back into a lingering depression that in-cluded months of insomnia and self-starvation. In all likelihood, antidepressants saved her life. They allowed her to sleep and eat, and then to put together a semester without sick days. She remained moody and apathetic. It was in these years that Eva looked like a Picasso, gravely beautiful, her face strained by the effort of living.

Like a character in a Borges story, Eva was memorious—seemingly incapable of forgetting a single detail of past misfortunes. Her year was filled with anniversaries: her mother's death, her sister's, the day each entered the hospice, the initiation of various cancer treatments, the exit from Eastern Europe, the arrival here, the sister's and mother's birthdays, and every holiday on the Jewish calendar. Each was the occasion for the return of overwhelming despair. Eva was battered regularly, from the inside. It was five years before she managed to reclaim a social life. At that point, she came off medication and cut back her visits to me. It was another five years before she marched through twelve months unscathed.

There is dignity in a prolonged recovery—but always, I would trade a bushel of sad grace for a peck of resilience. Despair and estrangement are understandable responses to loss. But if mourning lingers, it seems to me that we honor it in part because we must, because our ability to moderate hopelessness is limited. Often, what psychiatrists combat is not difficult emotion but an inability to emerge from it—not emptiness, but endless emptiness. An interval of grief followed by an increasing and finally a full turning toward the world—doesn't this sequence contain nobility enough?

This thought is doctorly, I know, but it is mine. It causes me to wonder about Picasso's intention. His is not the classic version of tragedy, with flaws of hubris punished. Picasso's sufferers are blameless and bereft. We are invited, so I imagine, to unite with these figures in their pain and to share their loss of direction. What are we to make of the man's unresponsiveness to the boy's touch? Is isolation what we triumph over or what we experience, when we see existence as it is? Should tragedy purge and uplift the viewer, as Aristotle imagined? Or are we meant simply to join these figures in devastation? Perhaps it is the gauntness of the man that worries me, an indication of chronicity, of the utter defeat that wastes body and mind. Standing before the image, seeing Eva superimposed, I am slightly nauseated by the notion that intractable despair is an ideal.

It hardly matters whether I am accurate about the history of art. I am dealing in autobiography. All I insist upon is that I did have (and then recoiled from) this immediate response in the gallery hall—profound! That, and the likelihood that awareness of profundity is the normative response, the one a curator has every right to anticipate in the viewer. The association of *despairing* with *deep* is so fixed, I am saying, so automatic that we scarcely realize that it *is* a pairing, a metaphor composed of two distinct elements.

Approaching the end of a corridor within an exhibition space, I glimpsed a cleft in a solid structure—a tiny fissure between deep and depressed. I confess that I was otherwise at a bad juncture, and not only as a writer. My clinical practice weighed on me—my failures with patients whose illness was obdurate. I saw in my patients' suffering not an enhancement of their humanity but the failure of my methods.

My doubts about the blue period were fleeting. One further glance at *Tragedy*, and the disturbance passed. How noble this family seemed— prototypically human, estranged from one another and the uncaring universe. A different mundane doctorly thought intervened: How grateful I would be for art as a memorial, or a vehicle for grief, were it my patient who had committed suicide, or my patient's friend.

When people hedge their answers to the eradication thought-experiment, part of what worries them is attitudes like the one I experienced momentarily. How far must it go, the opposition to depression? Will we no longer give despair its due? In discussion, I might have been inclined to say that depression can be opposed cleanly, without throwing into question our admiration for alienation or protracted grief. My interval of resistance to the obvious—to the depth of the blue period— gave me pause. Although it seemed like an adventure as well, to see where a new sort of awareness about depression might lead.

ii

A publisher invites me to contribute an introduction to a new edition of Carl Rogers's classic work *On Becoming a Person*. Conscious of the honor, I accept, but with misgivings. In his day, forty years back, Rogers was "The Psychologist of America." Now he is scorned, certainly in academia, as shallow.

My own experience in the public eye has made me mistrust reputations. I reread Rogers's books. The observations are precise, the arguments insightful. The science is advanced for its day. And I am left to wonder: how is it that Rogers is not an intellectual?

Rogers's essays are meticulous, informed by exquisite attentiveness to what patients say. I wish my sessions sounded more like his. And then, the theory is extraordinary.

Before Rogers, psychoanalysts tried to starve patients emotionally. The intent was to heighten the patient's anxiety, in order to motivate intense self-exploration. The resulting "free associations" would become the subject of tough interpretation, which would initiate change. But what if that process proved too harsh for most patients?

Rogers suggested that, in psychotherapy, optimizing anxiety usually means minimizing it. He observed that when you interpret an utterance, a patient will clam up; but if you support the affect—if you empathize—a patient will extend his line of thought. Rogers measured the differences between responses to interpretation and responses to empathy. He was the first to bring statistical rigor to studies of the process of psychotherapy, the first to use audiotapes and rating instruments.

Psychoanalysts have long acted as if they discovered the importance of empathy independently. They didn't. They stole from Rogers. In his day, Rogers was one of the great rebels against the prevailing orthodoxy of psychoanalysis. He said that the emperor had no clothes. Rogers did so from within clinical practice, on the basis of patient observation.

Rogers was remarkably effective. His writings changed beliefs within and without the professions. It was Rogers, not Benjamin Spock, who first envisaged a less authoritarian form of American public education, in which children would be trusted to find their own way. Pastoral counseling is mostly Rogerian. The concept of marriage that prevailed for much of the late twentieth century—the notion that an ideal relationship functions as a base for individual self-fulfillment, and not simply emotional merger—can be traced to Rogers's writing. Rogers's social positions can sound dated, but they were useful as a counterbalance to prior orthodoxies. In some future liberal resurgence, they might prevail again.

Popular audience aside, Rogers's credentials are sterling. He had sixteen books, two hundred articles, and numerous professorships to his credit. He drew on a range of social sciences to inform his work—animal ethology, anthropology, social psychology, and general systems theory. Rogers conversed in public with such figures as Martin Buber, Paul Tillich, Michael Polanyi, and Hans Hofmann.

The more I read, the more I wondered: How was Rogers not an intellectual? It did not help that Rogers was Midwestern, even rural, in his origins and mannerisms. (Rogers was born in Chicago but moved to the country at age twelve. He said his respect for the experimental method arose from his having, in adolescence, read a long text called *Feeds and Feeding*.) But the fatal impediment—so I came to believe, in the course of writing the introduction—was temperament. Rogers was cheery. He was comfortable with himself and others.

By convention, intellectuals are European pessimists. They are darkly complex. They are ill at ease in society. They struggle against inner demons. After World War II especially, Kafka became the model of an intellectual, or Kierkegaard.

Now, here is the strange thing. Rogers worshipped Kierkegaard. Rogers held alienation from the authentic self to be the core problem of modern man. The (difficult) goal of life, and the method of recovery in psychotherapy, according to Rogers, is "to be that self which one truly is." Rogers's most important book is named after the central task, becoming a person. *Rogerian therapy is applied Kierkegaard.*

Of course, Rogers's take on alienation differed from the existential version that prevailed in his time and ever since. Rogers agreed that alienation signals a problem, but he had hopes that the problem might be diminished. About this prospect, he was reasonably upbeat.

What is the relationship between alienation and gloom? In the wake of *Listening to Prozac*, an eminent medical ethicist tried to specify his unease with the new medication. Of an imagined prescribing psychiatrist, the philosopher demanded: "What could he say to an alienated Sisyphus as he pushed the boulder up the mountain? That he would push the boulder more enthusiastically, more creatively, more insightfully, if he were on Prozac?"

That question cut to the quick. Camus's Sisyphus has been my boon companion since first I met him, in solitary hours of reading in the high school library. I had been a sixties college student—if not a blazing radical, then a few steps shy. Had I now become a foe of alienation, or of resistance to arbitrary authority?

As an observer, I do want Sisyphus to understand his predicament. But what is the affect appropriate to subjugation? The gods intend for Sisyphus to suffer. His rebellion, his fidelity to self, rests on the refusal to be worn down. If Sisyphus is a hero, it is because he faces endless futility without succumbing to despair.

In the Prozac fantasy, of cosmetic psychopharmacology, we are to imagine a medication that lends confidence and resilience. Isn't that what Sisyphus has, what he exemplifies? Sisyphus is precisely creative and insightful, and he may have a measure of enthusiasm as well, once he understands the terms of his resistance.

That is the premise of Camus's essay. Because life engages him, Sisyphus can resist. For him, the walk down the mountain serves as an interval of freedom. In that momentary autonomy is his victory over those who would enslave him. "Happiness and the absurd are two sons of the same earth," Camus writes. "They are inseparable." It is not that discovery of the absurd allows for happiness, no. It's the other way round. Awareness of the absurd, according to Camus, "springs from happiness." That we feel joy despite our burdens is what opens our eyes to our condition. No again, Camus says, correcting himself in a memorable coda. It is not only during the downhill steps that Sisyphus exercises freedom. "The struggle itself toward the heights is enough to fill a man's heart. One must imagine Sisyphus happy."

I suspect that it was the automatic pairing of depth and depression that made the medical philosopher propose Sisyphus (if sarcastically) as a candidate for mood enhancement. We forget that the alienated can experience elation, that happiness can lead to awareness of absurdity. I want to reclaim Sisyphus, to set his image on the poster for the campaign against depression. Grief would be the rock's victory, or the oppressors'; joy is Sisyphus's and ours.

Sisyphus is who we (or my patients) might be if we could get the medication right, or the psychotherapy or the personal quest. Sisyphus is who we are when we are not hobbled by genetic handicap or brain cell atrophy, when we have withstood the traumas of childhood and stresses of adult life. Sisyphus exemplifies the capacity to remain whole in the face of adversity. Autonomy and authenticity and even awareness of absurdity, Camus says, rest on happiness.

I wondered whether the medical philosopher assumed that to mitigate depression or depressive traits is to dull awareness. Camus says that it is happiness that allows us to take the measure of our predicament. Like the story of Sisyphus, the example of Rogers stands in contradiction to the equation of sadness and complexity. Rogers is happy and observant. He builds a psychotherapy, a model of marriage, and a theory of education around the premise that our society distances individuals from experience of the self. Rogers dedicates his life to the problem of alienation, and yet he shows no signs of depression. He is provocatively stable, calm, reassuring, sunny, free of neurosis.

Taken this way, Carl Rogers is the answer to the question What if Prozac had been available in Kierkegaard's day? (Equally, Sisyphus is the answer.) Given resilience, given freedom from melancholy, a man can still see the central problem of alienation—can build a life around it, a life of the mind. I don't mean to put Rogers on Kierkegaard's level in term of originality or humor—only to say that it is not clear to what extent depression is a requirement for vision.

That was what I wrote in my introduction to *On Becoming a Person*. A sanguine Midwesterner can embrace alienation as a predicament without succumbing to pessimism. Enthusiasm should not be an absolute impediment to membership in the community of intellectuals.

iii

Another museum visit.

Some months after the Picasso encounter, I find myself in London. I am there for a medical ethics conference. The publisher of the British edition of *Should You Leave?* has scheduled a strategy session. She has piggybacked on visits with feature writers and magazine editors. In a spare hour, I duck out to the old Tate Gallery to catch a Bonnard retrospective.

Before seeing the exhibit, I would have said that Bonnard was a postimpressionist, and a minor one. That was the rap on him. That he was overfond of bright and even garish color, too sunny, too decorative. His work is the opposite of profound—a feast for the eyes, let us say.

At the Tate, the temporary exhibit requires a fee. In the ticket line, I stand behind a voluble woman who is trying to convince her companion, a buttoned-down man, that the show is worth seeing. It is one of those encounters everyone relishes when visiting abroad, the local types in action. The woman is large and loud, the man slight and meek, but seemingly not without his own unspoken opinions. The pair looks like something out of James Thurber.

The woman says, "The paintings aren't just beautiful."

Her companion persists in his quiet doubt.

The woman says, "They say it's not the way you think, all jolly. His wife was mentally ill. You don't see it at first, they say, but then you start noticing the wife. He stayed loyal to her, didn't he? In the paintings, he grows older but she stays young. All that turquoise, it's a reaction against terrible pain within."

I can vouch for the general content. The woman is defending the paintings on the grounds that they are not joyous simply but (which is better) joyous in response to suffering. Or perhaps not fully joyous. Cast over with melancholy, a quality that would confer worth—justify the time and money spent on attending the exhibit.

The man, if I can read the British right, is all the more discomfited at the prospect of visiting an exhibition whose virtue arises from the artist's loyalty to a difficult wife. It is a lesson he shrinks from. And yet he buys the tickets.

• •

Not then, but later, it occurred to me that the woman's pitch for Bon-nard echoed a contrast William James discussed, in his consideration of religious experience, between the once- and twice-born. The once-born are unreflectively happy, natural believers in God's beneficence and the world's beauty. They come to religion without struggle—without wrestling with the problem of evil. They are healthy-minded. In adoles-cence, they did not bask in woe.

In contrast, the twice-born begin as sick souls. John Bunyan is twice-born. So is Leo Tolstoy, when he comes to religion through an attack of melancholy. If Bunyan and Tolstoy find faith and happiness, it is of a sort in which sadness remains an ingredient. "Their redemption," James says, "is into a universe two stories deep."

As regards religion, it should make scant difference how one comes into harmonious union with the Eternal—James is obliged to say as much. But it is easy to see which children of God he prefers. He calls Saint Teresa of Ávila a shrew, because her self-doubt seems thin. The real interest for James is in those souls who begin in uneasiness and end in tempered zeal. James hints at a hierarchy of temperament, one that denigrates sanguinity.

I will add that James had suffered from depression. In my years of immersion, I began to ask what it meant that certain of our aesthetic and intellectual preferences have been set by those who suffer—there is no other way to put it—deeply. If the unacknowledged legislators of mankind (Bunyan, Tolstoy, James) are depressives, then we might want to examine the source of our value judgments when it comes to pes-simistic views of the human condition.

In the gallery, it becomes apparent that the woman in the ticket line was right. The selection of paintings is meant to clear Bonnard of the charge of innocence. Absent from the walls is any excess of pink and purple. There are many dark canvases, and then images of Bonnard's compan-ion and finally wife, the mysterious Marthe. Familiar paintings hang here as well, dining rooms giving onto gardens, but there is an air of oddness to the whole.

Where the hint of disturbance resides might be hard to say. In peculiar expressions on Marthe's face, perhaps. Or in the repeated renderings of her body, uxoriousness taken to the level of delusion or despair. "Proximate to the point of claustrophobia" is how the catalogue describes the relationship. Simultaneously, the text refers to a "mutual acknowledgement of separateness," even a preoccupation with it. The case is being made that Bonnard—imaginer of paradisiacal landscapes, arranger of enchanted still lifes, domestic artist par excellence, obsessive portraitist of his own wife—was a master of alienation.

The image of a conventional blonde beauty, Renée Monchanty, invades the imperfect Eden. Chanty (the name she went by—these relevant facts fill the catalogue) was Bonnard's mistress briefly. In a canvas hung here, Chanty, "surrounded in a glow of warm, golden colour, is seated in a garden looking out at the painter, smiling, one cheek supported by the palm of her hand, her round blonde head set against the flatness of a tablecloth rhymed with a plate of ripe fruit." From the edge of the canvas, Marthe stares at her.

The catalogue notes that Chanty committed suicide shortly after the portrait was painted. One essayist ventures that Chanty may have died in her tub. On Chanty's death, Bonnard begins painting Marthe in her own bath, obsessively—though here it may be a matter of something like hydrotherapy, a paranoid woman finding respite in warm water. The catalogue suggests a washing compulsion.

Bonnard is quoted as saying that the work of art is a stopping of time. But the eternal youth of Marthe, to the day of her death and after, seems excessive, as if the painter were indifferent to the strain inherent in life with an aging recluse, or intent on denying it. The apparently generous attitude masks anger, the catalogue argues, and a lament for transience. In Bonnard's celebration of life is a wrestling with horror and then with death. "The contemplation of loss," is how the essayist puts it, "the acceptance that everything in nature surrenders to time."

In this sad context, even the luscious still lifes become unsettling. The curator has made Bonnard into a Stoic or (if this attribution is not contradictory) an Epicurean—one way or another, through self-denial or hedonism, braced against loss.

To be bolder: The curator has made Bonnard into van Gogh.

Before setting foot in the exhibition, I thought of Bonnard as a congenital optimist, a man who lives amid sunshine, in Provence, in Normandy, on the Riviera. A man for whom fruit is always ripe. Who cannot get enough of the most vibrant hues paint chemists can put in a tube.

In this view, I was not alone. An article about the exhibit begins, "Though the public loved his happily colored landscapes [and] his well-lit scenes of domestic life, . . . when he died in 1947 at age 79, the French painter Pierre Bonnard was viewed by many critics as a primitive generator of color who belonged far more to the nineteenth century than to the twentieth." Of course, the essay has been written to familiarize readers with the critical revision, the case made by the exhibition in the gallery, that Bonnard was dark and deep.

I accept the curator's verdict. Bonnard is twice-born. He has had to struggle to capture the least taste of bliss. This assertion seems obvious. Judgments in art can be like that. Once in fashion, they strike us as simply true.

But viewing the canvases—and otherwise professionally immersed in depression—I care less about truth than this other issue, value. Why does it *rescue* Bonnard, from the status of minor artist, to say that his wife was paranoid? That he was preoccupied with separateness? Or that his still lifes are tinged with an awareness of decay? Why does that bit of biography or that attribution of aura make the ticket worth the price?

I stand before a quartet of (almost) still lifes. A basket of fruit bathed in gold. Flowers, sitting in ocher water, in a glass Provençal jug. (Here, Marthe's hand extends into the picture.) A table hosting a compotier and plates of fruit. (Now, the heads of a cat and dog are barely visible.) Another table with a bowl of oranges in the foreground, and in the distance one of those Edenic gardens.

Surely it is these very images that once informed the critical view-point. Now I try to conjure up the old Bonnard—Bonnard's twin in a parallel universe.

This Pierre (let us call him) is a man who chooses sagely in marriage. His wife, stable and endowed with exact taste, creates little scenes of homely bliss. Pierre loves her and them, in the manner of any fortunate husband. He does stray once—such things happen—into a pleasant af-fair, with an alluring mistress. The affair wanes, the mistress moves on. Pierre's wife has the maturity to forgive her husband this one indul-gence in the artist's license. He adores her all the more. He absorbs the influences of his time—impressionism, the mania for Japanese prints and primitive sculptures, contemporary novelists' experiments with perspective. Constitutionally contented, Pierre employs his talent in the celebration of light and form and color.

We know that this alternate Bonnard is imaginable—I mean, psycho-logically coherent—because for decades experts and the public did imagine Bonnard that way. But then the still lifes were less poignant. Al-together, Bonnard's art was dismissible.

I am incompetent to discuss questions about the object of art, whether it is best appreciated independent of history or biography or a larger body of work. I just take it that art rarely is seen that way, deraci-nated. I am asking something simpler. We look at the same canvas twice. On the first occasion we believe it to have been painted by a once-born optimist, in the second, by a twice-born soul who must struggle to earn or preserve his vision of beauty. Why has the canvas gained in depth? in value? Why is the still life relieved of the label *dec-oration* and welcomed into the realm of high art only when the (invisi-ble, implicit) shadow of decay falls across the (apparent, painted) sun-flecked peach or orange or apple?

The answer to these questions is obvious. But then, what came into play for me at the Bonnard exhibit, as at the early Picasso, was the nature of the obvious. How had the obvious come to be, and might it change?

One further thought: this attribution of worth or profundity applies not only to the object of art, or to the ideas implicit in art, but also to the artist, as a person. We think less of Picasso before he has dealt with the pain of his friend's suicide, before Picasso has brought awareness of loss to the center of his consciousness. We think less of Bonnard before we understand that his bright colors are applied in despite of his wife's affliction and his mistress's sad death.

This "thinking less of" refers to an incompleteness. We might say that Picasso or Bonnard would have been thin, or half-formed, or out of touch with aspects of the self, had he not encountered loss. Nor does the mere encounter suffice. Every life includes misfortune. It is the effect of misfortune, the grievous harm, that matters. One must be wounded, brought to earth; the injury must leave its scar.

But this claim is an odd one. Thinking of the other Bonnard, the parallel being who marries sagely, the Pierre we thought we knew—there are occasions when we would be content to say that such a man is fully human. Surely, marriage to a recluse is not a prerequisite to fulfillment, nor the loss of a mistress to suicide.

To put the same concern differently: the denigration of art that arises from joy and contentment merely—the insistence on grief as depth—struck me as a cultural equivalent to what I was observing in the consulting room, the conviction, among certain depressed patients, that the psychologically resilient must subscribe to a distorted—Pollyannaish—view of reality. As a clinician, I often wonder whether this contempt for the sanguine arises from an inability to see past depression or rise above it—from the pervasive effect of depression on the mind. Like Picasso's erotica, like Carl Rogers in his embrace of Kierkegaard, the (scorned and) optimistic spouse will own a measure of complexity, self-awareness, and passion; but from within depression, those qualities are hard to appreciate. In similar fashion, it seemed to me that the pervasiveness of depression—its prevalence and intractability, for the whole of human history—might have created the aesthetic assumptions that lead us to value a Bonnard above the same canvas painted by the science-fiction double Pierre and, indeed, to value one man above the other.

I never imagined that Picasso or Bonnard suffered a mood disorder. If biographers concluded that Casagemas's suicide threw Picasso into a state of depression, the validity of that claim was, for my purposes, beside the point. My petulant or resistant thoughts were limited to doubts about this matter of *depth*. Profundity had come to take on an odd cast for me—its meaning had begun to fade or fray.

This doubt or refusal simply came over me. It was not a matter of thinking a problem through. My failure to accept the obvious, in two museum visits, was more a premonition—a suggestion of what it would be like to be more immune to the charms of depression. Or a hint about what might be at stake in a quite thoroughgoing opposition to mood disorder.

The consequences seemed to me to extend far beyond the domains of medicine and public health. Immersed in depression, I had come to question perspectives we admire, in art and in life—the tragic, the despairingly alienated, the twice-born. I suspected that many conventional tastes and values would be at risk in a culture that stood foursquare against depression, as we do against all diseases. To rethink depression would alter our notions of beauty, worth, and the good life—if not just in the ways that my private experience foreshadowed, then in others, equally consequential. That was the conclusion I drew from my repeated difficulties with the ordinary ways of responding to art and to life stories. And to do without depression—there was a topic for science fantasy! How strange altogether our tastes and values might look from the vantage of a culture in which people were more resilient in the face of adversity and protected from depressions arising out of the blue.

From within psychiatry, it seemed inevitable that the first transition would take place, toward forthright opposition to mood disorder. In response to the probes of researchers from any number of disciplines—epidemiology, health care economics, behavioral genetics, neuroanatomy, radiology, cardiology, oncology, and immunology—depression had revealed itself as a particular disease, like multiple sclerosis or lupus, and not a proxy for suffering in general or the human condition. By some accounts, depression was a paradigmatic disease, a disease that might be used to illustrate the concept of disease. There was, it seemed to me, no going back, and there could be a good deal of movement forward, toward a position in which "the eradication of depression" would seem unremarkable as a phrase and as a social goal.

What It Is

Ten

❖

Altogether Again

M Y IMPRESSION IS that few people outside the research community appreciate the degree to which the scientific understanding of depression has changed in the past decade. For forty years, researchers had been focused on the role of neurotransmitters, like serotonin and norepinephrine, in setting mood. As new technologies became available—as it became apparent that depression involves abnormalities in brain anatomy—new hypotheses came to the fore, evocative new models of what depression is.

In discussing the work of Yvette Sheline and Grazyna Rajkowska, I had begun to outline one such model, our prevailing myth. It begins with the observation of depression-associated abnormalities in the hippocampus and prefrontal cortex of the brain. Those regions, along with the amygdala and some others, form a circuit that appears to govern the core symptoms of depression, the sadness, hopelessness, lack of energy, and difficulty with memory and concentration.

The hippocampus may be of particular importance. It is the area where Fred Gage first identified new nerve cell formation in the brain, an area especially prone to change, to cell atrophy and cell growth. The hippocampus has long been known to be a key location for stress regulation in the brain. Stress regulation is interesting for two reasons. Stress is intimately linked to depression. And stress is a central element in the leading model of brain cell death.

That model results from thousands of experiments by generations of scientists. The best known is Robert Sapolsky. Sapolsky works at every level of biology, from the gene to the social group. He has long split his professional time between laboratories at Stanford University and baboon homelands in Kenya. (When I asked whether his shaggy hair and beard help with baboons, Sapolsky said no, they help with fellow humans, by signaling loyalty to sixties nonconformity.) One of Sapolsky's important roles has been as a teacher to the professions—compiling and ordering fifty years of tangled findings on stress and aging. He performed this function in his influential book *Stress, the Aging Brain, and the Mechanisms of Neuron Death* (1992), an effort updated repeatedly, in review articles.

Most research on nerve cell functioning is performed on rodents. Life is stressful for rats—the proverbial rat race, perhaps. The average aging rat suffers hippocampal shrinkage and memory loss. In overview, it appears that the aging process involves a vicious cycle. Chronic stress leads to an excess production of certain hormones. The hormones injure brain cells and interfere with cell repair, particularly in the hippocampus. Ordinarily, the hippocampus puts a brake on the production of these same hormones. In the face of hippocampal injury, hormones continue to circulate, extending the harm and preventing recovery.

In their attempt to explain just how aging harms the rat brain, scientists looked first to other conditions that cause hippocampal shrinkage and memory loss. One such affliction is Cushing's disease, an excess of hormones produced by the adrenals, small glands that sit atop the kidneys (therefore ad-renal). Normally, the adrenals help mobilize the body in the face of challenge. They perform this task by producing "stress hormones." The hormones signal various organs to postpone inessential functions, such as storing energy, and instead to act in response to threat, through "fight or flight" behaviors. To the animal stalked by predators, the stress-response system is critical for survival. But it works best in the face of acute emergencies. When the mobilization lasts too long, this protective mechanism can cause harm, by (among other things) weakening cells in the hippocampus.

Today, naturally occurring Cushing's disease is much rarer than its imitator, Cushing's syndrome, the result of artificially made stress hormones—prednisone is an example—administered by doctors to treat various illnesses. Like the naturally occurring disease, Cushing's syndrome causes hippocampal shrinkage and memory problems. Since the varieties of Cushing's syndrome have only one element in common, chronic exposure to stress hormones, the cause of the harm to the brain is unambiguous.

So: aging (in rats) and chronic exposure to stress hormones both result in hippocampal atrophy. This similarity led researchers to investigate whether stress hormones are responsible for age-related changes in brain structure and function.

The rat research indicated that, when they don't kill neurons directly, the hormones can push cells to the brink of death. In the aged brain, strokes cause more injury than they do in the young brain, and so do infections, blood clots, inflammation, low blood sugar, seizures—you name it. Prior exposure to stress (and to stress hormones) is the critical factor in this age-related vulnerability. More stress in the past makes an animal more brittle in old age. Both neurons and their protectors, glial cells, are at risk.

Much of the damage done by stress hormones is to the stress-response system itself. The brain is a complex communications network, one cell reaching out to another. In the face of stress hormones, neurons lose connective wiring. In particular, cells in the hippocampus shed receptors for incoming messages about stress. The hippocampal cells also lose dendrites, the branches that connect a neuron to neighboring cells and transmit outgoing messages. Like overwhelmed people who withdraw from social contact, overwhelmed neurons in the hippocampus become isolated.

Ordinarily, the hippocampus signals the adrenals to end the stress response, but a damaged hippocampus does not send that message. A vicious cycle can result, as when you pull away from the phone and an annoying caller shouts ever louder. In stressed, aging rats, as the hippocampus shrinks, the adrenal glands grow beyond their usual size, pumping out ever greater quantities of hormones.

The model of harm is best worked out in the case of stroke, produced by briefly clamping off blood flow to a small region of the brain of a rat. If the rat has first been exposed to chronic stress, extra cells die, at the margin of the stroke. Repair mechanisms shut down. New cell growth does not occur. An injury that would otherwise be manageable turns catastrophic. The key defect is an inability to turn off the stress reaction—a "stuck switch" problem. The damaged hippocampus is a crucial element of the stuck switch.

So: chronic stress leads to the production of stress hormones. Stress hormones damage hippocampal (and other) brain cells, isolating them and pushing them to the brink of destruction. Further stressors push the cells over the edge. As damage progresses, feedback systems fail. Even minor adversity then causes the overproduction of stress hormones. What would otherwise be limited injuries extend, in the presence of stress hormones, into substantial brain damage. The hormones also dampen repair and regeneration functions, so that temporary injuries become permanent.

The Sapolsky paradigm had been elegantly elaborated, through exacting research that eliminates competing explanations and fills in details of causation. If the model sounds familiar in outline, it may be because it has been considered as an explanation for a variety of mental illnesses. These include the conditions that bear obvious relations to stress, such as post-traumatic stress disorder. The closest fit is to depression.

The relationship between stress and depression is particularly intimate: stress can trigger depression, and (physiologically, via hormone expression) depression acts as a chronic stressor. Many depressed patients have enlarged adrenal glands. Most have overactive hormonal responses to standard challenges.

The excessive production of stress hormones has widespread consequences. For example, women with past or current depression tend to have decreased bone density, a condition that can result from overexposure to stress hormones. (Cushing's syndrome patients have fragile bones.) In a study that looked at premenopausal depressive women in their thirties and forties, one third had (diminished) bone densities at a severity that ordinarily occurs only after menopause. The depressed women's stress hormone levels were 40 percent above normal.

The nerve pathways governed by stress hormones appear to be more resilient in humans than in rodents. Among humans, only two groups have damage similar to that in aged, stressed rats: the "old old," who have lived well beyond the average life span, and ordinary elderly men and women with a history of depression. Mood disorder ages the brain prematurely.

A substantial body of research suggests that the factors active in aging in rats shape the brain biology of depression in humans. The hippocampus is small. Stress responses become unduly prolonged. They act on neurons that have been made especially vulnerable. Repair mechanisms are less effective than they should be.

That last problem—failed resilience—has been of special interest to researchers. Why don't depressives bounce back? In an immediate sense, the answer has to do with the stuck switch—once depressives enter a negative state, they have unusual difficulty emerging. But why does an element of depression so often persist? Why (as in Yvette Sheline's findings) is the hippocampus small months or years after the most recent episode of depression?

When a bout of Cushing's syndrome ends, patients recover fully. The hormone levels fall, and the brain enters into a period of repair. The branchlike dendrites grow (the process is called arborization), and neurons establish new connections with other cells. Neurogenesis may occur as well.

But if research like Sheline's is right, the aftermath of depression is not like the aftermath of Cushing's syndrome. The brains of depressives are less resilient than they should be. How does depression become a chronic disease? Why is it progressive, with later episodes lasting longer than early ones? Defects in repair mechanisms may be as important to depression as the initial injury.

Thoughts along these lines have caused researchers to look at mechanisms of repair in the brain, as they relate to depression. The plasticity of the brain—its ability to compensate for the "pruning" of dendrites and re-arborize—is influenced by growth-promoting chemicals that filter into neurons from the surrounding environment.

One of the most prevalent growth promoters is brain-derived neurotrophic factor, or BDNF. For our purposes, it is easiest to think of BDNF as the opposite of stress hormones, in their long-term effects on brain cells. BDNF is an all-purpose resilience factor. In animal models, an abundance of BDNF encourages arborization and new cell formation. Absence of BDNF leads to pruning and cell atrophy. Infusion of BDNF into the hippocampus produces what look like both immediate and lasting antidepressant effects. In animal models in which antidepressants interrupt a stress response, the absence of BDNF makes the antidepressants lose their efficacy—perhaps because arborization and new cell growth are critical to recovery from depression.

Depleting an animal of BDNF does not lead to depression immediately. But scientists suspect that, over time, an animal with too little BDNF will be prone to a depression-like syndrome, because of an inability to protect, repair, or replace neurons. Work to test this hypothesis is in progress, using genetically manipulated mice whose ability to make BDNF can be shut off in the hippocampus at a time of the researcher's choosing, say, in the mouse's adolescence or adulthood.

And BDNF appears to be deficient in depressed human patients. For example, in the tissue samples from the prefrontal cortex in which Grazyna Rajkowska found disrupted cellular architecture, she also found a deficit in BDNF.

A person's level of nerve growth factors is set by a variety of influences—genetics, early trauma, and current stress and exposure to stress hormones. No one finally knows the importance of nerve growth factors in depression. But speculatively, the BDNF findings suggest a further mechanism for the stuck switch. In a simple version—and no one believes that the core deficit in depression will be anything so neat—depression (at the level of brain cells) just *is* a deficit of resiliency enhancers. A person might be born with a lower capacity to make those factors or might acquire an impairment on the basis of childhood trauma or chronic stress later in life. Without sufficient resiliency factors, the neurons in the hippocampus would be excessively vulnerable to atrophy and pruning. The hippocampus would become less competent to end stress responses as they arise. Other consequences would follow, including overproduction of stress hormones and (in another vicious cycle) a further lowering of neuroprotective factors.

This new research, linking depression to problems in stress responses and problems in repair mechanisms, meshes well with older research on neurotransmitters like serotonin and norepinephrine. Problems with neurotransmitters lead to decreases in neuroprotective factors, like BDNF. Whatever the line of investigation, the form of the resulting picture of depression is reasonably constant. Depression is characterized by frank abnormalities in the nervous system, such as the changes observed by Rajkowska and Sheline. These defects arise from failures in protection and repair of cells in critical brain regions. The overlapping models are working hypotheses in the fullest sense—they channel the course of research, and they influence clinical practice.

Like earlier hypotheses that have guided psychiatrists' approach to depression, the failed-resilience model of depression exists in the face of messy data. There are studies that suggest depressives have small or malfunctioning hippocampi early in life. Perhaps some hippocampal variation is genetic, a sign and cause of liability to depression. Early trauma, such as child abuse, may inhibit hippocampal growth, long before the onset of depression. First episodes of depression appear to be especially destructive, so that it may be that the relationship between days of depression and hippocampal loss is more complicated than Sheline's findings suggest. The data allow for different versions of a two-part story, in which inborn or early vulnerability is elaborated into progressive deterioration.

The overall picture, what I have called the myth of depression, is relatively stable. You might evaluate the evidence differently—disbelieving certain research results and placing more faith in others—and still you would conclude that failures in the modulation of stress and defects in neuroresilience cause or even constitute depression.

In the new model of depression, underlying physiological defects (like a deficit in resiliency factors or a small hippocampus) are made worse by stress. In this regard, depression would be like other diseases. Multiple sclerosis is now thought to work that way, as are eczema and asthma and hardening of the arteries—defects are expressed or exacerbated in the face of stress. Depression is a disease in which a host of injuries combine to cause a common downstream process that becomes self-sustaining. Certain cancers are like that—reasonably uniform, whether initiated by viruses, radiation, or toxin exposure. Depression affects multiple organs. So far, we have spoken of the brain, bones, and adrenal glands; later we will learn of problems with the heart, blood elements, and perhaps blood vessels. Many conditions that we fear (think of diabetes, with its effects on the pancreas, eye, heart, and kidney) are multisystem in this way. In terms of associated brain pathology, depression bears a resemblance to neurological disorders, like the dementias, with cell damage in particular layers of particular brain regions. The stuck-switch model of depression imagines that a system designed to protect the body, acutely, turns on chronically and begins to attack cells and organs it was meant to shield. In this regard, depression is like the autoimmune diseases, such as lupus. Altogether, the new myth makes depression look like an ordinary disease, conforming to ordinary models of causes and effects.

At the same time, depression is very much its own disease, distinctive in its form and expression. The disruptions to prefrontal cortex, hippocampus, adrenals, bones, glands, heart, and blood—these constitute a particular disorder.

There is, if we are open to seeing it, a disturbing beauty in the stress-and-impaired-resilience model of depression. For centuries, scientists and philosophers have yearned for a glimpse at the corporeal aspect of depression. In the 1620s, Robert Burton referred to earlier thinkers' beliefs about "how the body, being material, worketh upon the immaterial soul, by mediation of humours and spirits which participate of both, and ill disposed organs." Burton imagined correspondences back and forth, between mental and physical: "the chiefest causes proceed from the heart, humours, spirits: as they are purer, or impurer, so is the mind, and equally suffers, as a lute out of tune . . ."

As in the Renaissance model, in our contemporary myth anatomy and physiology reflect—poetically—the symptoms and traits that characterize depression. Hypersensitivity to adversity, vulnerability in the face of stress, withdrawal of intimate connections, premature aging, sluggishness in recovery, deteriorating course, chronicity of impairment, failed resilience—these phrases might apply equally to depressives and their neurons. The beauty, the poetry, does not mask a horrifying quality to the findings—a demonstration in the body of the fragility, "stuckness," and lack of reserve that blight the lives of the depressed.

Eleven

❖

Getting There

THE DENUDED NEURON, the disrupted brain architecture—
for all their metaphorical power, these injuries stand at the
wrong level. They are not the experience of illness, they are
not the person. And depression is the medical condition most closely
linked to the life story. Even from the realm of data we demand texture,
shading, detail. What makes a depressive? What is the setting, the origin, the narrative of depression?

My own understanding of the course of depression has been shaped
progressively by the work of a close colleague, Kenneth Kendler. Ken
and I came to the Yale psychiatry residency together in 1977. Each of
us had opted for an old-style, full-bore medical internship, I at Wiscon-
sin and Ken at Stanford. The sixteen other residents had chosen an "integrated" first-year program in Connecticut. Ken and I arrived as
outsiders.

Our trajectories could not have been more different. Ken was in the
"research track," churning out work on brain chemistry. In the "com-

munity track," I was set on adapting psychoanalysis to the realities of clinics in the inner city. But as newcomers, we were drawn together. We met on the racquetball or tennis court Saturday mornings when we were off duty. This arrangement lasted for the whole of our time in New Haven.

Ken was the genius in our residency group. He was never competing with the rest of us, only with other candidates for the Nobel Prize. He absorbed the Yale method of attacking a problem at every level, from neurotransmitter to cell, brain, person, family, and culture. Though psychoanalysis was a curiosity for him, he mastered its details as I never did.

The grand theory, in our residency years, was the monoamine hypothesis, the one that puts serotonin and norepinephrine at center stage. At a critical juncture early in his career, Ken turned his attention elsewhere. He dropped everything in favor of training in behavioral genetics—the statistical study of the inheritance of (in this case) mental illness.

Though he would have been welcome back at Yale or Stanford, Ken chose a position at the Medical College of Virginia. Although hardly a powerhouse in psychiatry, MCV did have a strong portfolio in medical genetics. Moreover, it had a twin registry, a large panel of pairs of twins born in Virginia (the registry was later expanded to include the Carolinas) and amenable to research. Ken had already published diagnostic studies that mined family data from Iowa and Denmark. He would go on to establish or tap into large registries in Sweden and Ireland. Using these populations, Ken began researching psychiatric disorders, again at every level, from chromosome marker to social behavior. Ken's main interest was in schizophrenia. But depression was a strong side interest, and his second level of attention can suffice to redefine a field.

Tending to registries is a demanding managerial and political task. It involves sending teams of collaborators into a community to contact the mentally ill and their family members, as well as control groups. Researchers then need to stay in touch with subjects over decades, maintaining a relationship that will keep them amenable to participating in surveys and biological testing. To give a sense of the magnitude of these undertakings: the Virginia Twin Registry began with a listing of all twins born in the Commonwealth since 1918. Research over the last fifteen years has extended to interviews with more than twenty thousand twin pairs and their parents, in an effort to tease out genetic and environmental influences for a range of disorders.

The rationale for building genetic studies around twins is apparent. Identical twins share all of their genes. Fraternal twins are like any siblings; they have about half of their genes in common. If a condition is entirely heritable, all identical twins will be "concordant" for it—when one has it, the other will. A lower percentage of fraternal twins will be concordant for the condition. If a condition is not heritable at all—if it arises purely from environmental factors—then genetic similarity will have no bearing. When a third of identical twins match up, so will a third of fraternal twins.

If you know the rates of concordance for a condition in identical and fraternal twins, and if you know how frequently the condition occurs in a given group of people, then you can calculate the relative contributions of genes and environment in producing that condition. That is, you will obtain an estimate of the *heritability* of the condition for that population. Because identical twins have all their genes in common, if you then look into the history of identical twin pairs discordant for the condition, you can hope to identify the environmental factors that matter.

For all but the simplest cases, the mathematics of heritability are complex. And the simple cases don't exist. No common mental illnesses have 0 or 100 percent heritability. Major depression turns out to have a heritability of 35 or 40 percent.

Heritability is not concordance. In most populations studied, and for most definitions of the illness, if one identical twin has been depressed, the odds are higher (sometimes much higher) than four in ten that the co-twin will have been as well. Heritability is a statistical attempt to look at all the factors that determine whether a person will be depressed and to determine the proportion of that influence that is due to genes. The figure 38 percent (for heritability) is reasonably consistent across different decades and across cultures. The one factor that raises the level of heritability is chronicity—long duration or frequent recurrence. If you consider only people who have remained depressed over periods of months or years, you find that persistent depression has a heritability of over 50 percent.

Some conditions that psychiatrists treat, like manic-depressive illness, schizophrenia, and attention deficit disorder, are more heritable than depression. But many common medical conditions, like high serum cholesterol and high blood pressure, fall in the 30 to 40 percent range for heritability, as do subtypes of diabetes. The 40–60 mix of heritability and environmental influence puts depression in the mainstream of highly prevalent diseases.

For conditions shaped by both nature and nurture, the interesting questions concern details. We want to know which sorts of genes create a liability to illness, and what sort of environment.

Psychoanalysis holds that the mind is shaped largely by psychological events—significant, emotionally evocative experiences that create inner conflict. But when biological psychiatrists speak of environment, often they are referring to mechanical influences on the brain. As recently as fifteen years ago, gung ho geneticists assumed that depression would turn out to look highly "biological" in its origins, as regards both genetics and experience.

For instance, in the uterus, just after conception, when a developing zygote, or fertilized egg, "twins," by splitting into two groups of immature cells, the division may be uneven. One twin begins with more cells than the other. This occurrence is "environmental," since it does not arise from the twins' genes. Still, any resulting differences between the twins are hardly psychological, in the sense of being caused by a thoughtful or emotional response to the state of the world.

Many chance events play a decided role in development. Working with simple worms—nematodes with fewer than a thousand cells—and raising them in cultures that are kept as constant as possible, scientists have observed decided differences in important traits. Some worms live three times as long as others do. Random small-scale processes—the drifting of atoms, molecules, and cells, along with subtle errors in genetic transcription—are probably responsible. The threefold difference is extraordinary. As one reviewer of the research on worms noted, "Astonishingly, the degree of variability they exhibit in longevity is not much less than that of a genetically mixed population of humans, who eat a variety of diets, attend to or abuse their health, and are subject to all the vagaries of circumstance—car crashes, tainted beef, enraged postal workers—of modern industrialized life." Imperceptible chance events evidently serve as vastly diverse "environments" for genetically similar creatures.

Then there is the matter of intrauterine growth. Counting the oocytes (the cells from which eggs grow) in genetically identical female mice pups born from a single mother, researchers find a threefold range—the range observed in unrelated humans. In the mice, some of this variation is due to position within the uterus—for instance, whether a female pup's nearest neighbor is a male. In general, subtle differences in prenatal experience—in nutrition, say—can cause variation between twins. Once small differences exist, then new insults, such as psychological stress on the mother, will have unequal effects on the fetuses.

Speaking of which: the link between prenatal stress (on the mother) and depression (in offspring) may be strong. In research on monkeys, seemingly modest challenges to pregnant mothers result in decreased hippocampal size and impaired neurogenesis in their young, accompanied by behaviors that look like anxiety and depression.

The hazards of childbirth confer risk as well. In a study conducted in patients with schizophrenia or a mixture of schizophrenia and mood disorder, childbirth complications seemed to lead to decreased hippocampal size and, over time, to emergence of the mental illness. Oxygen deprivation to the baby is probably the key factor. This study does not bear directly on depression; but it provides a model of an effect of the environment during childbirth on future mental illness, one that can hardly be said to arise from the person's emotional experience. Even though symptoms of depression (like those of schizophrenia) generally declare themselves in adolescence or later, researchers in the 1980s suspected that the course might be set early and through quite mechanical influences.

"Experience" of this nonpsychological sort almost certainly does play a decided role in depression. Often identical twins differ temperamentally, from early infancy—and of course, that difference is "environmental," since the twins' gene sets are the same. But geneticists who thought that psychologically significant events would prove irrelevant in the causation of depression were simply wrong. As it turns out, even some of the genetic factors that lead to depression have a psychological cast.

In discussing men who marry women who develop depression, I mentioned that moodiness is an early marker for vulnerability to depression. If you're anxious and emotional, you're at risk for depression. Evidence for those correlations comes from Ken Kendler's group.

Kendler's investigators studied twins' responses to questions from standard personality assessment instruments. Researchers rated factors like low self-esteem, pessimism, dependency on others, and the sense of lacking control over one's own destiny. They then looked at whether these tendencies precede or follow the onset of depressive episodes. All the expected traits bear some relationship to depression. The only one that *predicts* depression is neuroticism.

Neuroticism, in this circumscribed usage, is a tendency to moodiness. Neurotics answer yes to test items like "I feel miserable for no reason" and "I suffer from nerves." They give these responses even if they have never been depressed. Neurotics are irritable. They are prone to feeling hurt and to worrying for a long time after embarrassing experiences. Neuroticism is a robust trait. It lasts a lifetime. You get the same sort of scores if, instead of asking the subjects, you put the test questions (about the subjects) to their friends.

Kendler then investigated the nature of the interaction. Do episodes of depression heighten neuroticism? Does bad experience lead simultaneously to neuroticism and depression? It turns out that a history of depressed mood does bump up the neuroticism score. And negative events lead to both neurotic traits and depression. But these influences are minor. A different correlation turns out to be more important. About 60 percent of the genetic vulnerability to depression is shared with neuroticism, so that the two conditions develop in parallel, from a common biological cause. A gene, or set of genes, causes both moodiness and liability to depression. For some people (like Betty, perhaps, and not like Margaret), neuroticism and depression are two trunks off the same stock.

By the mid-1990s, scientists had identified genes that might lead to both conditions, neuroticism and depression. For example, separate research groups had discovered differing forms of a gene that affects the way the brain uses serotonin, one of the messenger chemicals that helps regulate mood states. This gene allows for the assembly of a protein, called the serotonin transporter, that fine-tunes cells' utilization of serotonin. (The scientific shorthand for the gene is 5-HTT—5-hydroxytryptamine is the chemical name for serotonin; the second T stands for transporter.) The serotonin transporter gene, or 5-HTT, comes in two forms, long and short. The long form makes half again as much of the transporter as the short form. Fewer than a third of humans have two long variants of the transporter gene. Fewer than 20 percent have two short genes. Most have one long and one short.

Studies appearing in the mid-1990s that looked at extended families found that relatives with two short genes were more likely to have neuroticism. This result was exciting—the discovery of a gene for a personality trait. The press dubbed 5-HTT the "Woody Allen gene." Some research suggested that the short gene also correlated with depression. But even the association with neuroticism was weak. The short gene conferred only a small increased risk. And some subsequent studies failed to replicate the original findings.

Research points to other genes that might cause both neuroticism and depression. But the 5-HTT story is particularly interesting because it contains suggestions about interaction of nature and nurture.

In 2003, an international team of scientists took a second look at 5-HTT, using a model of depression derived in part from Ken Kendler's work. The researchers were a husband and wife team at Kings College, London, Avshalom Caspi and Terri Moffitt. Once students of social aspects of mood disorder, Caspi and Moffitt had switched into behavioral genetics and gained access to an extraordinary database. In New Zealand, a representative sample of 837 white children had been followed from age three to early adulthood. Every two, three, or five years, the subjects and their relatives had been interviewed in detail, so there was an enormous store of information about the life challenges the children had encountered. The researchers tested the young men and women (now all age twenty-six) for the 5-HTT gene and questioned them about mood disorder.

The results were astonishingly clear-cut. In subjects where both 5-HTT genes were long, stress did not cause depression. It made no difference whether the subjects had been mistreated in early childhood; nor did it matter whether later they had encountered deaths in the family, ill health, or financial losses. Some of these young men and women did become depressed (presumably through causes unrelated to stress)—but among those with two long genes, the stressed and the unstressed looked nearly identical.

Among subjects with one or two short genes, adversity led to an increase in depression at age twenty-six, that is, current depression at the time the latest research was conducted. Those with more clear-cut early abuse were more likely to suffer depression. So were those who encountered a higher number of stressful events in their early twenties. And for each sort of adversity examined, subjects with two short genes were yet more prone to depression than those with one short gene and one long. More adversity led to more disordered mood, and at every level of stress, the symptoms were more severe for those with two short versions of the 5-HTT gene.

Think of the serotonin-as-police metaphor. Effectively, the long 5-HTT gene may mean more protection from stress. Perhaps relatively muted serotonin transmission (in people with the short variant of the gene) plays a permissive role when it comes to depression, conferring less resilience and allowing more damage. If the same gene plays a more direct role in the shaping of personality—if it leads to neuroticism—then people with the short version of the gene will have a slightly greater liability to moodiness, from early in life, as well as a greater tendency to contract depression in the face of stress.

It is almost the rule in behavioral genetics for later studies to weaken or complicate early findings. The New Zealand study has raised eyebrows on a number of grounds. Competing studies had found a less dramatic level of stress immunity in people with the protective variant of the gene. But even if its effect turns out to be less absolute than the Caspi and Moffitt study suggests, 5-HTT would be interesting as an example of one kind of gene that contributes to the heritability of depression. The gene has effects on personality (to the extent that it causes neuroticism) and it leads to depression via vulnerability to psychological stressors, like financial losses or the death of close relations.

The Caspi and Moffit findings, and others like them, point to a particular sort of liability to depression—extreme sensitivity to psychological disruption. This route is one long noted by observers of the disease. As Burton writes in *The Anatomy of Melancholy*, "that which is but a flea-biting to one, causeth insufferable torment to another; and which one by his singular moderation and well-imposed carriage can happily overcome, a second is in no whit able to sustain."

But the heritable part of depression is almost certainly mediated by a variety of mechanisms shaped by a variety of genes—and most likely by different combinations of genes in different people. Kendler's statistical analysis indicates that there must be genes that influence depression and do not give rise to the neurotic personality style. The primary effects of these (presumed) additional genes is uncertain. Some researchers have suggested that there may be genes for the stability or variability of a cluster of functions that includes both bodily cycles (such as daily and, for women, monthly hormone swings) and mood; people who are less "stable" physiologically may be more vulnerable emotionally. There may be genes that contribute to the protection of brain neurons. Defects in (or less active forms of) a gene that produces neuronal growth and repair factors, like BDNF, might predict depression. Genes that influence the prevalence of glial cells or the size of the hippocampus might play a role.

But neuroticism is a behavioral marker for some of the genes that predispose to depression. Much of the appeal of behavioral genetics lies in these detailed, seemingly incidental revelations that arise from data gathering. It's not (as the psychoanalytic theory has it) that your unresolved neurotic conflicts lead to disordered mood; it's that the genes that make you look conflicted happen also to be genes for depression.

The larger body of Kendler's work on depression leads to a comprehensive model of how illness develops. The research has points of interest all along the way. To turn to environmental causes: What sort of stressors lead to mood disorder?

In twin studies, geneticists divide events into "shared" and "nonshared." These adjectives sound self-explanatory. Certainly "shared" does. Much of what twins encounter they encounter together. But "nonshared" environment is a less intuitive concept.

Some experiences clearly happen to one person uniquely. A brick hits one twin (and not the other) on the head; the resulting brain damage leads to depression. But "nonshared" is a broader category, one defined by events' *effects*. Nonshared environment is any environment that just does influence two people differently, even if, from the outside, it looks as though both have encountered the same experiences and lived in the same milieus.

Religion provides an illustration. Sociologists have studied the effect of childhood environment on religious identification. If both your parents are practicing Catholics, and if in childhood all your peers and neighbors are Catholic, the odds are extremely high that even as adults you and your siblings will identify yourselves as Catholic. That result is reliable and it is independent of what each child brings to the environment in terms of temperamental endowment or early traumata. As regards the factors that affect religious identification, you and your siblings have experienced a shared environment.

But for most outcomes, the effect of experience on thought and behavior is more variable. If we look beyond identification and ask about church attendance, differences emerge. By late adolescence, some of your siblings will be churchgoers, and some will not. Personality factors may play a role. One sibling will be rebellious, another will be anxious in crowds, and a third will be left cold in matters of faith or attachment, while from early life you have been especially eager to please and also especially moved by religious feelings. Even if from the outside the environment looks uniform, for each of you internally it will have been distinct—off-putting to one, inspiring to another, constraining to a third, welcoming to a fourth, simply uninteresting to a fifth, and so on. For churchgoing, as observed in adult life, the seemingly uniform surround of practicing Catholic parents and neighbors will register as nonshared environment, an influence that differed for each child.

The measure for whether an environment is shared, for a given outcome, is whether identical twins respond to it identically—that is, whether they are concordant for the outcome. In many cases, discordant outcomes point to obvious differences in what the twins encounter. Parents may be accepting of one daughter and rejecting of the other, so that the nuclear family provides nonshared environments. But the same measure picks up the elaboration of subtle differences within the twins. For a host of reasons, from intrauterine incidents to the vagaries of fortune on the playground, by age five, even with a shared pair of 5-HTTs and every other gene, one identical co-twin may be confident and the other insecure. Then, a given level of parental support will be adequate for the first and insufficient for the second. In both the experiential and the statistical sense, the home environment is nonshared. That category applies even if the parents swear up and down that they have treated their children identically.

In Kendler's large-scale studies, it turns out that virtually all the environment that matters for depression is nonshared.

This result is unexpected. You might think that twins raised by neglectful parents would become vulnerable to depression, while twins raised by attentive and attuned parents would attain protection from mood disorder. Depression would be like religious identification: if you come from an abusive or perhaps a depressive family, you will be depressed. If you come from a supportive or upbeat family, you will avoid depression. Or you might imagine that being raised in poverty, or in a dangerous neighborhood, or in a bleak school environment will predispose to depression, and in almost any child.

But the influence of experience does not run along those lines. Studies of adults find virtually no persisting direct effects from shared environment. For depression, the environment that matters is the sort that affects different people differently. It is probably true that unattuned parents, indifferent schoolteachers, and poverty cause depression—but only in certain people. When depression is the outcome under study, the effect of overarching, seemingly uniform environments is always, always mediated by the perceiving mind and the predisposed brain.

Research groups from around the world have replicated this finding. The experience that causes or protects from depression is nonshared. This result has considerable power. One particular corollary is that when depression runs in families, the reason will usually involve genetics, rather than family culture only. More generally, the finding—that only "nonshared" events cause depression—highlights the role of the self in interpreting experience. Even bleak environments elicit depression only in the vulnerable. That shared environment rarely shows up in the chain of causation of depression pushes a good deal of what we call environment into the background.

Of course, family environments are not uniform. Often one child is picked out for neglect while others are coddled—as with Cinderella and her stepsisters. But even here, genes and early random events may have their impact.

I have a particular fondness for a minor finding in Kendler's work with twin girls discordant for depression. Interviewing the twins and their family members, researchers stumbled across an unexpected result: in the twins' childhood, the fathers were more protective toward the daughter who would later go on to develop a mood disorder. These were not abusive fathers—the main body of research examined that issue. Rather, they seemed to be fathers who had sensed emotional need in one daughter, and not in her identical twin sister. Early environmental differences had produced subtle contrasts in the twins' emotional makeup; fathers were keen enough observers to respond to that variation. Here is a trait that some people (like these fathers) carry: the ability to identify very early indicators of vulnerability and the impulse to nurture those who display them. Perhaps this finding points to one source of the "charm" of depression.

Of course, early signs of moodiness will often elicit less favorable responses. Teachers and classmates may show more warmth to sunnier boys and girls. From early on, resilient children may develop more extensive support networks, grow in self-assurance, and come to feel more in control of what happens in their lives. (With identical twins, the initial difference in personality traits would have emerged on the basis of nonshared experience, perhaps even in the womb.) In these and other ways, the environment is more benign for a luckier and less depressive child; early signs of emotional strength elicit encouragement and other social rewards. And compared to the depressive co-twin, the sanguine twin also experiences that environment as yet more benign, success building upon success.

Taking a different tack: an account of gene-environment interaction helps flesh out what it means to say that depression is about 38 percent heritable. Genes can act inside the body. On a genetic basis, a person may develop a minor anomaly in brain structure, like an insufficiency of the kind of receptors that help the brain turn off a stress response. Those variations might lead more or less directly to depression, through a (negative) potential that will play itself out in almost any environment. In schizophrenia, studies point to this sort of direct effect: the healthy siblings of patients with early-onset schizophrenia have brain abnormalities, and at a level gross enough to be identifiable on MRI scans. Brain abnormalities run in the family. Perhaps having a greater dose of those abnormalities—or a combination of abnormalities and fairly minor precipitants, like infectious disease—leads to mental illness in straightforward fashion.

A portion of the genetic contribution to depression may be of this anatomical sort; Kendler's studies find some direct connection between genetic predisposition and episodes of depression. But genes also act "outside the body." If your heredity leads you to look unattractive or behave unattractively, by the standards of the culture in which you live, and if you are then shunned and left friendless, you may lose confidence, approach stress unsupported, and develop depression. The statistical model would pick up much of that causation as genetic even

though as you recount your history, the narrative sounds eventful—
replete with memories that suggest a depression based on demoralizing
experiences.

This outside-the-body genetics is common in medicine. Imagine that
we calculate that a type of cancer, adenocarcinoma of the lung, is 40
percent heritable. We may discover that some of the genetic liability is
due to defects in the immune system. We might also find (as Ken
Kendler has) a genetic predisposition to addiction, and more specifically to nicotine addiction. That heritage leads to cancer, and it does so
via likely behavior in the prevailing social milieu, in which cigarettes are
available and marketed, and in which subcultures exist that welcome
smokers.

In *Listening to Prozac*, I discussed the hypothesis that depression en-
sues when the culture fails to reward people who are passive,
unassertive, and averse to risk. That theory is compatible with the view
that depression is partly heritable. The genes for the disfavored temperamental traits lead to unsuccessful behaviors that in time elicit a discouraging environment—fewer friends, less living space, and the rest.
Those with genes for (or early experience conducive to) traits that are
punished socially create a worse-than-average set of experiences for
themselves. And then a further interactive effect comes into play. If the
very people who suffer isolation are the ones who most need the protection that social integration affords—and if even common, expectable experiential blows are tougher for them than for others—then
the environment will strike them as especially hostile. This hostile environment is nonshared, worse objectively and experientially for the vulnerable than the resilient.

When people say that a given trait or illness results from "an interaction of genes and environment," sometimes they mean simply that both
nature and experience play a role. If on a genetic basis, you develop
malformed joints and if the only employment open to you is physical labor, you will contract wear-and-tear arthritis on the basis of two separate influences. Your joints did not determine your job, and your job
did not create your initial vulnerability.

But depression is one of those illnesses where the interaction is thorough. The genes create adverse environments, as when they lead to a temperament that the culture fails to reward. Ordinary environments become adverse when interpreted through personality shaped by the genes, as when someone needs more social stability and predictability than the culture tends to provide. Outcomes that evolve on this mixed basis in time affect which transmitters are and are not expressed in the brain, which receptors for those transmitters are protected, which cells flourish and which atrophy. Genes and environment interact at every level—behavior, feeling, chemistry, and anatomy.

And still we know that psychologically significant events simply do cause depression. After terrible losses, many people become depressed. No model that fails to acknowledge that connection is likely to convince us.

A portion of Kendler's work looks at the question What predicts an *episode* of major depression? Here, the target outcome is not a history of mood disorder but rather a distinct occurrence, depression in the past year. The narrow focus allows for an inquiry into immediate harm. Only then do the researchers pan back and trace a chain of causation.

The triggers are the expected ones. Stressful life events increase the risk for depression. These include the sorts of personal misfortunes generally understood to be depressing. The ones that show up in Kendler's data are: being robbed or assaulted, facing housing or financial problems, losing a job or encountering serious work problems, encountering major marital problems or undergoing divorce or separation, and losing a close confidant. Stressors in a social network can cause depression, too: encountering illness or death or a grave crisis in the life of a child, parent, or sibling, or entering into substantial interpersonal conflict with one of those relatives. Many of these effects are immediate. The stressor precedes the onset of a new depressive episode by a month or less.

The type of stressful life event matters as well, and in the expected direction. Events that involve an attack on self-esteem tend to lead to depression, and this result holds for both men and women. Being left or rejected by a loved one is such an event. Other sorts of losses also lead to depression—the death of a loved one, or a separation that you initiate. But the combination, *humiliating loss*, is especially harmful, worse even than loss by death. These effects are moderately specific. When a feared harm has not yet occurred, the mental illness that tends to arise is most often an anxiety disorder, rather than depression. Not the anticipation but the reality of a humiliating loss triggers depression.

This correlation—between stressful events and a depressive episode—is only the last step of a story. Looking at the big picture, we see that genes and experience are thoroughly mingled. We know, for instance, that people who carry a genetic liability for depression tend to "select themselves into high-risk environments." They drop out of school, marry unwisely, divorce often, abuse drugs and alcohol, and expose themselves to emotional catastrophes all along the line. The genes may act through temperament or by predisposing to mild forms of depression that then inspire bad choices—whose harmful outcomes result in worsening mood disorder and further stressors. The career of depression is dangerous.

In a study of women twin pairs, Kendler's raters looked at transcripts and listened to tapes of recent life histories and assessed the likelihood that given events had occurred independent of the subject's own actions. These ratings were checked and rechecked via judgments by second evaluators and through reinterviews of the twins. The results showed that "independent events" do trigger depression. But "dependent events"—where the depressive had a role in her own bad luck—had a yet stronger effect. A person may pick a fight with a supervisor and then find herself demoted at work—and become depressed as a result. Often what looks like an external event causing depression is an intermediate step in a complex interaction. The behavior of the depressive creates an environment rich in potential stressors.

Overall, between half and two thirds of the association between stressful events and depression is causal—the stress giving rise to the depression. At least a third of the causation runs the other way, and the proportion rises for later episodes of depression. The more often you've been depressed, the more you tend to contribute to your own misery. This result does not arise from acute depression—the stressful event almost always precedes a new episode. It is the ongoing, between-episodes aspects of the disease that lead depressives to complicate their own lives.

Some of the adversity can be traced to a genetic root. When a woman experiences certain stresses—such as divorce or serious marital conflict, or even disputes with close friends and relatives—her identical co-twin will likely be experiencing similar stressors, and at a rate that exceeds the correlation in nonidentical twins. The same relationship holds for the categories "job loss" and "serious financial problems." Stressful events occur in the lives of depressives on a nonrandom basis, related to their genetic heritage.

Kendler has pulled these varieties of causation together in an overarching statistical analysis that constitutes the best current model for the development of major depression in women. (Often research on depression focuses on women because women are twice as likely as men to become depressed.) The model is remarkably powerful. In technical terms, it accounts for more than half of the variance in liability to depression in the year under study. In effect, the model manages to take half of the causation into account—a very high figure for the behavioral sciences, and extraordinarily high given the narrow target, whether a woman will be depressed in one given year.

If we stop for a moment to think how coarse the measures are, in any statistical study of life events, we may be amazed at the ability of behavioral genetics to explain anything at all. Some apparent traumas are not especially traumatic. Think of an elderly man who has suffered a dense dementia for years and now succumbs quietly to death; in some regards, the event will be a relief for those close to him. Contrast a brutal death that befalls a vital person; its effect on those who loved him will be devastating. And then there is the matter of the quality of our relationship to the deceased. Freud believed that the most corrosive and lingering grief—pathological grief—follows the loss of someone we love ambivalently. Freud may have gotten the association right and the causation wrong; perhaps it is just that people prone to making emotionally complex attachments are also prone to depression. Still, what a person means to us in life will color our response to his death. Given the variety of human experience, it would not surprise us if inquiries into the influence of broadly categorized life events explained very little of the likelihood of depression. That Kendler's model accounts for half of what occurs might lead us to conclude that he is very much on the right track. If a finer-grained picture of loss could be obtained, throwing out those events that fail to touch us and emphasizing those that shake us to the core, we might discover that behavioral genetics explains depression very well indeed.

In his report of his overarching model, Kendler expressed his findings through a series of charts in which different ranks of influence are linked by arrows labeled with numbers representing degrees of correlation. A master chart looks like the wiring diagram for a poorly designed computer.

In the bottom row is the outcome, an episode of depression in the prior year. In the top row are early risk factors. There are four: genes, disturbed family environment, childhood parental loss, and childhood sexual abuse. These are the "upstream" causes that give rise to intermediate causes (like bad marriages) that then lead to depression in the year that is under study.

That abuse appears separately in the data—apart from general family turmoil—is a powerful indicator that the "environmental" causes of depression include particular, meaningful events. Childhood sexual abuse is quite as destructive as social researchers say it is. Independent of other influences, being abused leads to anxiety in childhood, future trauma, stressful events in adulthood, and (indirectly) depression. Breaking out sexual abuse in the model helps explain some of the "nonshared" quality of early environment; one sister may be abused and her twin not.

The rest of the chart is filled with intermediate influences, many of which we have already encountered. The early risk factors lead to a variety of personality traits and behavior patterns (neuroticism, low self-esteem, early-onset anxiety, and conduct disorders). Together, the risk factors and the personality traits then predict an increased likelihood of poor education, low social support, substance abuse, and traumatic events, such as physical assault. Those three ranks of factors—early risk, personality traits, and the negative events that cluster in adolescence and early adulthood—correlate with a divorce and depression by the subjects' middle thirties. Those four sets of factors then predict the likelihood of stressful life events in the year under study. And directly or indirectly, the five sets of factors predict the current episode of depression.

Some of the correlations were unexpected. In the model, childhood parental loss has no direct effect on the outcome, depression. The effect of loss is mediated by the other basic risk factors (disturbed family environment and childhood sexual abuse) and by low education. In other words, losing a parent (by death, divorce, or separation before age seventeen) has no discernible effect on depression if the child then enters a protected environment, with a supportive family, and if the child manages to stay in school.

Of the four early risk factors, only genetics has a direct causal link to depression. Disturbed family environment, like childhood sexual abuse and childhood parental loss, causes depression via downstream factors, like low self-esteem, later stressful events, and marital problems in adulthood. This sequence leave room for hope: if we can prevent low self-esteem and the rest, we may be able to minimize the effects of early events like loss and molestation.

For the clinician, Kendler's messy diagram has a familiar feel. It shows what appears in the office, a stream of consequences. Yes, the current episode of depression is preceded, often enough, by a precipitating event. But it is also preceded by past depression and past social difficulties. And these occur in an unsupportive social environment. Some of those events, and that environment, seem to flow from the patient's own behavior, arising from long-standing personality traits. At the root is a mixed series of predispositions—*I was always this way*—or early disasters.

From within the complexity, Kendler has pieced out three major pathways to depression.

The first, he calls "internalizing." Here, genetic factors are the core risk, active even when the social circumstances are benign. Neuroticism accompanies depression in a good number of these "internalizing" twins, the ones in whom genes create a marked liability to mood disorder.

A second pathway, "broad adversity," begins with a disturbed family environment, with childhood abuse and parental loss mixed in. This bad start leads to poor education, poor social support, recurrent trauma, and divorce, and then, via every sort of stressful life event, to depression. Here, genes play a lesser role.

A third pathway, "externalizing," leads from childhood conduct disorder to substance abuse to depression.

These "types" cover much of the clinical territory.

The third group, the "bad girls" who come to depression through disruptive behavior and drug abuse, are uncommon visitors to psychiatrists in private practice. Occasionally, I see "externalizers" early in the course of the illness. "Why can't I do drugs?" a young woman will ask. Her friends smoke weed or pop pills every night.

"You just can't," I say. "Luck of the draw. Some people can tolerate drugs—but not you."

The young woman smiles the bashful smile that got her through in younger years. She prefers not to hear the unwelcome news. For her, drugs lead to shaky social judgment, loss of motivation for important tasks, mistreatment by unreliable friends, and a tendency to crash when things go wrong.

"Give yourself a month off drugs," I say.

She nods vacantly.

I ask, "How about a day?"

If she had only two mixed drinks and three beers, she will tell me that she stayed away from alcohol last night, or almost.

As a doctor (or parent, or teacher), you can see the illness stretched out before you, all that hard luck to come.

I have worked with patients, men and women both, whose story revolves around a mixture of alcoholism and depression. Every psychiatrist has. Alcoholism clusters with depression in families. The combination is devastating. In Grazyna Rajkowska's studies, depressed alcoholics show the worst glial loss, as if the two conditions create synergistic injury, perhaps with liquor supplying toxic damage to a depressive's vulnerable brain.

As for other substances, it may just be that the drugs cause concrete harm—that addiction-associated depression involves its own distinct challenges to the health of the brain. Perhaps the toxins cause brain pathology directly, quite independent of stress and emotional vulnerability. I have little experience with drug-abusing depressives. For the most part, down the road, in full adulthood, they go elsewhere for care, in the public sector, if they seek care at all.

The first two pathways, internalizing and adversity, reflect a familiar clinical picture. Many patients come to depression through being beaten down by life—early trauma reinforced by bad fortune in adulthood, some of it of their own making. Others reach the same spot with less apparent reason; they arrive with a strong family history of mood disorder and a personal history of emotional sensitivity. Combined conditions, family history and adversity, are exceedingly common.

Kendler asked how the pathways intersect.

On its face, depression is a disease that arises in response to encounters with stressful events. Certainly it looks that way in Kendler's data, where (as opposed to what is implied in the New Zealand findings) severe and repeated stressors cause depression even for those with little genetic predisposition. Rodent models give the same picture. Stress a normal mouse early in its development, and then rechallenge it once it is mature, and you see what looks like a depressive syndrome. If we accept the stress model, we will then want to ask what genes contribute, when they cause depression reasonably directly.

Approaching this question, Kendler began with the notion that depression is a "kindled" illness. In kindled illnesses, each encounter with causal events, and each episode of a disease, makes subsequent episodes more likely. In the case of depression, a stressor may trigger a first episode of depression. That episode will leave a patient more vulnerable to subsequent events, so that now a lower level of stress will cause a recurrence, and so on. Later episodes tend to be more fully elaborated,

with symptoms that are more numerous, more severe, and less responsive to treatment. After a few episodes triggered by stress, the illness
may begin to occur spontaneously, in the absence of inciting events.
Kindling includes an early, inapparent phase. Here, stress affects the
brain without causing an episode of depression, but each event
nonetheless increases vulnerability. These hidden events and responses
are the kindling that precedes an open blaze.

Looking at women with recurrent depression, Kendler found that
each episode made it more likely that the subsequent episode would
arise independently of a stressful life event. Risk and experience became progressively dissociated—liability to spontaneous episodes
increased—up to the ninth bout of depression. The first few bouts of
depression are the most damaging, in terms of increasing future vulnerability. By the ninth episode, the pattern is set, and further episodes do
not add to the already high risk.

Kendler then asked how genes affect the kindling process. Looking
at genetic heritage, stressful life events, and episodes of depression,
Kendler tested three hypotheses. Genes might increase the odds for depression simply, without affecting the subsequent course; those with an
inherited risk would be more likely to experience a first episode—but
then their liability to future depression would match that of people who
come to a first episode purely through adversity. Genes might move a
person faster along the downhill course of depression, increasing the
speed of kindling, so that each stressful event is more than normally
harmful—counting, say, for two events in the damage it does. Or genes
might "pre-kindle" a person, so that she begins life (or enters adulthood) some distance down the pathway toward recurrence—just as if
she had already encountered a number of stressful events.

Kendler's data support the pre-kindling alternative. Looking at the
association between stressful life events and the onset of depressive
episodes, the curve for those at high genetic risk for depression looks
like the tail end of the curve for those at low genetic risk. Nature starts
you off farther down the road. In terms of social advantage, this inheritance is the opposite of the Bush family members' being born on third
base; the pre-kindled are born partway down a slippery slope. Your first

episode of depression looks biologically like someone else's third or fourth.

By this account, genetic depression is not a separate illness, distinct from post-traumatic or adversity-based depression. The different routes lead, at different paces, to the same unhappy spot.

Kendler's model meshes nicely with the results of a decades-long debate about the distinctiveness of the depressions. Repeatedly, researchers had tried to carve out depressions that are more "biological." These were the "endogenous" mood disorders; they came from within, on the basis of heredity, without obvious triggers in perturbing life events. Psychiatrists imagined that patients with endogenous depression would be more responsive to medication. They would be free of the neurotic personality traits (here we are speaking not of moodiness only but of the whole range of "Woody Allen" behaviors) that make black moods look like a lifestyle, not an illness. The notion was that the "uncaused depression"—the heritable, endogenous type—might be the core sort, the entity that "caused depressions" only imitate.

That distinction failed. Exogenous depressions, with evident external precipitants, often had the same course (in terms of duration and recurrence) as endogenous ones. The two variants responded to the same medications. Patients who experienced caused depressions went on to experience uncaused episodes, and vice versa.

Researchers moved from cause to form. Perhaps depressions that *looked* endogenous were the real ones, whatever their linkage to stressful life events. If the endogenous patients sometimes had stress-related depressions, still the episodes might be distinctive. It was said that endogenous depressions were characterized by constant, relentless negativity, combined with a fixed inability to anticipate future pleasure. Neurotic depressives (prone to respond to exogenous disappointments) were more flighty, less stable in their hopelessness.

But mood constancy turned out to be a marker of severity, not type of depression. Even high neurotics looked flatly despairing (that is, their disorder had the endogenous form) if their depression became sufficiently grave or protracted. Later, other diagnostic factors were added. One set of markers—increased sleep and appetite, instead of decreased—has proved modestly predictive of the type of antidepressant that is useful in treating an episode. But in the effort to define "pure depression"—depression that is more heritable, more responsive to medication, more strongly correlated with biological abnormalities—descriptions of form repeatedly failed the critical test of research, replication in subsequent studies.

The effort to subdivide depressions has continued into recent years. At any moment, there are always scattered promising findings that remain on the table. But for the most part, the effort to tease apart depression has been a failure. One of the great exponents of subtyping depressions titled a valedictory monograph "All Roads Lead to Depression: Clinically Homogeneous, Etiologically [that is, causally] Heterogeneous." He did not quite throw in the towel, but it was clear enough that late in life this researcher had come to see the resemblances among depressions, once they are under way, as more important than the differences.

To my way of reading it, the decades-long effort to divide the depressions (into core and peripheral types) often hides and reveals contempt for neurotic personality traits. *Real* illness should contain less humor, less drama—and less of daily life, with its humiliating losses. Real professionals should stand at a distance from the elements of neurosis, the shtick and the grand opera.

But in Kendler's model, and in the general opinion within psychiatry, it's all depression. There may well be distinctions, as there are in other diseases. Some breast cancers are familial, others are more environmental—but neither is the "core" or "essential" tumor. The concept sounds meaningless with regard to cancer—and now with regard to depression, too.

Ken Kendler's research in behavioral genetics provides a road map for the territory of depression. The results show how to get to serious illness from various starting points. The image is one of feeder parkways converging on a highway. The map is not without detail. The intermediate stopping points, the early minor depressions, are visible. Like an ancient cartographer warning "here be monsters," the genetics researcher has sketched in school and job failures, drugs, feckless lovers, divorce, and bereavement,

Under the gaze of the statistician, the form of the illness comes into focus. Depression has a firm biological basis. It is grounded in the genes and in early environmental influences that stand distinct from the psychological. It is progressive, with recurrence leading to heightened vulnerability and finally separation from external causation. At the same time, depression arises from experience. Stressful life events, such as child abuse, lay a groundwork for the sorts of deprivation and failure that lead to illness. Humiliating losses trigger episodes. For many sorts of harm, predisposition matters. The environment that leads to depression is nonshared. When background factors, like the tenor of family life, play a role, they do so via the manner in which they are experienced.

Depression is the model illness for gene-environment interactions. Depression puts sufferers at risk for stress, through the way the culture treats the moody. But not all causation runs in the direction we might at first imagine. The vulnerable expose themselves to harmful external events, by making poor choices at home and in the workplace. They bring on these "dependent" events even between episodes, when they are not depressed. And what looks like readily understood association—neuroticism leading to depression—is partly parallel causation, with both the result and its apparent precursor arising from a common pre-disposition.

The genetic findings mesh comfortably with neuroanatomy. Some are born more vulnerable, some are made vulnerable by early experience. Further stressful life events lead both sorts of depressives along the same slope. A short distance down, the brain is less sturdy in the face of a variety of insults.

Behavioral genetics takes a mechanical, statistical approach to depression. But if you stick with the research long enough, its uncomfortable terms of art become surprisingly resonant. Nonshared experience, outside-the-body genetics, humiliating loss, dependent event, broad adversity, internalizing, prekindling—these phrases tell different sad stories. Some involve inborn fragility. Some turn on cruel injuries. Some feature drugs and self-destructive behavior. Depression clouds lives in myriad ways. The depressed encounter more than their share of losses. Sometimes, depressives generate their own bad luck. Certain episodes of depression, complex and intractable, arise without apparent external cause.

This line of research goes some distance toward fulfilling our wish that science acknowledge the narrative aspect of mood disorders. At the same time, behavioral genetics locates a remarkably uniform illness. If depressives' life stories vary, they also intersect and overlap. Depression represents a distinctive vulnerability to harm. However it begins, depression leads to a brittle state in which minor adversity becomes catastrophic. That adversity includes episodes of the disease itself.

Twelve

❖

Magnitude

WHEN I SPEAK TO AUDIENCES about mood disorder—when I summarize Ken Kendler's model or the stress-and-failed-resilience hypothesis—they may concede that depression has the form of a disease. But inevitably, someone will express doubts about depression's gravity. Looking at the range of illnesses that afflict human beings, just how bad is depression?

This question has been answered with some decisiveness in the past fifteen years. Because public health dollars are scarce, statisticians have worked to quantify the harm diseases cause. Their findings have surprised even the researchers who devised the major studies: Depression is the most devastating disease known to humankind. This result holds across the board—in the developing world and the industrialized nations, in current surveys and in projections of future health care needs.

You might imagine that fatal diseases do the most damage. But researchers tend to rank-order conditions by asking questions like: How many good days does a given disease steal? Although there are obvious exceptions, like AIDS, most terminal illnesses arrive in old age.

They may account for only a year or two of lost life. In contrast, a chronic disease that begins in childhood or adolescence will blight many decades.

Since the late 1980s, researchers have relied on a standard measure of burden of disease, called "disability-adjusted life years." This figure takes into account a variety of calculations. It begins with problems with mobility, self-care, and daily activities, such as work and study. It rates cognitive dysfunction, pain, and discomfort, including severe mood alteration. These factors contribute to a summary estimate of the severity of a typical bout of the illness under study—in this case, the severity of an episode of depression.

Researchers then look at the data on prevalence—how often does a disease occur, and how long does the illness last? Combining estimates of severity with estimates of prevalence, it is possible to calculate the "burden" attributable to a disease, in terms of time lost to disability. That figure is then added to years of life lost due to premature death. Various adjustments are factored in. (A year in young adulthood is valued slightly more than a year in late adulthood.) The intention is to create a number that represents the difference between the health status resulting from illness and an ideal situation in which a person lives free of disease to a ripe old age.

Assume that, under benign circumstances, women live to age eighty. Then, consider a young woman who at twenty succumbs to a severe, early-onset arthritis and suffers a one-third disability for the next sixty years. Her burden of disease is twenty good years lost—roughly the same as the loss suffered by a previously healthy woman who dies suddenly at sixty. Since the actuarial discounting values early years more, the final calculation will rate the crippling illness as slightly more disabling, over the course of a lifetime, than the premature death. Researchers check results of this sort against people's actual preferences: Which fate would you prefer? The first trade-off data came from health care experts, almost none of them psychiatrists; current studies pose the questions to patients and the general public.

Groups around the world have undertaken the same effort using different assumptions and weightings. The results of these analyses are similar. Varied assumptions lead to a single conclusion: Not AIDS, not breast cancer, but depression is the major scourge of humankind.

The most extensive global-burden-of-disease study is one conducted by the World Health Organization, the World Bank, and the Harvard School of Public Health. The study was massive. Its results began appearing in 1996 in volumes of almost a thousand pages each; six of a projected ten have been published. The findings are often quoted to the effect that by the year 2020, depression will be second only to ischemic heart disease—narrowing of blood vessels and related cardiac problems—in terms of disability caused.

Astonishing though it is, the estimate for 2020 serves to mask the current reality. As of 1990 (the year for which data was analyzed), the afflictions that stood ahead of depression were ones that steal years by killing children young—respiratory infections, diarrhea, and the illnesses of early infancy. These conditions are grouped—they represent not one disease but many—while major depression stands alone, independent of bipolar disorder (manic depression), minor depressions, and alcoholism.

Among the chronic diseases of midlife, depression was (by 1990) already the most burdensome, and not by a small margin. Major depression accounted for almost 20 percent of all disability-adjusted life years lost for women in developed countries—more than three times the burden imposed by the next most impairing illness. The story was similar in developing regions: depression was still the fourth most burdensome disease (after conditions that affect the very young) and the most disabling disease for both men and women age fifteen to forty-four. In the 2020 projections, depression becomes the single most disabling disease in developing regions.

These findings may be counterintuitive, but they hold up solidly in the face of a variety of approaches to the evidence. In fact, the global-burden data on mental illness were calculated conservatively; they probably underestimate both the loss of life due to suicide in depressives and the indirect harm depression causes when it complicates other diseases, such as diabetes or stroke. Looking at depression, the study considered only full-blown acute episodes; periods of residual symptoms were excluded. The undercounting probably amounts to tens of millions of life years lost annually to disability caused by depression.

There is room for concern in the other direction as well: The disability-adjusted life years measure is necessarily inexact. Still, it is impressive when internists, surgeons, and public health officials conclude that depression is the disease that injures patients most. And the numbers are overwhelming. Cut the estimates for depression in half, and it would still cause much more disability than asthma and diabetes combined. Make what adjustments you will, the result is the same. Depression has no rival as a disabling disease.

The impact of depression in these studies is not only a matter of prevalence—how common depression is. The data create an estimate of the disability caused by a single instance of illness, in this case, an episode of depression. There are seven categories of severity. The depressive episode is in the second group, next to the top. The highest ranking, most severe group includes conditions like dementia and quadriplegia.

An ongoing study is updating the global-burden data on mental illness. In the meanwhile, indirect measures support the original findings. In studies of days lost in the workplace, depression is usually in the lead, just as it is in the disability-adjusted life years estimates. And observations of workers as they are here and now, at midcareer, understate the impact of mood disorder. Without depression, those workers would already be at more productive jobs.

Estimates put the annual workplace cost of depression in America at over forty billion dollars. Forty billion dollars is 3 percent of the gross national product. In terms of losses to productivity, depression is far more expensive than any illness we might name. It is more expensive than heart disease taken as a single category. It is more expensive than the many cancers, grouped as one disease.

Beyond absenteeism, depression plays an important role in what employment specialists call "presenteeism," substandard participation on the job, as a result of the impairments in concentration, memory, and energy. When they show up, workers with major depression are more than six times as likely as workers without to underperform. Detailed samplings of performance in the workplace suggest that being depressed on the job is equivalent to calling in sick half a day or more each week; in comparison, ongoing arthritis, asthma, and headache had no such effect.

Depression creates additional costs. It causes missed days not only for patients but also for the relatives who tend to them.

And to a large degree, the apparent costs of other chronic illnesses are finally costs of depression. If you look at which arthritic patients are most disabled in the workplace, it is not those with the greatest objective harm to joints but those who have arthritis complicated by depression. Similar results have been found for a variety of illnesses, from hypertension to migraine. The combination of diabetes and depression is especially common and especially disabling. These more subtle or indirect costs are not factored in to the standard estimates of depression's economic effects and its tendency to disable—they are excess injuries.

In terms of the harm it causes, depression has a "perfect storm" quality. It is common. The best studies show that over 16 percent of Americans suffer major depression in the course of a lifetime. In a given year, between 6 and 7 percent of Americans suffer major depression, about the same percentage who suffer diabetes.

Most chronic ailments, such as arthritis and hypertension, have their onset in midlife, the forties or early fifties. Heart disease and stroke typically occur even later. Depression has its first effects early—and then it persists or becomes recurrent. Half to two thirds of people who have ever been depressed will be depressed when interviewed in a given year down the road. And depression spans the life cycle.

Depression often begins in adolescence. A recent study looked at children between the ages of twelve and seventeen, a stage of life when illness is rare. In the prior six months, more than 7 percent of boys and almost 14 percent of girls had met the full criteria for major depression.

Some of the injury from adolescent depression is immediate. Suicide is the third leading cause of death among American adolescents, after accidents and homicide, and many of the suicides arise from depression.

Depression interferes with every aspect of a young person's life. Depression correlates with failure to complete high school, failure to enter college, and failure to complete college. Adolescents who have experienced depression show impairments in verbal performance and in social functioning that persist after the episode remits. Depression decreases the odds of using contraception and increases the odds of teenage pregnancy. It predicts teenage marriage and early divorce.

Depression in adolescence casts its shadow forward. One study found that almost 8 percent of depressed adolescents commit suicide in the first ten or fifteen years of adult life. Those depressed in their teens are more likely to experience career failures and to appear on the welfare rolls. Teenage depression is correlated with high rates of hospitalization in the adult years for both psychiatric and other medical reasons. One study (as yet unpublished) found that a single diagnosis of depression in adolescence conferred an increased risk of heart disease throughout life

These health economics data—often based on one-time interviews in the workplace or correlations between payrolls and insurance records—confirm the behavioral genetics findings, which arise from the evaluation of individuals over decades. However you approach the issue—twin studies, employment studies, public health studies—depression accounts for extraordinary levels of pain and disability.

The most disabling illness! The costliest! The public health studies underscore the gap between what we know and what we feel about depression. Reading a dramatic claim in the newspaper—one, say, to the effect that only 15 percent of depressed patients receive appropriate care—we may think, well, "depressed," "appropriate," it all depends. But how much could it depend? The magnitude of the harm depression causes is unimaginable; discount it by 50 percent, and depression remains at the head of the pack.

Studies that focus on cost and lost productivity tell only part of the story. Those approaches ignore or minimize consideration of the effects of depression in late life, after the conventional retirement age. In old age, depression becomes a straightforward risk factor for shortened life, not through suicide but through ordinary ill health.

The most carefully controlled study of death and depression in the elderly comes from data gathered to investigate heart disease. Researchers evaluated more than 5000 men and women age sixty-five and older in four communities over a six-year period. Those with high depression scores were over 40 percent more likely to die than those with low depression scores.

The researchers then looked at the usual contributors to mortality: social class, health risk factors (such as smoking), and other concurrent disease, as well as minor indicators of heart problems, below the level of outright illness. Poverty can act as a stressor; heart problems can deplete energy or lower mood. But after controlling for those variables, depression still accounted independently for a 24 percent increase in deaths—from such causes as heart attack and pneumonia. This increase put depression at the level of high blood pressure, smoking, stroke, and congestive heart failure as a risk factor for death in the elderly.

Think of it: a cardiac study that finds depression as deadly as congestive heart failure. I mention this research because its statistical analyses are so painstaking. Less well constructed studies suggest that, throughout life, depression can double or triple the death rate. Only a small minority of the excess deaths are suicides.

No one is certain how depression shortens life. Depression leads to poor health behaviors, through apathy—that problem may account for the high death rates found in the less carefully designed studies. The better studies control statistically for poor health behavior—they set it aside—and still they find that depression kills. Depressives have abnormalities in hormone regulation, blood vessel and heart functioning, and immune responses to infection. Adult-onset diabetes occurs more often in the depressed. A body of research suggests that tumors may grow faster in the face of depression, and that in cancer patients depression at the time of diagnosis predicts bad outcomes from the malignancy.

If it entailed none of the disabling consequences analyzed in the international public health studies, if it had no effects on schooling and work and marriage and parenting, if it never resulted in suicide, if it caused no daily suffering, if it were as invisible as high blood pressure, depression would still earn its place among a brutal and elite group of chronic illnesses, those that act throughout the body and across the life cycle to lead to early death. But of course, depression does harm on all those levels. The public health findings of the last decade consitute another change in our understanding of *what it is*. Depression is a disease of extraordinary magnitude—one of the most devastating diseases human beings suffer.

Thirteen

❖

Extent

MONSTROUS IN THE EXTREME CASE, *no doubt. But every-one gets the blues. Depression exists across a wide spectrum.*

Today, that objection has it backward. Yes, a hundred years ago, as the psychoanalytic model was making its ascent, it was possible to say that we all have inner conflicts and melancholia is only a sign of especially intense ones. By that account, mood disorder is an exaggeration of the normal condition.

Once depression takes its place among the ordinary diseases, we are bound to read the spectrum in the other direction. It's like blood pressure or serum cholesterol: since the high readings are understood as dangerous, the important question is at what (lesser) level the risk sets in. Taken on their own, the low-level versions of most spectrum illnesses—think again of arthritis or asthma—might strike us as scarcely worth noticing; it is in the light of major cases that the minor manifestations earn their classification as pathology.

I wonder in any event whether the spectrum metaphor isn't overdone when it comes to mood disorder. The emptiness, paralysis, and terror of depression have only a modest connection to the sadness of everyday life. That's why a memoirist like William Styron can spend a whole book wondering at the ineffable quality of his suffering, different in quality from anything he had encountered before.

Because health is distinct from depression—because the spectrum is limited in its extent—the most useful way to explore continuity is to start with major depression and work outward toward less severe conditions, at each stage paying attention to the harm that minor depression represents or causes.

The standard definition of depression is built around the major depressive episode. Episodes are identified via symptoms. There are nine: depressed mood, problems experiencing pleasure, low energy, disrupted sleep, diminished or increased appetite, mental and physical agitation or slowing, feelings of worthlessness or guilt, difficulty concentrating, and suicidality. For a major depressive episode, you need five of these symptoms, including one of the first two, sadness or anhedonia. The symptoms must have lasted two weeks. They must be substantial enough to cause you distress or impair your functioning—that is, they must be of at least moderate severity. (There are further refinements; for example, uncomplicated bereavement does not count, even if it lasts two weeks and involves five symptoms.) Generally, if you have a depressive episode, you qualify for the diagnosis of one or another subtype of depression.

This sort of operational definition, progressively refined, has been in general use for about twenty-five years. Its effect has been revolutionary.

In the middle of the last century, most forms of depression, major and minor, were lumped into a catchall category, "depressive neurosis." Depressive neurosis included patients immobilized by what today would be termed a major episode. But reasonably healthy psychoanalytic patients also qualified, if their complaints featured moodiness more than anxiety.

The grab bag was hardly problematic in the days when, for a broad range of conditions, there was only one treatment, psychotherapy. But for research, the category was useless. Because groups of doctors disagreed about the nature and boundaries of illness, neurotically depressed patients in New York City, where psychoanalysis was in vogue, bore scant resemblance to neurotically depressed patients in St. Louis, where hospital-based, medical-model psychiatry prevailed. You could not reasonably test a remedy for depressive neurosis and expect the result to hold across sites.

By quantifying distress, in terms of type, number, severity, and duration of symptoms, diagnosticians were able to identify a group sufficiently uniform for the purposes of research. The diagnoses were much more reliable—that is to say, more stable and reproducible—than diagnoses grounded in prior, vaguer definitions. Someone diagnosed depressed *here* would be diagnosed depressed *there*. Someone diagnosed depressed *then* would likely be diagnosed depressed *now* and in the future.

It is impossible to overstate the influence or the success of the operational definition. It has been a more important scientific tool than the PET scan. Almost every research result regarding depression in humans refers to people with at least two weeks of five symptoms of moderate severity. The altered neuroanatomy, the genetic risk, the excess disability—all are liabilities of major depression, operationally defined.

The operational definition of depression gained its initial standing from its correspondence to clinicians' impression of "caseness." The criteria picked out patients whom psychiatrists considered ill. Most people who qualified were well within the boundary; they had been profoundly incapacitated repeatedly, for months at a time. If you ask either patients or doctors to rate symptoms and role impairment from very mild to very severe, you find that most patients who meet the minimum criteria for depression are at the severe end of the range. Most depression, operationally defined, is severe illness.

But there are exceptions. Imagine that in the face of terrible losses, you spend two weeks struggling with disturbed sleep, poor appetite, low energy, disrupted concentration, and sad mood. The thought of suicide never crosses your mind. Despite your unhappiness, you remain optimistic. You remain curious about your children's progress, want to live to a ripe old age to see how their stories turn out. You've been through slumps before. The fact that this one is deeper and longer does not have you shaken. Why shouldn't sadness wash over you? There's reason enough.

It is the eve of day fifteen. Are you depressed?

Here, the answer might depend on your future course. Imagine that the next morning you waken recovered—if not yet full of vim and vigor, nonetheless revived and ready to face the world. You remain upbeat thereafter, despite the persistence of the adversity. We might not want to style you depressed—resilient, rather. If then you never in your life experience another day of disordered mood, we will be disinclined to say that you had been ill ever.

For you, the diagnostic criteria were invalid. You did not have the disease.

This problem has little clinical relevance. A temperamentally hopeful person faced with an obvious challenge is not likely to find his way into psychiatric care within two weeks, even if he experiences moderate psychic disruption. In twenty years of practice, I have never seen a new patient who complains of just two weeks of moderate depressive symptoms. If such a patient were to consult me, I might tread water—extend the period of evaluation. If the despair lifted, my thought might be that the episode was self-limiting. More likely, I would tell myself, *He was never really depressed.*

This glitch—an instance when a person meets criteria but would not qualify as a patient—helps to reveal the dual nature of the operational definition. One reason that the "Chinese menu" approach to diagnosis (one from column one, four from column two) tends to work is that the scenario we have considered is uncommon. It is just unlikely that if you are depressed for two weeks straight, you will waken recovered on day fifteen or that you will live a life free of mood disorder. Given a certain level of psychic disruption, a person is at high risk for the real thing, the career. Here, "depression" applies prognostically. The diagnosis has predictive validity.

The two-week period of depression is illness because, untreated, it tends to lead to very substantial mood disorder—in the way that moderate high blood pressure is an illness because it predicts heart attacks and strokes. If you have high blood pressure for three years and then are hit by a car and killed, a friend would be justified in saying you had never been ill a day in your life. Did you have "a medical condition"? In terms of what doctors treat, you did. But there is also a sense in which to call high blood pressure a disease is to conflate risk with the thing itself.

Many medical conditions have this second aspect. Chest pain, if it originates in the heart, is both a symptom—painful and disabling in itself—and a predictor of serious cardiac disease. You can't write off even quite mild angina, because it represents risk.

Like angina, early depression is both disease and risk factor. If you are depressed for two weeks, the odds are that you will continue to meet criteria for at least four months, and more likely nine months or a year. Most people who meet the minimal criteria will then suffer recurrences of the full syndrome or experience symptoms on an ongoing basis.

Actually, the two-week episode "predicts" the past as well. It predicts that investigators will discover that you have a family history of depression, and a genetic predisposition (judging from the state of your identical twin), and memories of a difficult childhood. It predicts that you will look vulnerable in a variety of ways, that you have a broad syndrome, extending beyond the five recent symptoms and beyond the recent episode.

Our understanding of prognosis derives from longitudinal research—observations of patients over time. One such study, funded by the National Institute of Mental Health, began in the late 1970s. It looked at over 500 patients identified as depressed when they sought treatment at any of five medical centers. The subsequent work was "naturalistic"—researchers followed patients as they received or (mostly) failed to receive treatment.

Depression turns out to be a tenacious condition. Two years after the initial episode, 20 percent of patients had not yet recovered. Ten years out, 7 percent remained depressed. At fifteen years—6 percent. These were not especially treatment-resistant patients. Few had received an adequate course of medication or psychotherapy before entering the study; half of those who remained persistently depressed went on to receive almost no treatment.

When they did recover, the vast majority of patients experienced subsequent episodes: 40 percent at two years, 60 percent at five years, 75 percent at ten years, and 87 percent at fifteen years. With each recurrence, the time to recovery lengthened and the time to the next recurrence shortened. After a second episode, the two-year recurrence rate was 75 percent. After a fifth episode, the *six-month* recurrence rate was 30 percent. With each recurrence, about 10 percent of patients remained depressed continuously for five years.

These findings testify to the undertreatment of depression. In the 1980s, only 3 percent of those depressed for six months had received even one full-dose, four-week trial of antidepressants. The results also indicate the limitations of treatment and the stubbornness of the illness.

Diagnosis is prognosis. The criteria had identified patients with a serious, protracted, recurrent condition. If anything, it looked as if the researchers had set the bar too high. In restricting their attention to subjects with five moderately severe symptoms, doctors might be missing people with substantial levels of risk and disability.

In terms of how psychiatrists treat depression, the main effect of the research findings was to emphasize the importance of complete remission—the elimination of all symptoms—as a goal.

In the heyday of psychoanalysis, therapists had been content to end an episode of depression—if they considered that task important at all. Therapy had more fundamental aims. Character change was the gold standard. Without character change, a person is not yet master of his demons, and so a remnant of melancholy is only natural. Quite mainstream theories held that certain depressed patients were not depressed enough—their moderate depression arose from a failure to understand how deep their moral crisis ran. But even pragmatic psychotherapists were content to see a patient rise from frank depression to low-level pessimism and self-doubt.

Pharmacologists had similar standards. A patient who, on medication, halved his burden of symptoms was said to have responded to treatment. Generally, such patients no longer met the episode-based definition for major depression. Technically, they had recovered, so long as they now had, say, three symptoms rather than five.

But in the past decade, it became clear that patients with residual symptoms suffer recurrences sooner and more often than patients who become fully "themselves again." The findings of the NIMH study were particularly stark. The researchers looked at subjects whose depression had remitted to the point that they had only one or two mild symptoms. Even that seemingly trivial degree of depression left subjects at risk. Patients with minimal residual symptoms were 30 percent more likely to relapse into major depression than patients who, on recovery, were symptom-free. Patients with residual symptoms relapsed to an episode of major depression three times as fast as patients with no residual symptoms. And for patients with one or two residual symptoms, additional symptoms began to accumulate almost immediately; these patients— unlike patients with a symptom-free recovery—slid back toward depression as soon as the prior episode was declared over.

These findings caught the diagnostic experts flat-footed. In 1991, some years into the NIMH study, a consensus group had proposed a definition of recovery from depression that allowed for the persistence of a moderate degree of symptomatology. That definition was wrong. Even modest disruptions of sleep and appetite, for example, signal a substantial increased likelihood of future episodes and all they imply in terms of harm. By the late 1990s, it had become clear that symptom-free recovery is the goal in the treatment of depression.

In its attempt to characterize what occurs in nature, psychiatry had defined less acute, less protracted, or milder depressive disorders. We will turn to these lower-level depressions presently; they, too, cause substantial disability. Once the minor depressions were taken into account, another conclusion became unavoidable: depression tends to be chronic. Even among patients who recovered completely, only a third remained free of depression ten years out. If you took a first episode of depression and then looked nine years down the road, the average patient would have been in one or another form of depression half of the weeks for the entire interval. Starting with a second episode, patients had substantial symptoms more weeks than not, in any interval the re-searchers chose to look at.

Patients who suffer depressive episodes are prone to minor depres-sions. Between illnesses, these patients may experience chronic, low-level symptoms that shape what looks like a morbid personality style. Depressive episodes serve as markers for a career of waxing and waning mood disorder.

Even this description of the course of depression recognizes too many boundaries. The life histories of depressives led researchers to ask about the intervals of lesser symptoms. How distinctive, really, is the depressive episode? How minor are minor depressions? What is the fu-ture of a patient who has endured something like the career of depres-sion without encountering two weeks of five moderate symptoms?

Ken Kendler, the behavioral geneticist, took on the depressive episode. It turns out that the criteria for major depression are arbitrary in every regard. Patients who have only four moderately severe symp-toms of depression for two weeks do badly down the road. Suffering five moderately disabling symptoms for ten days confers a poor prog-nosis. Five mild symptoms, endured for two weeks, predict substantial risk as well. Every criterion—number, severity, and duration of symptoms—sits on a continuum of risk. Suicide, work and social prob-lems, future full-blown depression, depression in your identical twin—all these misfortunes are only very slightly less frequent in people who pass through episodic states that sit on depression's edge. In fact, in Kendler's data, major depression (a full five-symptom episode lasting more than two weeks) is as common in those who a year prior reported three or four symptoms as in those who had reported five.

Nor does ratcheting up the criteria help. Researchers have tried to find a solid core, the true illness, depression, by adding requirements to those that define a major episode. If you consider only patients who also have active suicidal thoughts, for example, you miss large num-bers who go on to quite serious outcomes, from self-destructive acts to hospitalizations for mental illness—and the (apparently) suicidal group still contains some patients who have benign subsequent courses.

Over a broad range of severity, you can expand or contract criteria as you please, and still you will not manage to corral all those and only those people who by a reasonable understanding are seriously depressed. Depression is solidly continuous, in the manner of high blood pressure. Less depression is better and more is worse, in terms of disability and future risk; but everywhere, good- and bad-outcome cases are admixed.

These results leave researchers hoping to find biological markers— tests that will correlate directly with progressive harm to the brain. A valid test might show in one case that what symptomatically looks like a minor or residual depression is part of a physiological process that is eroding the hippocampus, endangering the heart, and so forth; in another case, testing might show that what looks like a full-blown episode will have no likely residual consequences, in an especially resilient person. Often in medicine, we hope for these more valid predictors—we might want to know which people can live safely with high blood pressure in the absence of treatment.

For now, any practical approach to depressive illness will rely on operational definitions of apparently continuous conditions. Two weeks of five moderate depressive symptoms correlates with brain abnormalities, general health risk, and marked disability. What looks like low-level depression is often a stage of major depression or a risk factor for it. And low-level depression has risks of its own.

For clinicians, both in mental health care and in general medical practice, the standard definition of depression had been problematic from the start. Most people who complain of hopelessness and low energy fall short of the diagnosis, even when their discomfort is substantial. These despairing-but-not-depressed patients are the ones who cost the medical system the most. They show up in doctors' offices with physical complaints that are expensive to work up—and that turn out to arise from minor mood disorder.

That is why the professions moved, with some tentativeness, to test criteria for less severe disorders. The research identified symptom clusters that form a halo around depression. Psychiatrists gave these

syndromes names like *dysthymia* (which refers to low mood of long duration), *minor depression* (like major, but with fewer symptoms), and *recurrent brief depression* (repeated episodes of full intensity, none of
which lasts two weeks).

Because even these diagnoses miss a large number of patients of
concern to their doctors, psychiatrists began to study research subjects with quite limited complaints. These people had two symptoms
for (at least) two weeks but did not complain of depressed mood or
the inability to experience pleasure. They might, for instance, discuss
obsessive thoughts of death and express feelings of worthlessness in
the course of an interview: "I don't know what's been wrong these
past months. I've come to believe that I've never been any good at
anything and never will be. I keep thinking of walking in front of cars.
Sure, I still like spending time at the track. If my horse comes in, I get
a good feeling. And yet, I wish it would happen to me, something to
end it all. I'm no use to anyone." Even if such a person retains normal
patterns of sleeping and eating, even if all the other signs and symptoms of depression are missing, still this condition is dangerous and
debilitating.

This least substantial depressive variant—two symptoms—was
called *subsyndromal symptomatic depression*. The awkward word *subsyndromal* was meant to signal awareness on the part of researchers that
so limited an impairment necessarily lacks shape—but then what is the
word *depression* doing in the phrase? Is the condition illness, or not?
Both the name and the concept evoked sniggering when they were proposed in the mid-1990s.

When it occurs in a career of profound depression, low-level depression is clearly an element in a chronic illness. Low-level depression can
precede major depression (in which case it is called prodromal), it can
follow it immediately (as residual illness), or it can appear belatedly, as
a minor recurrence. These instances of depression are part of a single
picture. But what is the significance of the low-level depressions on
their own? Are they mere stumbles, in the course of a healthy life? Or
do they resemble mood disorders in the harm they predict?

It turns out that in every respect, lower-level depressions look like attenuated forms of major depression. The biology of minor and major depression forms a continuum. For instance, on falling asleep, the time to enter the rapid eye movement, or REM, phase is substantially decreased in major depression; it is somewhat decreased in low-level depressions. Low-level depressions cluster in families where major depression is prevalent. Low-level depressions can progress to major depression, or they can be dangerous on their own. In one study, almost a quarter of patients with recurrent brief depression had attempted suicide. Even the subsyndromal state, the merest hint of depression, confers a suicide risk three or four times that of the general population.

And low-level depression is disabling. We have already considered the finding that, in old age, quite modest levels of depression predict early death. In fact, every disability that follows on depression also clusters with the subsyndromal state: excess physical illness, excess medical cost, excess days out of work. Welfare benefits, disability benefits, emergency room visits—name a social cost, and it correlates with low-level depression.

Although the criteria may seem minimal, the minor depressions are hardly universal. To experience even two symptoms of depression for two weeks would feel foreign to most people who are otherwise in good health. I consider myself reasonably depressive, in terms of my personality style. I am easily upset. I brood over failures. I require solitude. I have a keen sense of injustice. In the face of bad fortune, I suspect that I might well succumb to mood disorder. In medieval or Renaissance terms, I am melancholic as regards my preponderant humor. And yet I have never qualified for a diagnosis of a low-level depression. I don't hold on to even isolated symptoms, like insomnia, for days on end. Thinking of the patients I see for marital counseling, many are the same way—grumpy, uncomfortable, and in a bind, but not depressed at any level, now or ever. Depression, across a broad spectrum, remains a distinct disease, separate from the various personality states it sometimes accompanies.

In one careful study, the incidence of the depressions, at a moment in time, was 10 percent, with major depression and dysthymia in the

2 to 3 percent range, minor depression between 1 and 2 percent, and subsyndromal depression close to 4 percent.

Of course, many of the people identified in one category will go on to experience the other forms of depression or have suffered them already. The long-term studies of depression and depressive symptoms forged a particular understanding of depression: it is a unitary illness. Most minor depression is depression. A good deal of subsyndromal depression is depression.

It could have been otherwise. The data might have shown that one subtype of depression clusters in particular families, to the exclusion of other diagnoses. It might have shown discontinuities in the level of risk conferred, for work disruption or suicide attempts or future depressive episodes. It might have shown that episodes lead mainly to future episodes and not to the minor states. But studies of the form and course and consequences of depression suggest a single disorder.

On first consideration, this result may seem unexceptionable. Severe depression arises in people who have been mildly depressed. Severe depression can lead to mild depression. Even mild depression is burdensome.

But on second thought, the notion of a unitary disease may be unsettling. Will we call it all depression? Even two symptoms? Sadness, guilt, feelings of worthlessness—surely those are part of who we are, as we pass through life. Doesn't legitimating a range of "depressions" play into the hands of the drug companies? Or, alternatively: Don't psychiatrists know that we live in a capitalist system? Extend the range of depression, and employers will stop offering mental health coverage altogether.

These concerns bear addressing, but perhaps the first thing to say is that they come from spheres—moral, aesthetic, political, and economic—that, while they enter into medicine, stand at a distance from the issues of symptom and prognosis that doctors consider when they formulate a diagnosis. Medicine asks, *What is the phenomenon?* If depression is a unitary disease and if even minor variants carry risk, then it is and they do.

Besides, in the office, a good deal of minor depression feels like major depression. Dysthymia can be a devastating condition. Imagine being sad on most days, for years. There are mild cases of dysthymia—

dysthymia that has the texture of everyday unhappiness, being worked out slowly, say, in psychotherapy. But most dysthymia looks like the behavioral, lived-out representation of the stuck switch—relentless stress, constant fragility, battering and bruising from without and within. If someone is plagued by sadness, hopelessness, mental slowing, and low self-worth, it is small comfort that he eats well. Sitting across from dysthymia, it is not hard to imagine that you are in the territory of depression.

For most of the twentieth century, under the rubric of "neurosis," yet more minor depressive states might be labeled illness. I suspect that what seems sinister, in the reclaiming of part of this territory, is the mode of treatment. In retrospect, we may have tolerated a loose understanding of mood disorder because we did not imagine psychotherapy to be radically effective. About psychoanalysis in particular, there was always doubt—it might be more self-exploration than medical intervention. Contemplating treatment via more hard-edged means—think of genetic engineering, think of a campaign of eradication—demands that we own our beliefs regarding minor depression and its status as disease.

But here again, our finickiness seems to reveal an inclination to treat depression differently—as if it were not the equal of diabetes or epilepsy. Spectrum diseases are common in medicine, and we understand their manifestations as pathology all along the spectrum. All psoriasis is psoriasis. Discover a dime-sized patch of psoriatic rash, and you will carry the diagnosis *psoriasis* for the rest of your life, whether or not you go on to suffer the joint pain or life-threatening skin exfoliation that can arise in that underappreciated affliction. Nor are incidence and prevalence factors in the demarcation of disease. One hundred percent of the population get dental cavities, and no one denies that these constitute pathology. Following the ordinary standards of medicine, low-grade depression is just that, low-grade depression.

Someday, our unease may be alleviated by the discovery of accurate biological markers. We might find that certain low-level depressions are benign, along with a small percentage of cases that meet our current operational definition of the major episode. But my guess is that such a resolution would entail the same reevaluation of the significance of mood states that we are facing today. We would find that a good deal of what we had once been content to write off as personality style is, in biological terms, ongoing illness, creating damage throughout the body. We might become convinced that our former tolerance for low-level depression had been *faute de mieux*, a function of limitations in our ability to identify, prevent, or cure disorders of mood.

For now, psychiatrists work, as doctors generally do, with probabilities. We make judgments, matching symptoms with choices: intervene, recommend lifestyle changes, do nothing. Given the data on the harm and risk attaching to residual symptoms and low-level depression, our efforts at treatment are reasonably vigorous. To accept depression as disease is to see pathology or risk in minor versions.

Fourteen

❖

Convergence

IN THE LATE 1980S, when advanced brain scanning was still a novelty, Duke University obtained one of the first magnetic resonance imagers, a machine capable of creating detailed pictures of brain anatomy. As K. Ranga Rama Krishnan tells it, no one knew what to do with the new technology, so he sent some of his elderly depressed patients along, to see what would turn up. What the radiologists found were "unidentified bright objects," small white patches clustered in critical areas of the brain. Krishnan continued to request scans on patients with "late-onset depression"—those with a first episode after age sixty-five. Over 70 percent showed the bright spots.

Krishnan, now the chair of psychiatry at Duke University, is an enthusiast with a wide range of interests. He wandered into psychiatry via curiosity about the workings of the eye. A growing awareness of how the visual system constructs the world, inductively rather than through precise reproduction of light signals, led to questions about how mind and brain work altogether. Krishnan has always been a complete doctor, aware of the effects of mental illness throughout the body, and curious about the influence of peripheral illness on disorders of thought and behavior. His claims of random discovery are not to be trusted; Krishnan has well-informed instincts.

Once he observed the bright spots, Krishnan encouraged a pathologist to scan brains at autopsy and then dissect them to characterize the lesions. The bright spots signaled changes in blood vessels—empty spaces that ranged from 1 cubic millimeter (a "punctate lesion") to 70 cubic centimeters (think of a sphere with a diameter of over 2 inches). The holes were the result of "silent strokes"—injury to parts of the brain that do not govern movement or sensory functions like vision. Such strokes go unnoticed because they result in no dramatic, immediate changes in experience or behavior.

Silent strokes turn out to be reasonably common after age sixty. But among elderly patients with silent strokes, those with late-life depression have the most extensive damage. When Krishnan first reported this finding, it met opposition. Editors of professional journals were reluctant to have *depression* appear in the title of articles about blood vessel disease. They suggested that Krishnan waffle with such formulations as *depression-like syndrome*. For the most part, Krishnan held his ground. "Vascular depression" (as he came to call the subtype) *is* depression—depression associated with blood vessel disease.

Like many discoveries in contemporary psychiatry, vascular depression is a fresh encounter with an old concept. A hundred years ago, a German psychiatrist and (as we would now call him) geriatrician named Robert Gaupp proposed the category "arteriosclerotic depression." In the era of psychoanalytic dominance, that concept faded. And now present-day psychiatrists were showing reluctance to embrace a blood vessel disorder as a mental illness. They imagined that Krishnan was merely seeing depressed mood in the context of a dementing disease or normal aging.

As a mood disorder, vascular depression has its distinctive features. Anhedonia is especially frequent—patients tend to be unable to look forward with pleasure to future events. Compared to other elderly depressives, patients with vascular lesions come to the illness with less family history of mood disorder or substance abuse, and less experience of depression in their own earlier lives. Late-onset depressives tend to be more impaired and harder to treat than are patients who first encounter depression early in life. But these differences are subtle.

Vascular depressives meet full criteria for the depressive syndrome—altered sleep and appetite, excessive guilt, impaired self-image. Often their condition responds to standard antidepressants, and it improves reliably with electroconvulsive therapy, ECT. In general, in terms of course of illness and likelihood of recovery, the depressed older patients with silent strokes resemble depressed older patients who have no lesions. Episodes of vascular depression tend to arise or worsen in the face of stressful life events. Episodes occur more often in patients with poor social support. Vascular depression acts like depression, except that by the time the syndrome emerges, sufferers are already a fair distance down the common pathway—a first episode of vascular depression might look like a second or third episode of the sort of depression that begins in youth or at midlife.

And vascular depression is a disorder of the same parts of the brain implicated in depression in general. We may recall, from the studies that made Rajkowska turn her attention to depression, that run-of-the-mill, nonspecific depression has a vascular aspect. Often, depressed patients show decreased blood flow to the prefrontal cortex. In her postmortem studies, Rajkowska found anatomical damage—cellular disruption—in this region. In time, Krishnan was able to assemble a series of elderly patients with silent strokes, some with major depression and some free of depression. He could then have a computer examine their brain scans and "subtract out" the incidental lesions—the ones that occur in the control group and cause no mood disorder. Presumably, the remaining lesions, the ones that appear only in the depressives, constitute the damage specific to late-life depression. These bright spots show up in limited regions. Prime among them is the prefrontal cortex.

Anatomically, vascular depression looks like the depressions that occur earlier in life; only the cause of injury to the relevant areas differs—strokes, rather than genetics and the cumulative effects of stress. The result from Krishnan's "subtracting out" experiment—the finding that, among all the patients with silent strokes, it is those with damage to the prefrontal cortex who experience the syndrome of depression—suggests a causal role for the abnormalities that Rajkowska identified in younger patients on autopsy. The silent-stroke research provides strong support for the current myth of depression, the hypothesis that, at the level of neuroanatomy, depression is disruption to a defined circuit of regions of the brain.

Through his work with the elderly, Krishnan was able to add information about the function (and malfunction) of the prefrontal cortex. One part of the prefrontal cortex is especially implicated in depression, both in Krishnan's work with the elderly and Rajkowska's postmortem studies of glia. This section, which sits just behind and above orbits of the eye, is called the orbitofrontal cortex. The orbitofrontal cortex integrates incoming information including "performance feedback"—awareness that one is succeeding or failing at a task.

Krishnan's group gave a "trail-making" test to elderly subjects half of whom did, and half of whom did not, suffer vascular depression—and none of whom showed signs of dementia. The test is like a child's dot-to-dot game. The goal is to connect in sequence (1 to A to 2 to B, and so on) a series of numbered and lettered circles scattered on a page.

This task is not one that depressed patients do well. Even worse than the initial error rate is depressives' response to correction. In the test, if a subject makes an error, the administrator gently points out the problem and suggests how to proceed. After correction, virtually no control subjects make a subsequent ("perseverative") error. But depressed patients do—many more than controls even when the baseline error rate is taken into account. Some depressives have catastrophic reactions; after a correction, they go on to connect dot to dot in random fashion, as if they had lost all hope of succeeding at the task.

Krishnan repeated the test one and two years after the initial administration. Even as they aged, the nondepressed elderly got better and better at the initial puzzle. The depressed patients did not improve, and their perseverative error rate continued to worsen. These problems persisted whether or not the patients remained depressed—indeed, the errors did not correlate with the active level of depression but seemed to signal an ongoing problem in responses to mild challenges. ("Processing information with a negative valence" is what the postcorrection portion of the trail-making exercise is said to test.) Krishnan was then able to use functional brain imaging—the kind that follows energy utilization in different parts of the brain. When test administrators suggested corrections, the subjects' orbitofrontal cortices lit up.

This result—perseverative errors—is interesting in light of the common claim that depressives are realists. It is true that the adaptive state for human beings involves a degree of unrealistic optimism. In gambling experiments, where subjects are asked to evaluate the odds of winning at a given level of risk, the nondepressed tend to give optimistic estimates, even in the face of mounting losses. The depressed are more accurate—well, what else would they be? But in these same trials, depressives continue to make bad bets. Even when depressives perceive accurately, they lack the motivation to heed their own judgment and alter their behavior.

In interviews with depressives, including those in remission, Krishnan found that a similar problem explained the performance on the trail-making test. The depressives understood the correction but paid more attention to self-fulfilling prophecies—that they were fated to fail anyway, that they were screwups. In cognitive terms, vascular depression sounded a good deal like run-of-the-mill depression as seen by a cognitive therapist. Depressives had fixed, negative views about themselves. These attributions governed their behavior and led to failure, in the face of reasonably easy tasks.

The vascular depressives looked like Betty, with the anomaly of the will that prevented her from attempting even a small art project. They were overwhelmed, inhibited from trying—only here, there were clues as to the physical basis of that inhibition. The vascular depressives' lack of mental resilience appeared to arise in direct fashion from damage to the orbitofrontal cortex of the brain. To put the same result in reverse fashion, many run-of-the-mill depressives resemble elderly depressives with small lesions in the orbitofrontal cortex.

Awareness of vascular depression colors the debate over whether depression is an honest-to-goodness disease, and where along the spectrum it attains that status. Consider a person who, through silent strokes, sustains injuries to parts of the brain implicated in assessments of the world and the self. On scan, the orbitofrontal cortex reveals bright spots, as do the hippocampus and amygdala. If an additional minuscule stroke then precipitates an episode of major depression, does that episode constitute an instance of illness? What if the ensuing problem is not major but minor depression—is a disease in action here?

I have posed these questions in discussions with various groups, including philosophers. Any level of stroke-based brain damage constitutes disease in almost anyone's book when that damage produces symptoms. Indeed, most people are inclined to grant full disease status to such a condition even in the presence of quite limited lesions and quite trivial alterations in mood or judgment. Our focus on the physical is such that evidence of holes punched in the brain proves decisive. The entire spectrum is illness; treatment of both the blood vessel disease and the resultant mood state seem justified, even pressing.

Now (I have asked diverse groups), imagine that the damage to the cortex and the reduction in regional blood flow are caused not by stroke but by a combination of factors—genes, stress, prior depression. Does the ensuing mood disorder have a different status? When they approach the problem in this fashion, most audiences are inclined to classify even minor depression as illness.

If not in logical, then in practical terms, vascular depression reinforces the claim that run-of-the-mill depression constitutes pathology. And here the direction of cause seems not to matter. Whether depression results in brain damage or results from it, whether the damage is permanent or reversible—beside this striking model, vascular depression, mood disorder in a variety of imagined shapes attains legitimacy.

• •

So far, we have assumed that strokes set the stage for depression, but the picture is more complex. Krishnan's observations revitalized a field whose results have been tantalizing for some years—the overlap of depression and cardiovascular disease. Some of the causation runs in the other direction. Depressive symptoms seem to increase the risk of stroke and heart disease.

Numerous studies confirm depression's link to poor heart health. By middle age, depression becomes one of the strongest, by some measures the strongest, of independent risk factors for cardiac disease. Minor depression increases the risk of cardiac death by half. Major depression triples or quadruples the risk. Those liabilities apply both to people with heart disease and to those with no disease (at the start of a four-year study). Looking only at coronary artery disease—abnormalities associated with restrictions in flow in the vessels that nourish the heart muscle—depression quintuples the risk of death.

Perhaps that statistic bears repeating: mature men and women with depression are five times as likely as those without to die of coronary artery disease. These risk rates have been adjusted for the presence of smoking, drinking, high blood pressure, diabetes, and a variety of other factors. The unadjusted rates—taking account of both direct and indirect harm from depression—are yet higher. A high level of risk applies across the range of heart disease. In other studies, depression has been shown to double, triple, or quadruple the death rate from unstable angina, coronary artery bypass surgery, and congestive heart failure.

Perhaps the best-studied phenomenon is the excess risk that major depression confers (also two- to fourfold) in those who have suffered heart attacks. Even a few scattered symptoms of depression can increase mortality. And such symptoms are not rare. Studies have shown that as many as 60 percent of patients with heart attacks show at least a modest level of depression. Major depression hovers in the 10 to 20 percent range.

The discovery of the link to cardiac disease brought depression a level of attention it had never received on its own. The largest study of psychotherapy ever undertaken—over 1700 subjects were enrolled—

addressed the effect of psychotherapy on depression in patients who had suffered an initial heart attack. Actually, the study enrolled almost 2500 subjects; the additional 800 received training aimed at helping them cope with loneliness or isolation—"low perceived social support"; most of this group also received psychotherapy for depression. The study was funded by the National Heart, Lung, and Blood Institute. By contrast, the influential Treatment of Depression Collaborative Research Program of the National Institute of Mental Health was considered ambitious when it studied 250 patients.

For the cardiac study, patients were enrolled within a month of their heart attack. The sample was divided in two. Control subjects received routine medical care from their cardiologist; subjects given the active intervention received six months of both individual and group psychotherapy and up to an additional three months of group treatment. In the event, the therapy (a cognitive-behavioral model was used) diminished patients' level of depression somewhat in the first six months. By thirty months out, depression rates in the treatment and control groups were identical. And the therapy had no effect on the death or heart attack rate.

Perhaps this result should not have been surprising. Interventions with cardiac patients are excruciatingly delicate. A prior study of enriched nursing care, conducted in Canada, had been a disaster. The nurses had contacted patients at home and worked on the way they handled negative emotions. The nurses also helped patients establish good cardiac health behaviors, like proper diet. Over 1300 patients were enrolled—at which point the study had to be stopped because too many patients were dying in the *active intervention group*, the group receiving additional nursing care. In particular, it was uneducated, anxious, elderly women living alone who showed the excess deaths.

The result shocked the researchers. They came to believe that the elderly women could not handle the extra attention. To be educated and put in touch with their feelings sent these patients into a panic. In unintended fashion, the study demonstrated that psychosocial approaches can affect the death rate in heart attack survivors; leaving depressed, anxious, isolated women alone is an effective strategy—at least when contrasted to coaching by nurses. The Canadian results suggested that selecting the right psychological approach for depressed cardiac patients would not be simple.

The Heart, Lung, and Blood Institute trial of psychotherapy may have suffered from a similar problem; perhaps the cognitive approach was simply wrong for some patients. But in that research, an additional complication muddied the findings. A number of patients had received antidepressant medications.

A pilot study conducted at Columbia University had suggested that certain antidepressants—the ones that affect serotonin pathways—could lower the rate of bad cardiac events in patients who were depressed following a heart attack. The research involved 389 research subjects, of whom 186 were given Zoloft. The researchers reported that the medication was "robustly superior to placebo" in treating depression, a result that was most apparent in the severely and recurrently depressed patients. But the effects on heart disease were more impressive. At the end of six months, 7 patients had died; 5 of these were in the group that did not receive Zoloft. Results were in the same direction for repeat heart attack, heart failure, and severe angina. None of these findings was statistically significant—the study had been too small—but there was only one chance in nine that the trend was a fluke. Zoloft seemed to prevent between a quarter and a third of bad cardiac outcomes.

As a result of the Columbia study and others, ethicists ruled that the Heart, Lung, and Blood study could not exclude antidepressant treatment. The protocol required that severely depressed patients and any patients who failed to respond to five weeks of psychotherapy be sent for psychopharmacologic evaluation. Again, Zoloft was the drug most used. By the end of the study, 28 percent of the intervention group had taken antidepressants, for an average of twelve months. So had 20 percent of the control group.

The medicated patients had a 30 or 40 percent reduction in deaths and in recurrent heart attacks. The serotonergic antidepressants in particular appeared to reduce the death rate by 40 percent. The researchers reporting the results downplayed the link between antidepressants and survival, because the study had not been designed to study that connection. Ideally, you would have wanted to assign patients randomly, to receive medication or placebo. Still, it was the severely depressed and the refractory patients (those unresponsive to the initial treatment) who had received medication; they might have been expected to have an especially bad outcome—and they did especially well.

The simplest explanation for a link between depression and heart disease—and for poor outcomes in depressed cardiac patients—is behavioral. Depressives take less good care of themselves than the nondepressed. In particular, the depressed exercise less. But in the case of patients who have had heart attacks, self-care is probably not the issue, given that extra attention from nurses confers no benefit.

Another leading hypothesis concerns blood clots. Depression is a multi-organ disease. Depressives have thinned bones and enlarged adrenal glands. It turns out that depressives have blood platelet abnormalities as well (platelets are small corpuscles that help with clotting). Depressives' platelets tend to be too sticky—more likely to become activated, more likely to form clots along the walls of blood vessels, including the thrombi that block vessels. Some of this corpuscular stickiness appears to arise from stress. When hormones create a state of alert—anticipating fight or flight—they prepare for possible blood loss by making platelets better able to clump. Serotonin plays a key role in this process. In depression, neurons in the brain show abnormalities in the density of serotonin receptors. So do platelets in the bloodstream.

Overall, the clotting system, like other aspects of the stress response system, is chronically hyperactive in patients with depression. This excess responsiveness appears to take place on three or four different levels, involving both platelets and circulating chemicals that serve as clotting factors. Here we complete a (vicious) cycle in the story of vascular depression. It is not only that small strokes cause depression and a loss of resilience in the face of stress; depression and stress may act through the clotting system to cause small strokes in vulnerable regions of the brain.

A second set of observations may help explain the association between depression and heart problems. Depressives show less moment-to-moment speeding and slowing in the heartbeat, in response to minor stimuli such as inhaling and exhaling. This "invariant heart rate" is thought to be a result of overly persistent nerve stimulation to the natural cardiac pacemaker. The evenness is problematic. According to a general principle in engineering, systems that show proportionate or even random responses to small perturbations are less likely to suffer catastrophic responses to large perturbations. More flexible is more stable. An overly stable heart rate puts you at risk for serious arrhythmias. An invariant heart rate, at the level that is common in cardiac patients with depression, more than doubles the risk of death in the two or three years after an initial heart attack. Research suggests that an invariant heart rate may be a sign and result of disregulation in stress pathways. Problems in heart rhythm can lead to problems in clot movement and disturbances in blood flow to the brain.

These problems are not incidental. Depression is not a brain disease merely. It is a neurologic, hematologic, and cardiovascular disease. Overactivation of stress pathways causes a liability to clots and arrhythmias—and alone or together, these predispose to heart attacks, silent strokes, disturbed mood, and sudden death.

It happens that the serotonergic antidepressants, like Zoloft, act on both clotting and heart rhythm. Zoloft (and Prozac, Paxil, Celexa, and Luvox) make platelets less sticky. Perhaps the benefit to heart attack victims has nothing to do with these medications' ability to reduce depression. The antidepressants may be acting as blood thinners merely—like the aspirin routinely dispensed in the aftermath of heart attacks. (The antidepressants act through a different mechanism and can be given alongside aspirin.) The same group of antidepressants can also improve heart rate variability. In cardiac patients, Zoloft and the others may work not through treating depression, the disease of mind and brain, but through treating depression, the disease of heart and blood. Or they may act more nonspecifically (as blood thinners merely), so that they would improve the death and recurrence rate in all heart attack victims, not only those who are depressed.

But there is reason to believe that the central effects of the antidepressants matter. For one thing, in the major studies, recovery from depression, by any means, results in a better cardiac prognosis. For another, even the older, less serotonergic antidepressants (like Elavil) confer some advantage. In a community survey of smokers in and around Philadelphia, the older antidepressants reduced the risk of heart attacks by half. These antidepressants do not thin the blood, and they can actually *worsen* arrhythmias. Their positive effect on cardiac health almost certainly comes from their action on the brain, probably through treating mood disorder and muting excessive responses to stress. That is to say, antidepressants probably protect the heart through their main effect, combating depression.

Stroke victims also benefit from antidepressants. In one remarkable study, researchers at two teaching hospitals in Denmark randomly assigned patients with recent strokes to either Zoloft or a placebo. To join the study, the patients needed to be free of depression and heart disease. Otherwise, the researchers merely recruited patients from 137 consecutive admissions for stroke. Depression is frequent in the wake of stroke. One year out, about a quarter of the placebo group and 10 percent of the Zoloft group were depressed. The differences were similar for the neurologic and cardiac outcomes. The placebo group was three times as likely to be rehospitalized and two to three times as likely to suffer severe cardiovascular events. The numbers were small, but the placebo group also had two to three times the number of recurrent strokes.

In replications of this study in Iowa and Argentina, antidepressants or placebos were administered for twelve weeks to over a hundred patients recovering from strokes. Two years later, over two thirds of the patients who had taken antidepressants were alive, but only 35 percent of the patients who had taken the placebo. The results were best for the patients who began antidepressant treatment earliest; overall, it looked as if prompt administration of antidepressants might halve the mortality from strokes. The meaning of these findings is muddied by the "all-rounder" nature of the new antidepressants. They seem to treat everything. But it is clear enough that, in addition to its effects on bones and endocrine glands, depression presents a risk for heart and blood vessel disease.

Depression is a derailing of functions. The regulation of heart rhythm is a bit off. Platelets are out of control. Strokes and heart attacks become more likely. These results testify to the *pathologic* nature of depression. It's nothing like a normal state. Imagine a culture that has no concept of mental illness, a society in which despair and psychic paralysis count for nothing and the medical profession attends only to organ damage, such as heart attacks and strokes. Given access to what we know, the doctors in that culture would still treat depression vigorously, as a multisystem disease.

But of course, such a culture is unimaginable. Psychic pain intrudes on the work of medicine continually. Cardiologists and neurologists are not the only doctors who encounter depression. In recent years, depression has added new complexity to the work of doctors who treat cancers and infectious diseases. Here, the problem is mood disorder that arises in response to commonly used medications. The prime offender is interferon.

Interferon is a mainstay of treatment in a variety of serious illnesses, from multiple sclerosis (a nervous system disease) to multiple myeloma and malignant melanoma (cancers) to hepatitis C (a viral inflammation of the liver). The drug—there are actually seven or more variants in use—is an artificially produced form of a naturally occurring substance released by white blood cells in the face of viral infections. In the treatment of cancers and infections, interferon can be lifesaving. But if it is to be effective, interferon needs to be taken for months. Interferon can cause unbearable depression, and it does so with a high frequency. As a result, patients drop out of treatment.

Interferon-induced depression is a risk factor for relapse and even death. In one study, 45 percent of melanoma patients suffered full episodes of major depression during twelve weeks of treatment with interferon. In another study, fully a third of hepatitis patients had to be withdrawn from interferon treatment because of intolerable depression—and this figure does not include patients who were lost to follow-up, some because depression caused them to drop out of the protocol.

The hepatitis figures define a public health crisis. Hepatitis C, a liver infection spread sexually and through needle use, is epidemic. In the developed world, more people are likely to die of hepatitis C over the next decade than of AIDS. Interferon is the principal treatment for hepatitis C. Practitioners refer to the 80/80 rule. If a patient can tolerate interferon for 80 percent of the optimal duration, taking 80 percent of the optimal dose, he stands a good chance of entering a remission, by inducing a decrease in the viral load. Less than 80/80 spells failure. The drug-abusing population in particular is impulsive and intolerant of discomfort, and therefore unlikely to follow through with a treatment that induces mood disorder.

Here is an instance where the risk of depression is high, the onset is predictable, and prevention is a matter of life and death. As a matter of some urgency, researchers set out to characterize interferon-induced depression.

The results of that research will sound familiar. In response to interferon, depression tends to occur as a full syndrome—changes in mood, sleep, guilt feelings, and the rest. Depression is more common in those who enter treatment suffering scattered symptoms of depression. Past history and family history of depression are also predictors in some studies, as are current social stressors and lack of social support. Elevated stress hormone levels prior to treatment predict depression during treatment. On PET scans, which measure the brain's use of energy, hepatitis C patients on interferon show marked decrements in activity in the prefrontal cortex. This change occurs in proportion to the subjects' level of depression, with the most depressed showing the greatest prefrontal suppression. The prefrontal slowing appears to be mediated by interferon's effects on the way cells handle serotonin.

Interferon treatment also increases activity in stress hormone pathways. Researchers measured stress hormone levels in melanoma patients throughout a twelve-week treatment with interferon. The patients who became depressed were those who showed high stress hormone responses in the face of interferon. Because the resulting syndrome looks so typical, in animal studies of mood disorder interferon is sometimes employed to create model depressive syndromes.

Both the depression and many of the intermediate brain changes can be prevented by premedicating patients with antidepressants (often Paxil) that act via serotonin. In a study of melanoma patients, Paxil reduced the risk of depression from 45 percent, in the placebo group, to 11 percent, in the group given the antidepressant two weeks before the first dose of interferon. The depression-related dropout rates were 35 percent in the placebo group and 5 percent in the Paxil group.

Theorists have proposed that interferon plays a villainous double role. First it creates vulnerability through disrupting the functioning of the prefrontal cortex, and in particular harming serotonin pathways; then, interferon pushes unprotected brain cells over the edge through the effects of stress hormones. The result is a typical mood disorder—afflicting those with typical risk factors, responsive to typical treatments. Interferon-induced depression is depression. And here again, depression is not a normal behavioral variant or personality style; it is a clear abnormality of brain and behavior caused reliably by a toxin.

There are depressions that arise naturally, in the course of other illness, that resemble the interferon-induced version. Interferon is a cytokine. Cytokines are signaling molecules in the immune system. White blood cells, our protection against infection and other intrusions on the body, produce cytokines in response to various threats. Much of the cytokines' activity is cell to cell, coordinating responses to infection and inflammation. But cytokines also affect receptors in the brain and the stress hormone system—the presumed route for their effect on mood.

Cancer patients often get depressed. As in the case of heart disease, this association may seem obvious. But certain types of cancers—

cancer of the pancreas is notorious—are associated with especially high rates of depression, when compared with other cancers similar in their prognosis and their tendency to cause physical pain. The cancers that elicit depression are the ones that stimulate the release of high levels of cytokines. And the individual cancer patients who become depressed tend disproportionately to be those with high plasma cytokine levels. Biochemically, interferon-induced depression and the depression that accompanies these cancers are probably indistinguishable.

Experientially, the cytokine-induced depressions appear to be identical to ordinary depression; but few would argue that they constitute, in Poe's phrase, a "dropping off of the veil" that stands between humans and life's reality. Are sufferers from pancreatic cancer wiser than sufferers from lung cancer? Do the medically depressed attain some signal benefit, in terms of mature worldview, when compared to other patients, those whose illnesses do not give rise to mood disorder? If they retain some shred of legitimacy, still these questions may arouse queasiness.

The medical depressions clarify the nature of depression altogether. Effectively, to be depressed is to be in the condition of a person who has suffered small strokes in the brain or a person exposed to high doses of interferon. To be depressed is to risk heart attack and stroke. To be depressed is to suffer an impairment that would qualify as disease if it had no effect whatsoever on mood.

Like the stress-and-aging model, the perspective that arises from the medical depressions makes the disease look like failed resilience. After all, half of patients with pancreatic cancer do not suffer depression. Even without antidepressants, a majority of patients with myeloma or hepatitis manage to take adequate doses of interferon for an adequate interval. Forty percent of patients with heart attacks show no evidence of depression. In the face of quite overwhelming harm, these patients can (presumably) still make neurons and neuronal connections in the hippocampus.

Myths give rise—usefully, generatively—to fantasies. Our myth's attendant fantasy is resilience. The opposite of depression is not indifference to the human condition. The opposite of depression is a resilient mind, sustained by a resilient brain and body. Resilience implies an ability to face threats and persevere. In resilience, the heart and the blood vessels function reliably in the face of physical and psychological challenges. In resilience, nerve cells stand far from the verge of destruction, and new connections grow and sprout, allowing for new learning and further vigor in the face of future stressors.

Fifteen

❖

Resilience

WHAT IS TO BE DONE to fulfill the fantasy of resilience? The answer would seem simple: everything. Programs that target childhood sexual abuse have the potential to protect mind and brain. So do initiatives to prevent blood vessel disease. We might adopt a utopian view that improvements in social organization will result in less stressful environments for children, or for humans in general; by this account we could claim that political action, of whatever stripe we favor, is part of a campaign against mood disorder.

But attempts to prevent depression through social or general medical interventions have their limitations. Some people are born with a marked predisposition to depression. For them, routine levels of stress will prove excessive. Even for people who are not especially fragile, there are just too many pathways to mood disorders. Often, societal change is slow; and the swing of the pendulum is not always in the right direction—we can easily imagine life getting more stressful rather than less.

If you had to specify one direct response to the modern understanding of depression, it would be an effort to devise *general* tools that interrupt the pathway leading from stress to brain injury. The interventions would afford protection to neurons at risk, even for people in adverse social environments. Ideal treatments would catalyze repair and new cell growth.

This goal has, in fact, driven the psychiatric research of the past decade.

For the last fifty years, pharmacologists have worked on modulating the brain's handling of norepinephrine and serotonin. The results have been disappointing. New medications like Prozac and Paxil and the others have their advantages—they do especially well, for example, with social anxiety, and they have improved the treatment of low-level depression. But the early antidepressants, developed in the 1950s, are as effective at ending depressive episodes.

Besides, throughout that half century, scientists have understood that serotonin and norepinephrine play at best supporting roles in the biology of mood and mood disorder. Research into stress hormones has been a refreshing alternative. It builds on a substantial knowledge base—decades of studies of endocrine diseases, stroke, and aging. And it holds the promise of prevention, even in the absence of complete knowledge about the nature of depression.

Depression may be mediated by a number of genes. Social sensitivity might cause depression, and so might social insensitivity, if it leads to loneliness. But so long as you cut the link between life stresses and resultant neuronal fragility, you will be minimizing the translation of that genetic potential into illness. If certain "medical" depressions—such as the depression caused by cytokines—act via the stress hormone pathway, then a treatment that interrupts that pathway might protect against them as well.

One way to shield the brain from stress hormones is to stop cells from producing them. Medications that do that job are called antiglucocorticoids. (The first stress hormone discovered was made in the adrenal *cortex*, and its first known function was modulating the way cells use the sugar *glucose;* so from early on, stress hormones as a group were called *glucocorticoids.*) Doctors already have access to a number of antiglucocorticoids, developed to treat cancers, infections, and hormone disorders. Antiglucocorticoids tend to have dangerous side effects. Even their main effect, dampening the fight-or-flight response, is reasonably worrisome: for how long would we be inclined to impair the body in its ability to react to acute challenges? Still, it was hard not to wonder how these readily available drugs might affect the course of depression.

Psychiatric researchers began by giving short courses of antiglucocorticoids to patients whose depressions had failed to respond to conventional regimens. In most trials of antiglucocorticoids, 50 to 60 percent of patients experience a marked diminution in their level of depression; additional patients show partial responses. This result is astonishing. Conventional antidepressants are said to have a 60 to 70 percent response rate, but this figure applies to a broad range of patients. The research subjects in the antiglucocorticoid studies have disease that is refractory to other treatments. What makes the results more remarkable is that it is hardly obvious that the antiglucocorticoids should resolve depression at all.

Some antiglucocorticoids block the production of steroid hormones. Usually, patients feel better on steroid hormones. Patients given cortisone, for ailments like poison ivy, often report a sense of euphoria, or even a degree of mania with irritability. This response can be especially marked in people prone to mood disorders. And a brief infusion of glucocorticoids can induce a sense of well-being in depressed patients, one that may last for days. In theory, the benefit of medications that block stress hormone production should be limited to prevention of further deterioration in vulnerable neurons. In terms of immediate bodily effects, antiglucocorticoids should make people feel run-down.

But refractory depressed patients experience no worsening on antiglucocorticoids. The patients do better, and the change can be rapid. Apparently, relief from stress hormones is so important that the effect overwhelms any discomfort the antiglucocorticoids might cause. The unexpected upswing in mood in response to antiglucocorticoids suggests that stress hormone abnormalities might be a central aspect of depression.

The gross approach to the stress hormone system—shut it down—may lead to useful treatments for mood disorders. But researchers hoped to craft finer interventions. Perhaps it would be possible to alter the brain's response to the stress hormones without harming the body's overall ability to respond to acute challenges. By 1990, the cutting edge of research had moved from modulation of serotonin to the selective blockade of the brain effects of stress hormones. The prime target was corticotropin releasing factor, or CRF.

Corticotropin releasing factor was characterized half a century ago as a hormone that causes the adrenal gland to produce other stress hormones. But CRF has a second set of functions—it acts directly in the nervous system. In a variety of animals, if you introduce CRF into the brain, or if you create a genetically altered individual that produces excess CRF, you see behaviors that look like depression. A number of research results pointed to CRF as a suitable target for intervention in humans. Depressed (human) patients often have elevated levels of CRF in the spinal fluid, a marker of excess CRF in the brain. Studies of untreated depressed patients at autopsy found a tripling of CRF-secreting brain cells, in a pattern suggesting that neurons that normally do not produce CRF had been transformed to do so. Many of the (deleterious) brain effects that we have attributed to stress hormones are put into action by CRF.

The campaign to block the effects of CRF began with work in rats. In rodents, the stress model of depression has been elaborated in detail. Depriving rat pups of maternal care at critical points in development results in chronic changes in the stress hormone systems. The behavioral effects of the early stress appear later in life. If the previously stressed animal is challenged in adulthood, a behavioral syndrome emerges that looks like depression. The restressed rats are listless, socially withdrawn, uninterested in ordinarily attractive stimuli like sweetened water, and prone (as unstressed rats are not) to consume alcohol solutions when offered. Exposure of grown rats to chronic mild stress has similar effects. As they age, stressed rats do poorly cognitively, on maze tests. The depression-like syndrome can be reversed or prevented by the administration of antidepressants. And on all of these measures, some rats prove, on a genetic basis, to be relatively immune to the challenges that generally cause symptoms.

In rats, the depression-like syndrome is accompanied by the activation of genes that cause the production of excess CRF. The rats sprout receptors for CRF in parts of the brain where these receptors are otherwise absent. These same rats show disregulation in their handling of the transmitter chemicals implicated in depression, serotonin and norepinephrine.

And here is another point where hippocampal damage may play a role. The hippocampus can act as a brake on stress hormone activity within the brain. If hormone levels are high, the hippocampus sends out "negative feedback," discouraging other parts of the brain from making CRF. When the hippocampus is damaged, it loses this ability to fine-tune stress responses. Then other parts of the brain produce CRF and CRF receptors, even in the presence of high circulating levels of stress hormones. The animal models provide detail for the hypothesis that the damaged hippocampus is an element in the stuck switch, the abnormality that exposes brain and body to an excess of stress hormones.

Scientists identified—and sequenced and cloned—CRF receptors in the parts of the rat brain implicated in the maintenance of mood. The researchers then worked to create "antagonists" meant to sit on a specific type of CRF receptor and interfere with its functioning. The theory was that with an antagonist in place, even if the brain produced excess CRF, it would find few open receptors. Cells would not get the message to produce excess stress hormone. The hormone production would diminish. If the antagonism was specific enough, the drug would produce this hormone-suppressing effect locally in the brain, without shutting down stress responses throughout the body. The rat would be made relatively immune to psychic stress while remaining able to mount a response to an infection or a wound.

In the rat models, the effort succeeded at every stage. CRF antagonists interrupt the vicious cycle of stress and harm. When these chemicals are administered, pre- and restressed animals display neither the symptoms of depression nor the indicators of progressive neuronal damage. And yet the rats can still produce the general fight-or-flight response; these rats react appropriately to acute stress, but they do not display the depression-like syndrome.

Drug companies competed to create CRF-blockers that would prevent depression in humans. Much of the research was carried on in secret. But in the spring of 2000, a group from the Max Planck Institute in Munich, Germany, reported the results of a "proof of concept" experiment.

They had given twenty depressed patients a medication designed to block a particular CRF receptor, CRF-1. CRF-1 receptors are not so specific a target as researchers would like—they are widely distributed in the brain and body. But the drug trial proved reasonably successful. One subject had a dramatic bad outcome—he became suicidal and dropped out of the study. Almost all the other patients tolerated the medication for the length of the trial, thirty days. They remained able (in the face of a standard chemical challenge) to mount a normal stress response. And their depression improved, sometimes dramatically. In further safety trials, the drug in the Planck Institute experiment appeared to cause liver damage. But in principle, selective CRF receptor blockade worked. You could interrupt CRF transmission in the brain, maintain the acute stress response elsewhere, and diminish depressive symptoms or end an episode of depression outright.

Had the medicine caused fewer side effects, we might well be in the decade of stress hormone blockade. In theory, CRF antagonists should work to prevent post-traumatic stress disorder, stress-related sleep disorders, and a host of anxiety syndromes. And of course, they should prevent the progression of depression, by interrupting the effects of stress hormones on vulnerable parts of the brain.

Six pharmaceutical houses have patented compounds that block the effects of CRF. In lower mammals, these drugs pass into the brain and block the effects of stressors that otherwise produce depression-like syndromes. Barring disaster—and disasters (suicidality, liver damage) have been common in research on CRF antagonists—the day will come when we get to see these substances in action, in the treatment or prevention of depression in humans.

In the meanwhile, some research teams are shooting the moon. Robert Sapolsky, in particular, is pushing science to its limits. He is using genetic engineering to moderate the effects of stress hormones on the brain.

Sapolsky's primary target is stroke. In the aging rat (we may recall), the damage from stroke takes place in two waves. First there is the acute injury, caused by an interruption of blood flow to a part of the brain. Then comes secondary damage, the elaboration of the stroke, caused by the outpouring of stress hormones. Sapolsky's work centers on preventing that elaboration. The ideal preventative would act as close to the vulnerable cell as possible. The stress hormones would exert whatever effects they are meant to exert throughout the brain and body, but neurons would not die.

Sapolsky's work involves altering neurons so that, when stressed, they make substances that guard against cell death. Sapolsky begins with genes that manufacture neuroprotectants. He attaches these genes to viruses and lets the viruses carry the genes into the neuron. The viruses have been modified so that they cannot commandeer the cell to cause further infection. But Sapolsky ensures that the virus retains certain of its special properties.

For the most part, Sapolsky works with herpes simplex, the class of virus that produces cold sores. Herpes viruses invade nerve cells—an essential requirement for the task Sapolsky wants them to do. Ordinarily, the viruses then multiply to cause acute infections—this is the capacity that genetic engineering eliminates. And then the viruses lie dormant in the nerve cell, until the organism is stressed—at which point they leap into action. That's why you get a cold sore just when everything else in your life is going wrong. How do viruses know when to turn on? They monitor your stress hormone levels.

In the Sapolsky model, the herpes virus, stripped of its infectious power, sits in nerve cells until its switch has been tripped by exposure to high doses of stress hormones; then the virus causes the cell to manufacture and release not viruses but neuroprotectants. The system is a thing of beauty. Under normal conditions, the rat is unchanged—the virus lies dormant. Stress the rat briefly, and again nothing happens. The virus's activation is subject to a lag time. But if you clamp an artery and deprive the rat's brain of oxygen, then within hours, the rat's brain cells are churning out protective chemicals. The stroke in the rat's brain remains local. In the face of the same initial insult, a control rat (not protected by the reconfigured virus) sustains extensive brain damage.

These Rube Goldberg inventions actually work. In the face of a variety of stressors, mimicking stroke, heart attack, and seizure, the protected rats suffer half the expected cell loss. In some models, where unprotected rats lose almost 40 percent of the nerve cells in a given brain region, the rats who have been administered the gene therapy lose almost no cells at all.

Sapolsky is engineering increasingly complex means of fighting brain injury. For instance, he has created a molecule that looks like a stress hormone receptor on one end and like estrogen on the other. In the rat model under study, estrogen causes repair through the growth of new neurons and through arborization. Now when a stressor comes along, the rat brain produces this dual-purpose molecule. The "rear end" of the molecule soaks up stress hormones. And then the "front end" sets repair processes in motion. The more stress it encounters (this is the theory), the more resilient the rat becomes.

Sapolsky is well aware that his model might equally be used to protect the mammalian brain against the causes and consequences of depression. He is extending his research to look at neuroprotection in mental illness. For technical reasons, he has begun with syndromes in which anxiety predominates. But he has already produced virus-borne genes that can break down glucocorticoids or interfere with the action of glucocorticoid receptors in the brain. That is to say, he has made a start on antiglucocorticoid gene therapy. In slices of rodent hippocampus, these inserted genes protect against stress hormone damage without interfering with cells' ability to form new connections, through arborization. And the viruses that carry these genes are ones that come into action only after exposure to chronic stress.

There is a vast distance between theory and practice. No time soon will anyone inject genetically rejiggered viruses into patients vulnerable to depression. There are too many hurdles—safety issues, technical issues. Certain genetically engineered viruses, though their main effects are beneficial, confer a risk of cancer. Viruses don't always go just where you hope they will. For now, Sapolsky resorts to drilling a hole in a rat's skull and introducing viruses locally into relevant regions of the brain.

Still, for a concept that sounds like science fiction, Sapolsky's brain-protection project is remarkably far along. And because it addresses an uncontroversial problem—reducing the harm strokes do—it is a sort of genetic engineering that stands a chance of moving forward unimpeded.

The Sapolsky work allows us to imagine a future in which depressive patients, or people with a pronounced liability to depression, might be protected through the insertion of genes that, at critical moments, would kick in to prevent cell damage or promote resilience. The result might be, if not the extirpation of depression, then a dramatic interruption of its progression. When you came to adulthood, you might choose to adopt neuroprotective or resilience-inducing genes. Thereafter, your level of depression would not worsen, even in the face of dramatic stresses and humiliating losses. The vascular depression of old age might be delayed. Depression would be ever less common; in the face of a single bad episode, preventive measures would be employed, to prevent recurrence.

There is a sense in which the preventive models we employ here and now are especially intrusive. I am thinking first of psychotherapy, but antidepressant medications, to the degree that they modulate personality, have a similar problem. They ask us to change who we are, in a fundamental way, in order to fend off a particular disease. If we stop to think about it, we may find this approach quite odd. Beyond the admonition that is a staple of Western medicine, moderation in all things, for the most part doctors do not ask that patients alter their personality to prevent illness. Medicine's function is to keep patients free of disease, so that they can live their lives in the fashion they choose, expressing their personalities freely. The ideal of neuroprotection or neuro-resilience allows psychiatry to join the rest of medicine in this unobtru-sive posture.

The beauty in this fantasy, the fantasy of resilience, is that it takes place at the level of anatomical pathology, the level of vulnerable cells in selected regions of the brain. A gene is inserted that remains dor-mant most of the time. Only in the face of stress is it activated—and even then, after a time lag. The brain's reaction to transient stressors is unchanged; the stress-response "switch" works as it always has, permit-ting emotion in the face of challenges. It is only when stress threatens to overwhelm and injure neurons that the altered cells produce neuro-protective factors. Protecting neurons should also protect the stress-response switch.

In this model, you are who you are most of the time—glum or perky, empathetic or clueless. You may experience unease, anxiety, alienation, and despair. But even after a humiliating loss, your stress switch will not stay stuck in the "on" position. In due course—and before they shrink your hippocampus or disrupt your prefrontal cortex—your stress hormones will abate. They will not take you farther down the road to chronic depression.

Sapolsky's genetic engineering is especially appealing because it acts close to the neuron at risk. But even the less elegantly tailored research efforts, the ones aimed at blocking the production or reception of glu-cocorticoids, respond nicely to our account of what depression is. The specific CRF inhibitors are meant to keep much of the stress-response system intact, and still to shield the brain from the effects of stress hor-mones. The goal is to keep the hippocampus fit, to lubricate the stress-response switch, and indirectly, to permit brain cells to grow and make new connections in response to events in the world.

Sixteen

❖

Here and Now

THIS VISION, modulating the effects of stress hormones, is either utopian or dystopian according to one's valuation of depression. In either case, it is a matter of science fantasy. But it is equally accurate to say that the imagined capacities, to protect neurons and promote their capacity to form connections, are ones we have already, in rudimentary fashion.

Today, for the most part, doctors treat depressed patients with medication or psychotherapy, or both in combination. We use the same modalities to prevent recurrences. Our interventions have grave limitations. They fail with some patients. They injure others. Often they work by halves, making patients better but not well. But when they succeed, antidepressants and (more speculatively) psychotherapy may be agents of the very changes investigators aim for in cutting-edge research. This theory, that psychiatric treatments work through conferring neuro-resilience, represents a change in the scientific orthodoxy.

From the early 1950s to the early 1990s, the leading model of depression and of antidepressant treatment involved neurotransmitters like serotonin and norepinephrine. Though it clearly contained part of the truth, that model became ever more problematic.

By the late 1980s, a chemical called tianeptine had become a fly in the ointment for psychopharmacologists. Structurally, tianeptine is a variant of the tricyclics, the medications, like Elavil, that were among the first modern antidepressants. Developed as an anti-anxiety agent, tianeptine turned out to work for depression as well. (In Europe and South America, it is used to treat both anxiety and depression, under the trade name Stablon.) What was known about tianeptine challenged the neurotransmitter doctrine, where more is better. Prozac and its cousins are serotonin reuptake inhibitors—they make more serotonin available by slowing the rate at which nerve cells sop it up for repackaging. Tianeptine was a serotonin reuptake enhancer—a drug that ought to dampen serotonin-based communication in the brain. In my talk in Copenhagen, about how theories of mood disorder flourish in the face of contradicting evidence, I included tianeptine's efficacy on the list of examples.

Subsequent studies found that tianeptine does not interfere with serotonin transmission in critical regions of the brain. But before that evidence emerged, researchers had tried to pin down the mechanism of action of this "atypical antidepressant." Using a rat model, they discovered that the medication promotes neuroresilience. Tianeptine protects nerve cells in the face of stress. In some studies, stressed rodents pretreated with tianeptine actually showed hippocampal growth, instead of shrinkage. Pretreatment with tianeptine also prevented stress-induced impairments in learning to navigate mazes. The increased hippocampal volume (in rats and shrews administered tianeptine) is due to two factors: the sprouting of connections between cells and the proliferation of new cells—neuroplasticity and neurogenesis.

A group in the Yale University psychiatry department, headed by Ronald Duman, a molecular biologist, wondered whether tianeptine was atypical after all. Perhaps many antidepressants enhance nerve cell growth. Working with adult rats and employing the same marker for cell proliferation, BrdU, that Fred Gage had used in his demonstration of neurogenesis in the adult brain, the Yale group looked at conventional antidepressants. They selected a drug from each standard class—one that primarily affects serotonin pathways, one that affects norepinephrine pathways, and one that affects multiple neurotransmitters. These dissimilar medications, acting initially on different circuits in the brain, had this effect in common: each increased neurogenesis. The new cells were both neurons and glia, in normal proportions.

Subsequent research looked in detail at antidepressants, like Prozac, that increase the brain's access to serotonin. In animal models, these medications stimulate hippocampal growth through blocking the effects of stress hormones and increasing the levels of nerve growth factors.

One scientist (René Hen, at Columbia University) tried to isolate the neurogenesis function. He gave mice irradiation to the hippocampus in a low dose that blocks new cell formation but otherwise does not injure cells or alter behavior. The key experiments involved a measure for anxiety—the increased time it takes mice to venture out to feed in a strange (that is, new to them), brightly lit area. In mice that have not been irradiated, Prozac stimulates neurogenesis and lowers the time to feeding—it makes mice less anxious. In irradiated mice, neurogenesis is impossible—and the Prozac does not work. Even on medicine, the irradiated mice hold back. The difference in effect has nothing to do with appetite; in a dark, familiar area, irradiated mice chow down normally. And it is the hippocampus that is crucial; irradiating other parts of the brain leaves the action of Prozac intact. Various tests of mood alteration in the mouse give similar results: Prozac offers protection only when it can stimulate new cell formation in the hippocampus.

Hen's results suggest that the action of antidepressants may depend on the growth of new nerve cells. His findings may lead us to ask whether neurogenesis is critical to recovery from depression altogether.

We may also wonder whether these mechanisms of protection, repair, and nerve cell growth apply to humans—to patients we treat now, with current methods. A hint that they might comes from a reanalysis of Yvette Sheline's study of duration of depression and hippocampal atrophy. Sheline went back to the records and, from the total number of days that women were depressed, she subtracted out the days that they were on antidepressants. That modification led to a yet better "fit" of the data. The loss of hippocampal volume correlates with the number of days a woman is in a depressive episode. It correlates better with the number of days she is depressed and off medication.

If this line of research holds up—that is, if antidepressants mute the effects of stress, protect the hippocampus, and encourage neuroplasticity and neurogenesis—then for all their imperfections, the medications we use today bear a surprising resemblance to the treatments researchers are working to develop. In effect, the antidepressants are (highly flawed) neuroresilience factors.

Parenthetically, this model of medication action has been used to explain why antidepressants are relatively ineffective for adolescents. Traditionally, this difference was attributed to diagnostic uncertainties; in the young, depression does not have the predictable form it has in adults, the syndrome built around dense sadness, sleep disturbance, and the rest. But that symptomatic variation may reflect chemistry and anatomy; very young depressives often do not have the reduced hippocampal volume, disturbed prefrontal organization, elevated stress hormone levels, and dampening of neurogenesis common in depressed adults. As a result, the brain may require a different form of repair. This train of thought is highly speculative; after all, studies show that Prozac can be useful in the treatment of adolescent depression, and in some studies, hippocampal differences are apparent from an early age. But researchers' engagement in this discussion indicates how seriously they take the hypothesis that antidepressants work through enhancing neuroprotection and neuroresilience.

Whether psychotherapy can claim those benefits is yet less clear. And here I should perhaps admit to certain prejudices. I am a psychotherapy enthusiast. My first book, *Moments of Engagement*, celebrates the beauties of individually crafted therapies in an era when treatments have become standardized. My third, *Should You Leave?*, shows off out-of-fashion therapies I have collected and continue to utilize. For fifteen years, I taught a required seminar that introduced individual psychotherapy to psychiatry residents at Brown University. Even with patients like Margaret, who complained that I had negotiated with an alien—even when I fear I am blundering—I consider psychotherapy to be an essential element in the treatment of depression. But I have mixed feelings about recent research on psychotherapy. It seems limited—not nearly so creative as research on medication, not nearly so important in its contributions to our understanding of what depression is.

Most psychotherapy research in the last decade has focused on efficacy. A typical study will demonstrate that a brief course of a conceptually simple therapy can shorten an episode of depression. In aggregate, the research suggests that in mild depression, psychotherapy works about as well as medication. For patients traumatized in early childhood, psychotherapies may play an especially important role. In severe depression—more symptoms, longer duration, greater risk of suicide— the psychotherapies work less well than medication, though still they may have a contribution to make. The combination of antidepressants and psychotherapy is especially effective. Like those of medication, the benefits of psychotherapy can wear off once treatment ends; follow-up or continuation psychotherapy—a series of refresher sessions—helps prevent relapse and recurrence.

But the findings are not uniform. In some of the major studies—the one funded by the National Heart, Lung, and Blood Institute is a good example—psychotherapy has produced only mediocre results.

And conceptually, the research of last decade has been pedestrian. By the late 1980s, it had already been established that psychotherapy helps mildly depressed patients. Much of the recent research seemed to be a response to political necessity—the need, repeatedly, to persuade health insurers of the importance of a modality they don't like paying for.

Only recently have researchers tried to integrate psychotherapy into the failed-resilience model of depression. The most important study found that after fifteen to twenty sessions of a therapy focused on altering self-critical modes of thought, those depressed patients who improved showed increased energy utilization in the hippocampus. The changes in the brain were different than those seen in antidepressant treatment—perhaps indicating a distinct sequence of recovery, and thus suggesting a reason that medication and psychotherapy complement each other in the restoration of health. This and similar studies look at brain function, rather than changes in anatomy.

Of course, psychotherapy research is limited by the absence of a good animal model. What, in mice and monkeys, corresponds to an apt interpretation? Elizabeth Gould, the researcher who discovered neurogenesis in primates, has looked at the effects of "enriched environments," most recently in marmosets, softball-sized monkeys convenient for laboratory research.

The standard caging of research animals is isolated, drab, constricted, and unstimulating. Gould gives her marmosets more space, more toys, and more peers to play with; she hides food, so that the little monkeys get the pleasure of foraging. The research model involves traumatizing a pregnant mother with startling noises. The conventionally caged offspring show impairments in neuroplasticity and neurogenesis—and the enriched environment helps prevent or correct these deficits.

As Gould herself says, it is hard to know whether we ought to think of enrichment as psychotherapy or whether (as is reasonably likely) we should assume that standard caging constitutes further stress imposed on monkeys made vulnerable *in utero*. But Gould's work is suggestive. It seems to support what we hope is true, that benign environments hasten recovery. Psychotherapy might constitute, or help patients to create, such an environment.

To know some of what we would want to know about psychotherapy might require new technology—imagine an imaging device that can follow detailed developments in the brain in real time. But seemingly simple lines of inquiry have only recently entered the research agenda. For example, when psychotherapy helps to prevent recurrence in depression, is it because the patients behave differently and therefore provoke fewer humiliations? Or is therapy strengthening, so that a given stressor is now less likely to cause relapse? One thoughtful study does suggest that therapy may "decrease the potency of life events in provoking recurrence." But for the most part, psychotherapy research has slighted questions of mechanism. If therapy makes people resilient, we don't know why.

In relation to our myth of depression, perhaps the important unanswered question is mechanical: Does psychotherapy affect brain structure, and how?

I recognize a sour-grapes quality in my attitude toward psychotherapy studies. Therapy worthy of the name, I have always thought, should lead toward a clearing away of lies and defenses, an enriching of emotional life, and a new discovery of self. The techniques for those tasks would be hard to capture in operational manuals. Truly intimate treatments might require the therapist to assume an attitude of active not-knowing; the crucial capacity might be an ability to modulate interpersonal distance, so that the therapist might now supply empathy and now pull back and provide room for the patient's private exploration. I have always favored naturalistic, "process" research on the mechanisms of action of psychotherapy as it is generally practiced. But the profession has put its energies into tests of treatments that are easy to teach and evaluate.

I worry about the applicability of psychotherapy research to the patients I see. Many of them already live in supportive and stimulating environments; they seek help because their mood does not correspond to their circumstances. These same patients may be familiar with the insights and exercises of simple therapies. Indeed, these patients may have failed at a course of treatment—cognitive therapy—aimed at training them to avoid self-undermining habits of thought. Do our additional efforts—the long and detailed inquiry, the attention to hard-to-acknowledge aspects of feeling and memory—provide further or different help? There is so much we would wish to know.

In practice, in the treatment of major depression, I almost always combine medication with psychotherapy. I imagine that by loosening the stuck switch, and permitting dendritic arborization and new cell growth, the antidepressants allow for the learning that psychotherapy guides. Theorists working on neurogenesis have suggested that therapy may help direct the placement of new neurons, and so make medication-stimulated cell development more useful to the person recovering from depression.

For depressives, I imagine that psychotherapy has diverse benefits. It uses a modality that many of them know well, self-examination, to help them moderate self-destructive thoughts and feelings. It offers skills and coaching that allow depressed patients to create a more reliable social environment and thereby encounter fewer losses. It provides a setting in which the depressed can let their guard down and fall apart—so that they can "hold it together" at home and at work. Cynics have suggested that psychotherapy is the human equivalent of grooming behaviors in monkeys, a chance for primates to sit together peaceably and feel the benefits of social integration. I do not discount that possibility.

Overall, future scientists, looking back on our contemporary treatments for depression, may judge them to be Rube Goldberg devices. A patient enters into a psychotherapeutic relationship. The treatment makes him feel safer and more socially competent. In animal terms, his brain reads that result as an increase in social integration or status hierarchy. That change allows for the release of serotonin, a chemical that is elevated in socially dominant primates. The serotonin boosts the production of neurotrophic factors like BDNF. Those factors protect hippocampal neurons from the effects of stress hormones. The same factors allow for dendritic sprouting and new cell formation. The hippocampus and other brain areas in the mood circuit begin to recover. Feedback mechanisms come back into play. Stress hormone levels fall, a new equilibrium is reached, and the episode of depression ends. Antidepressant medication—for instance, the sort that allows for more efficient use of serotonin in the brain—begins only half a step closer to the requirement for effective treatment, neurogenesis.

This strange account (of psychotherapy in particular) puts neurogenesis at the center of the recovery process. It may be. In a bold theoretical paper, Fred Gage and his colleagues have suggested that "the waxing and waning of neurogenesis in the hippocampal formation are important causal factors, respectively, in the precipitation of, and recovery from, episodes of clinical depression."

This speculation may place a limit on our fantasies about progress in the psychotherapies. If the talking cures are effective, still we are unlikely to imagine an approach that is vastly more useful than ones already developed, in terms of its power to induce neurogenesis. Given the many causes of depression, more substantial progress may require a biological intervention that has a direct protective effect, downstream, close to the vulnerable neuron.

Still, it is interesting to think that our current medications and psychotherapy may work—if at a remove—through enhancing neuro-resilience. The utopian project, eradicating depression by protecting vulnerable parts of the brain, may be only an extension of what we do now, when we do it well.

❖　❖　❖　❖

In this account of what depression is, I have presented a single myth, one that leads from stress to cell damage, via problems with feedback mechanisms and neuroresilience factors. In truth, this model coexists with competing ones. Other regions of the brain may be as important as the hippocampus in the depression story. A variety of neurotransmitters are receiving attention. But I think it is fair to say that some version of the hypotheses flowing from the studies we have reviewed—the work of Rajkowska, Sheline, Sapolsky, Kendler, Gage, and others—informs most concepts of depression under serious consideration today and most research in progress. Any viable account will include attention to genetic predisposition, early-life trauma, later adversity, varied insults to brain cells, anatomical damage, neuronal pruning and sprouting, and new cell growth

To call the stress-and-resilience model of depression a myth is to concede in advance that any number of the details will require revision. How we treat or prevent depression will change as the evidence and our tools do. But for many purposes, it is the *form* of the story that counts. Only a very extensive revision of our myth would change the practical implications for public policy—the imperatives for early identification, vigorous intervention, and the like. Those issues (and more openly political ones like accommodation in the workplace and parity with other illness in insurance coverage) will be debated in the context of a version of *what it is* that resembles the one before us.

Likewise for the issue that interests us here, the social role of depression. If depression arises from or causes abnormalities in the brain, if it entails predictable suffering, if it results in progressive impairment in mental function, if it produces enormous economic costs, if it leads to substantial illness in what psychiatry calls peripheral organs, such as the heart, if depression shortens life, if it has substantial genetic underpinnings, if it is a disorder of failed resilience, if is treatable or preventable—then depression will pass, as I believe it is doing already, fully into the category of disease. Not only in medicine but also in daily life, to understand depression as pathology will become a habit of mind.

What It Will Be

❖

Seventeen

The End of
Melancholy

ONE WAY TO INDICATE THE IMPORTANCE of the recent research findings is to say that they settle a debate that is as old as Western medicine. In the fifth or fourth century B.C., Hippocrates attempted to define as medical a series of complaints that might otherwise be understood as spiritual. Among them was a disorder of the humors, an excess of black bile (or melancholy), that when it affected the body caused epileptic seizures and when it affected the mind caused dejection. Hippocrates was arguing that melancholy is illness.

Hippocrates' diagnostic categories are not ours. Melancholy went beyond depression. Melancholy was responsible for hemorrhoids, ulcers, dysentery, certain eruptions of the skin, and diseases of the lungs and chest. Melancholy included the frenzy of mania and schizophrenia.

One by one, each of the conditions Hippocrates included under the rubric "melancholy" proved to be as fully medical as any other disease he might have named, or that we might name now. The last piece, depression, has fallen into place.

· ·

The opposite position, the belief that Hippocrates was contradicting, has taken many forms, religious and secular. Its most influential expression occurs in a document that is itself largely scientific, the *Problemata Physica*, or *Problems*. The *Problems* is a discussion, in question and answer form, of conundrums of mathematics, biology, astronomy, and physics. It was long attributed to Aristotle, but the surviving version, from the second century B.C., is now believed to be by his followers, perhaps incorporating some of Aristotle's writing. The *Problems* includes questions poorly answered to this day: "Why do young men, when they first begin to have sexual intercourse, hate those with whom they have associated after the act is over?"

In the thirtieth book of the *Problems*, the author asks why it is that outstanding men—philosophers, statesmen, poets, artists, educators, and heroes—are so often melancholic, some to the point of illness. Among the ancients, the strongmen Heracles, Ajax, and Bellerophon were melancholic; more recent examples cited in the *Problems* include Socrates and Plato and the Spartan general Lysander. The answer is that too much black bile leads to insanity, but a moderate amount creates men "superior to the rest of the world in many ways." The overarching argument in this section of the *Problems* has a standard form, alluding to the golden mean that contains the good. But the convoluted effort needed to make theory (of moderation) fit observation (of great men) suggests that melancholy was troublesome for Greek philosophy; the answer is one of the longest in the collection of problems. Seen simply, melancholy is an extreme, not a mean. A good number of the "outstanding men" listed as examples actually went mad; not moderate but *excessive* bile may confer superiority.

Thus is born the tradition of heroic melancholy. Surely some version of this idea existed earlier. Hippocrates seemed to be answering a claim that melancholy is inspiration or possession. But the specific formulation in the *Problems*, the melancholic as exceptional—brave and imaginative—has had a long reach. When husbands attribute refinement to their depressed wives, and when those depressed women credit themselves with superior judgment that is intimately connected to their mood disorder—that homely sequence echoes the *Problems*. The *what if* question dates back two millennia. If melancholy were preventable—if the stars were differently aligned—would Ajax have stood off Hector in single combat?

Following the publication of *Listening to Prozac*, I imagined that if I returned to writing about mood disorder, it would be to trace the course of classical notions of melancholy—and in particular the belief that melancholy is more or less than an illness. This project appealed to me because often I had a sense, when I spoke about treating depression, that I was debating two thousand years' worth of elaboration of heroic melancholy.

The Greeks, and the cultures that succeeded them, faced depression unarmed. To tease apart the mental illnesses, to locate their distinct pathologies, and to document their harm—these tasks require complex technology. Even now, we barely possess the means. Treatment has always been difficult. Depression is common and spans the life cycle. When you add in mania and schizophrenia and epilepsy, not to mention hemorrhoids, you encompass a good deal of what humankind suffers altogether. The impasse calls for the elaboration of myth. Something must be made of melancholy. And then that something takes on a life of its own. Poets style themselves melancholic. They write about their depressions. They accord worth to poems written from the melancholic standpoint. Two thousand years is a long time.

Depression becomes a universal metaphor, standing in for sin and innocent suffering, self-indulgence and sacrifice, inferiority and refinement. The face and habit of depression become standard poses in portraiture, informing images of beauty, wisdom, and maturity. Narrative structures are built around the descent into depression and recovery from it. Romantic poetry, religious memoir, inspirational tracts, the novel of youthful self-development, grand opera, the blues—depression is an affliction that inspires not just art but art forms.

We stand within the tradition of heroic melancholy. We are fish judging the ocean. That is why it is so hard to know what to make of claims in favor of depression. Perhaps the *what if* question should be asked more broadly. To what extent have we judged art according to its success as a talisman against or comfort in the face of this feared state, melancholy? To what extent have our tastes been colored by two thousand years of therapeutic impotence? What would art look like if depression had been easier to treat or prevent?

The cultural history of depression is the history of culture. Academics have approached the task repeatedly, in their painstaking ways. The result is many big books, each on a tiny topic. Only a mosaic of big books, only a library, would cover the territory.

In 1964, the art historians Raymond Klibansky, Erwin Panofsky, and Franz Saxl published a work that became a model for the writing of intellectual history. Their *Saturn and Melancholy* is an extension of an early monograph (1923) by Panofsky and Saxl on a single image, an engraving from 1517 by Albrecht Dürer called *Melencolia I.* The length of the expanded text, 400-plus oversized pages about meaning in this one image by Dürer, speaks to the density of symbolic motifs prevalent by the sixteenth century: purse, keys, drooping head, clenched fist, dark complexion, dog, compass, magic square, molding plane, polyhedron, bell, sand timer, scales, angel. Hidden and apparent are references to melancholy's links with sloth, avarice, wealth, power, weariness, hubris, anger, delusion, intellect, imagination, judgment, literature, geometry, astrology, handicraft, isolation, constancy, lovesickness, procrastination, success, aging, Christianity, and genius. Although the portrait is of a woman, hints of self-reference show through. Dürer was a heroic melancholic. The engraving is autopathography.

Four hundred pages, then, to explicate one depiction of melancholy. And then there are the grand acts of scholarly synthesis. The great German sociologist Wolf Lepenies pored over Renaissance and Enlightenment medical and political tracts to make the case that notions of utopia derive, via negation, from theories of depression.

Robert Burton wrote his *Anatomy of Melancholy* in early-seventeenth-century England, when the monarchy was in transition. For Burton, depression is disorder in the mind linked to disorder in the self and the state: vice, impiety, and uncertainty. Burton's utopia is regimented, with "few laws, but those securely kept, plainly put down, that every man may understand." Where political life is well arranged, melancholy will not flourish. But in mid-seventeenth-century France, when the monarchy used the tedious routine of the salon to hold the aristocracy in a golden cage, utopian thoughts turned to the wildness of nature, or to solitude, contemplation, individualism, and political resistance. In the writing of Duc François de La Rochefoucauld and others, order injures the spirit, and disorder stimulates healing. These are the poles of social solutions to melancholy—labor or leisure, obedience or rebellion, integration or alienation, credulity or cynicism, calm or turbulence.

The gist of the scholarship is this: that fantastic forms grow on this irritating grain of sand. Ideals of civics, beauty, wisdom, religion, and morality take shape around theories of mood and mood disorder.

The great flowering of melancholy occurs in the Renaissance, as humanists rediscover the *Problems*. In the late fifteenth century in Florence, a cult of melancholy flourishes, among the followers of the humanist Marsilio Ficino. His treatise on health, *The Three Books on Life*, links melancholy to intellect. Learned people tend to be melancholic by birth; if not, they become melancholic as an occupational hazard, through inactivity, solitude, study, and agitation of the mind.

The melancholy to which Ficino referred was at the first level a medical illness, well described by the ancients. The specific disease we call depression was a prime element. Rufus of Ephesus and Galen of Pergamum, writing in the second century, produced impressive works of observation, describing depressed patients we would recognize today. Of course, melancholy encompassed flatulence and distended veins and coldness of the extremities on the mild end and, at the other extreme, coma and paralysis. Hypochondria (the affliction of organs, like the spleen and liver, that sit below the chondrium, or diaphragm) was melancholy. Hysteria, an affliction of the uterus, began as a separate disease but soon merged into melancholy. By the Renaissance, almost any form of madness was melancholy.

Accounts of mind and brain remained grounded in notions of the humors, bodily fluids produced by the digestive and circulatory organs in response to both diet and the motions of the planets. A single theory encompassed pathology, normal psychology, physiology, astrology, political economy, and spirituality, so that in every era, notions of civil hierarchy, sin, and planetary influence pervaded accounts of morbid melancholy.

But the course and syndrome of depression were very much present. Doctors understood that melancholic episodes recur and worsen over time. They knew that melancholy causes premature aging, that distinctive forms of melancholy emerge in old age, that melancholy leads to afflictions of the heart. If we look for it, and of course, we can look too hard, there in the messy accounts of melancholy is modern depression, along with solid wisdom about its management.

One detail from this literature appeals to me especially. While preparing an essay about federal regulations that require employers to treat depression like any other medical disability, I came upon a passage in the works of Saint Teresa of Ávila. This is the same Saint Teresa, the sixteenth-century Spanish Carmelite nun, whose practicality would later offend William James. Writing about the administration of nunneries, Saint Teresa is moved to discuss depression. For minor versions, in which sisters disobey, she recommends punishment, to restore conformity. But Saint Teresa considers melancholy to be the severest illness. Since the gravely afflicted are not at fault, she suggests something like accommodation in the workplace:

[T]he prioress can refrain from ordering them to do what she sees they will be unable to do because of their not having the strength within themselves. She should lead them with all the skill and love necessary so that if possible they submit out of love. . . . And she must note that the greatest remedy she has is to keep them much occupied with duties so that they do not have the opportunity to be imagining things, for herein lies all their trouble. And even though they may not perform these duties so well, she should suffer some defects. . . . And strive that they do not have long periods of prayer, nor even those established in the constitutions, because, for the greater part, their imaginations are weak.

Spiritual discipline is paramount, but a skillful leader can avoid crises through advance and concurrent adjustment of requirements. Teresa of Ávila explains that she devotes so much time to this illness because it is chronic and progressive. She sees terminating the current episode as a preventive measure, to avert future deterioration.

Humane approaches to mood disorder appear and vanish. But the other tradition, heroic melancholy, becomes ever more elaborate, ever more an element of the obvious—what we just know about human nature. From Florence (and the school of Ficino), the cult of melancholy enters England through "Italianate travelers," foppish aristocrats who style themselves artists and scholars and affect the melancholic attitude and dress.

Sometimes, they are lovesick. A century ago, a literary sleuth drew academics' attention to a wonderful confusion, from medieval times onward, involving the word *hereos*. It derives from Eros, the Greek god of love, but *hereos* becomes misread as *heros*, so that the malady of Eros merges with the malady of heroes, to create a form of melancholy that encompasses lovesickness and nobility alike. Afflicted by lovemelancholy, a man sees through surface to the vanity of the human condition. "The bile," one commentator notes, "is a corrosive substance that strips off the veil of human pretension and allows the sufferer to see the world as it truly is." Melancholy is a divine gift that confers consciousness of surface and depth.

A second classical tradition merges with heroic melancholy. Adherents of the ancient Greek schools of moral philosophy—Stoics, Cynics, Skeptics, Epicureans, and Aristotelians—were looking for ways to avoid the pain that follows on loss. Philosophers were early psychotherapists, and their preventive prescription for depression was *ataraxia*, serene detachment. The thoughtful man avoids the disruptive passions by limiting his emotional investments. Ataraxia is a state of contentment, but just barely. It involves a sober mistrust of intimate commitment and a constant awareness of life's pains. To be braced against misfortune is to be aware of the injustices, misunderstandings, and impossibilities that corrupt our relationships to one another, to nature, and to the self. By the time of the Renaissance, this prophylaxis against decompensation looks a good deal like depression. The melancholic merges with the self-possessed philosopher, so that depression becomes the image of wisdom.

In truth, the Renaissance texts are self-contradictory. Lawrence Babb, the great authority on melancholy in Shakespeare's England, argues in *The Elizabethan Malady* that this confusion is not one we impose on the work looking backward. The Elizabethans' difficulty is an extension of the Greeks'. The case for moderate amounts of black bile coexists with examples in which an excess of black bile leads to greatness.

In the fashion of the times, thoughtful melancholy cedes place of pride to an irritable variant. The vogue for melancholy demands sourness. London witnesses a plague of "melancholic malcontents." They are so numerous that Thomas Nashe, the sixteenth-century satirist, calls on the devil to "take some order, so that the streets not be pestered with them so as they are." Young men study melancholy "as one learns a game or dance."

According to Babb, the "malcontent is usually black-suited and disheveled, unsociable, asperous, morosely meditative, taciturn yet prone to occasional railing." He may be rebellious and seditious, drawn to political intrigue. And he may have picked up any number of social vices abroad. Often his discontent arises from society's failure to reward his exceptional talents. There are many variants: the cynic, the scholar, the religious melancholic (either sinfully slothful or divinely inspired), the miser, the crafty politician, and the scoundrel or criminal. Villainy is a prominent, even dominant component of melancholy. In dozens of stage dramas, the principal character is a melancholic malcontent. *The Revenger's Tragedy* is a drama of melancholy; and so is *Lust's Dominion*. For that matter, so is *Hamlet*.

Hamlet is much else, of course. Even the critics who analyze the play through its use of the conventions of melancholy agree that Shakespeare transcends the genre, in particular by juxtaposing appearance and essence, gesture and interiority. ("I know not 'seems' . . . I have that within that passeth show.") But the drama plays off the stereotype.

Before he speaks, Hamlet's "inky cloak" invokes the malcontent. Hamlet's quip that he is "too much in the sun" is a punning rejection of

Claudius's claim of fatherhood, but it also makes reference to melancholics' preference for dark retreats. (Robert Burton, in his extraordinarily influential *Anatomy of Melancholy*, in part a summary of earlier opinion, writes that the melancholic *"loves darkness as life, and cannot endure the light*, or to sit in lightsome places.") Hamlet's wit is itself a badge of melancholy, as is his opposition to the king.

As soon the title character takes the stage, an Elizabethan audience would understand that it is watching a tragedy whose hero's characteristic flaw will be a melancholic trait, in this case, paralysis of action. By the same token, the audience would quickly accept Hamlet's spiritual superiority, his suicidal impulses, his hostility to the established order, his protracted grief, passionate loves and hates, wise speech, bitterness, solitary wanderings, erudition, impaired reason, murderousness, role-playing, passivity, rashness, antic disposition, "dejected havior of the visage," and truck with graveyards and visions. Scholars find botanical, zoological, mythological, astrological, and medical references to melancholy throughout the play. To the Globe spectator, these allusions would be evident, even insistent. Social and theatrical convention lent Hamlet a coherence that, as a psychologically motivated character, he may lack for modern audiences.

Hamlet, arguably the seminal text of our modern culture, is the product of an era rife with melancholic discontent, as an affected posture. Seeing *Hamlet* in its social setting might make us mistrustful of the literary tradition of melancholy as it develops. How much of the association between melancholy and its many attributes—from introspective wisdom to artistic genius—arises from the nature of the condition? How much is artistic conceit? *Hamlet* provides a strong template for the narrative of melancholy: the explicit message is that melancholy is a character flaw. But melancholy confers depth and a fascinating, complex sense of self. Implicitly, the melancholic is attractive.

There is, perhaps, in our acceptance of *Hamlet*, a hardening into fixed form of what might otherwise be fluid or fleeting. The virtue of the melancholic becomes obvious. Hamlet is the modern man, troubled and contemplative, paralyzed and alienated.

• •

In what I have called my years of immersion, I wondered what prevented a reconciliation between medical and popular views of
depression—what prevented a resolution of the dialectic that has been
with us for two millennia, now that we know so much more about *what
it is*. Particularly when I spoke to university audiences about depression,
it struck me that what was at stake was some version of heroic melancholy. Surely, I would be asked, you see the value in *alienation*. And I do,
that is, I see the value of standing apart from social institutions and cri-
tiquing them. I see the value in wondering at our place in the cosmos, or
feeling dislocated in the face of life's absurdity. But I have no worry that
alienation will disappear if we become better at treating or preventing
depression. The contrary notion, that alienation might vanish, appears
to flow from a cultural myth, in the most complete sense—a tale built up
to take account of what science could not yet explain.

And so it seemed to me important to consider that tale, to define
what we are afraid of losing, as we sharpen our understanding of depression. I am that model (and foolish) amateur, the doctor who loves
to read; even so, I thought that I could see a pattern of development, a
movement in the myth of melancholy. Increasingly, the admirable portion was limited to the depressive traits. Frenzy and hemorrhoids had
been set aside, so that the heroic melancholic was merely anhedonic,
alienated, apathetic, ruminative, and sad.

The Renaissance sustained several simultaneous traditions of melancholy. Cervantes began his literary career with a long pastoral poem, full
of pining and tearful shepherds suffering from unrequited love. *Don
Quixote* makes use of a different version of melancholy, the comical inspiration of the madman. These traditions flourished for centuries, but
they have not had the lasting force of melancholic malcontentment, or
rather they have been subsumed by it. Jean Canavaggio, the great biog-
rapher of Cervantes, writes that:

> [M]adness—as Michel Foucault has brilliantly demonstrated—
> is now a source for uneasiness for us: it is incongruous, even inde-

cent, to make fun of a madman, as our ancestors loved to do; and we perceive as tragic the loneliness of the hero that Cervantes shows us misunderstood by everyone. In a word, the distance that separates our view of *Don Quixote* from the one that classical Europe formed of him reflected, beyond any doubt, a profound evolution of customs and sensibilities.

In the case of insanity, *what it is to us* changed to meet the medical understanding. And then what emerged in our reading of the *Quixote* was the hero's loneliness and his alienation from his fellows.

The eighteenth and nineteenth centuries have had the most marked effects on our current selection of traits to admire, from within the universe of the melancholy. I remember in college reading T. S. Eliot's complaint that as a critic, Goethe "made of Hamlet a Werther," referring to Goethe's effete, love-struck, depressive hero. Goethe had described Hamlet as a flowerpot planted, mistakenly, with an oak tree. "A fine, pure, noble and highly moral person," Hamlet is too good for the task fate imposes on him.

I don't suppose I could stomach *The Sorrows of Young Werther* today. The Hamlet dispute led me to it, at an age when I was more open to high romance. Even then, Werther struck me as moony and immature. He lacks the boldness and taste for intrigue that might cause greatness in a soldier or statesman. He lacks even Hamlet's energy and cunning. Melancholy has lost its vigor, turned fragile. But it is clear enough that, in terms of literary genealogy, the sensitive depressive is a lineal descendent of the Renaissance malcontent.

Werther resembles *Hamlet* formally as well. Werther's disorder is presented as pathology. But the sufferer's appeal is evident. In the late eighteenth century, young men declared their identification by wearing the fictional hero's outfit: blue tailcoat, yellow waistcoat, and high boots. Some committed suicide in costume, and in the manner of Werther—a bullet above the eye.

The curious transformation begun in the Renaissance reaches its completion in Goethe. It is no longer that melancholy leads to heroism.

Melancholy *is* heroism. The challenge is not voyage or battle but inner struggle. The rumination of the depressive, however solipsistic, is deemed admirable. And this value applies even in cases when the interior examination fails due to a lack of moral courage. No matter that the protagonist remains callow and self-deluding. Melancholic sensitivity is noble by definition. So is the melancholic's sense of outsider status. With Goethe, the aspects of depression we continue to value have come to the fore: sensitivity, alienation, and creative genius. By implication, this greatness of soul attaches to the author as well.

From Werther, it is a straight march to high romanticism and then modernity. I am thinking now of Thomas Carlyle's fictionalized spiritual autobiography, *Sartor Resartus*, a book that made a particular impact on me. A college friend recommended it at a moment when I was teetering between majoring in the social sciences and majoring in the humanities. Carlyle gave the final push, with his demonstration that literature is a moral undertaking, fully "relevant" (the decisive criterion in my undergraduate years) to the conduct of a life.

Carlyle writes purposely overblown prose, but his pain shows through in ways that are endearing. He styles himself a follower of Goethe; the mock memoir borrows motifs from *Werther* and Goethe's later writing. In the wake of a failed love affair, Carlyle's fictional stand-in enters a state he calls "the "Everlasting No." ("I lived in a continual, indefinite, pining fear; tremulous, pusillanimous, apprehensive of I knew not what . . .") Unlike Werther, Carlyle's hero rejects suicide and embraces the "Everlasting Yea." The choice is existential, to accept the restricted comforts of work, faith, and communal attachments. Still, the attractiveness of the sorrow makes a case for the twice-born.

Sartor Resartus was extraordinarily influential for most of the nineteenth century. The novel was well known to Dickens and Tennyson, and to the many writers of rebellious anti-Victorian memoir late in the century. It was a particular favorite of Wilhelm Dilthey, the philosopher and literary scholar who helped popularize and define the term *bildungsroman*. Together with *The Sorrows of Young Werther*, Carlyle's book establishes a formula that is nearly invariable: failed romance, dark night of the soul, transcendent insight, reconciliation with life's limitations. This trajectory continues to inform our notion of the shape of a life story.

For the poet especially, the recovery may be less impressive than the original affliction. Kierkegaard is only stating the obvious when he begins *Either/Or* with the equation of depressive pain and poetry:

> What is a poet? An unhappy man who in his heart harbors a deep anguish, but whose lips are so fashioned that the moans and cries which pass over them are transformed into ravishing music. His fate is like that of the unfortunate victims whom the tyrant Phalaris imprisoned in a brazen bull, and slowly tortured over a steady fire; their cries could not reach the tyrant's ears so as to strike terror into his heart; when they reached his ears, they sounded like sweet music. And men crowd about the poet and say to him: "Sing for us soon again"—which is as much as to say: "May new sufferings torment your soul, but may your lips be so fashioned as before; for the cries would only distress us, but the music, the music is delightful."

Poetry is the anguished outcry of the melancholic—Kierkegaard could not be clearer. Implicitly, Kierkegaard identifies himself as the poet-sufferer. He may even be making reference to *The Anatomy of Melancholy*, where Burton describes the pain of depression: "No torture of body like unto it! The tyrants of Sicily have contrived no greater torment, no strappadoes, hot irons, Phalaris' bulls." And of course, Kierkegaard is heroically lovesick as well.

Of course, *Either* is followed by *Or*, in which depression is a sign of spiritual weakness and self-indulgence. But who can forget the opening howl?

I have mentioned my early affinity for Kierkegaard. Perhaps I am playing favorites, but his writing strikes me as the meeting point between melancholy and the contemporary sense of personal identity. Kierkegaard places himself in the classic tradition, the exceptional man who translates his suffering into art. But he picks out an element of melancholy that has had special meaning ever since, the alienated consciousness, always aware of its distance from authenticity, immediacy, and single-mindedness.

The sociologist Harvie Ferguson puts Kierkegaard at the center of a thoughtful review of the topic, *Melancholy and the Critique of Modernity*. By Kierkegaard's time, Ferguson writes, "The modern, disenchanted, disillusioned, wholly secular individual is expected to be melancholic." If the ancient philosophers considered the absence of passion to be the goal of the wise man, their descendants—Pascal, Descartes, Kant, and Hegel—take melancholy to be something like a given, the coloration of life under which we all operate. Melancholy is no longer one temperament among four or five, but a universal condition. At the same time, melancholy is a mark of insight—a sign that a person is in touch with his surroundings. The isolation that one feels in depression is the isolation people ought to feel in a mechanical, chaotic, and uncomprehending universe.

Where once melancholy caused rebellion, now melancholy *is* rebellion, a form of resistance to the seductions of bourgeois satisfactions. Outright depression, in its constancy and intensity, stands as a reproach to the modern era. Melancholy is awareness, of our distance from God, meaning, and purpose. Melancholy is a sin, or many sins—sloth, a lack of caring—but since we are all sinners, it is also a useful sign of our condition. Melancholy is, moreover, an intellectual gift, a spur to writing and imagining. These beliefs lead to the formulation that melancholy is the depth of modernity.

From the romantic period onward, this rebellious and alienated melancholy becomes a central subject of literature. It is no great leap from *Either/Or*, in 1843, to Baudelaire's *Fleurs du Mal* in 1857 and Dostoevsky's *Notes from Underground* in 1864. The fin de siècle memoir is updated Carlyle, in its celebration of depressive mood. The Parisian bohemians are melancholics. I have mentioned Jean Rhys's novels, in which a passive, vulnerable, lonely, anhedonic, alienated feminine ideal emerges. Rhys's heroines live and eat and meet up with abusive men in the bistros and hotels of the prewar Left Bank and Montmartre. Simultaneously Sartre's heroes indulge their nausea, and then Camus's Stranger claims sympathy for the emotionally depleted. The themes implicit in Kierkegaard become commonplaces. Intense emotional sensitivity and social alienation are a requirement for authenticity in a whole line of fiction and poetry, and sometimes in life as well. Does it surprise us when we read, as I just have in Diane Middlebrook's joint biography of Ted Hughes and Sylvia Plath, that when the two met, he wore shabby, shapeless black clothes? He dyed the cloth himself, Plath's jaguar, her "black marauder."

In Joseph Skibell's recent novel, *The English Disease* (the title refers to melancholy), the narrator puts it this way:

> . . . in the West, in the wake of the Enlightenment, we've taken what is essentially a state of psychological pathology—the alienated, isolated ego—and conflated it with the archetype of the hero, so that each one of us is now expected, as though he were Ulysses or the Lone Ranger, to live heroically divorced from a defining culture, without a history or a community or a hierarchy of shared values, and to make of this solitary, muddled wandering a meaningful and exemplary life.

How remarkable that a confusing ancient speculation should hold sway for two thousand years, each generation's version serving to update, to retailor, what comes before. How strange, we might say (with our changed habit of mind), to have made so much of a disease. So much and so little.

Over time, the claims for melancholy expand and diminish. To speak first of diminishment: as the definition of melancholy has narrowed, more modest benefits have been ascribed to the affliction. The result is dullness. To say that phobia predisposes to achievement on the battlefield, or that the contemplative life has ties to sedition, greed, and villainy—these are remarkable correspondences. We are charmed to learn that the statesman's skill in diplomacy has the same roots as lovesickness. The ancient apparatus of heroic melancholy had its appeal—the astrology, the warmth and coolness of the blood, the dual links to sin and religious inspiration, the repeated reflection of inner life and political economy. So much of what made the topic worth discussing, over the centuries, has fallen away.

This diminishment results in part from the fragmentation of melancholy. Hemorrhoids, ulcers, phlebitis, dysentery, and skin diseases have lost their signal functions. Likewise for phobias, paranoia, alcoholism, mania, epilepsy, obsessive-compulsive disorder, and schizophrenia. To us, none of these is melancholy. Each has its own explanation, its own effects, none especially mystical or admirable. In the past few decades, in thinking of melancholy, we have had to make do with depression and its minor variants.

Once you cleanse melancholy of mania and paranoia and the rest, you lose a good many of the impulsive, creative, frenetic, sardonic, villainous, and vigorously malcontented types. Altogether, taking into account the variety of disorders that once were packaged into melancholy and the number of outcomes that were associated, we may come to see the linkage with heroism as a humane delusion. Inexplicable suffering was so substantial and so widespread that necessarily the portmanteau category, melancholy, had to be understood as saintliness or deadly sin, equanimity or agitation, timidity or valor, inspiration or befuddlement, virtue or vice. Melancholy was a compelling condition, the condition of humans *in extremis*; it had to be something.

The thinning out of causes has led to a narrowing of expected effects. Active, battlefield-style bravery is no longer part of the equation. The modern version of heroic melancholy, if we are honest, involves intense self-examination that leads to writing or fine art. If we want to be more specific, and a little mean-spirited, we may say that depressives are successful at composing depressive verse, or depressive memoirs, or philosophical works that turn on depression. This small hypothesis carries some interest, but it is a pale descendant of the thesis of the Aristotelians' thirtieth problem, that melancholy leads to superiority in diverse undertakings, feats of physical strength as much as poetry.

And even the small hypothesis may describe a contingent outcome, one that has arisen from historical happenstance. Cultures sustain and elaborate customs, through what the critic Harold Bloom calls the anxiety of influence. What a wonderful detail—that when pub crawling, Ted Hughes dressed like a Renaissance malcontent—like Hamlet! Once the vogue of the melancholy is enshrined in literature, once the depressive perspective is identified with the poetic, once the pattern of narratives of self-development is set—art accepts and plays with these forms. As depression, like dysentery and epilepsy and the rest, declares itself a disease, our valuation of depressive art might seem an anachronism, the remnant of a tradition required to mitigate and justify otherwise inexplicable sorrow.

That is to say, it might seem an anachronism but for the expansion of melancholy to encompass the human condition. When we are in touch with ourselves, we are all melancholics. Alienation and hypersensitivity are states of awareness. This is the grand hypothesis of melancholy—not that it creates art, but that it describes our place in the universe. And here, too, our understanding of depression gives us reason for doubt.

The examples of the alienated man in modern literature are, for the most part, genuine depressives. Werther is a suicide; Carlyle's alter ego, Teufelsdröckh, escapes narrowly. Kierkegaard's fictional stand-ins would meet any reasonable definition of chronic major depression, as would Kierkegaard himself. If we look to the end of the twentieth century, to the novelist Walker Percy and his many heroes who exemplify alienated man, these admirable rebels are depressed, certified as such by their fictional doctors. Percy uses the word: "You are depressed because you should be. You are entitled to your depression."

But surely, given what we know about depression now, given *what it is*, the state is not one we would choose to inhabit. One way to think about this problem is to look past the fragmentation of melancholy to the fragmentation of depression.

The depth of modernity is not contained in the sort of depression that results from multiple strokes in late life. Memory loss, learning deficits, and decompensation in the face of trivial failures—those defects are not wisdom. The depressions stimulated by interferon, or by various cancers or infections, seem too mechanical to elicit admiration. The people who, on the basis of cytokine-induced depression, decide to stop taking medication, the ones who lose all hope in the face of disease—we consider that they are robbed of something crucial, *élan vital*. Their viewpoint is bleak, but it seems less a matter of profundity than of depletion—as soon say that blood loss or vitamin deficiencies constitute depth.

It's not that you *mightn't* learn from a bout of medical depression. Sometimes we make use of suffering, fear, and pain. But—to answer an earlier rhetorical question—for the most part we do not attribute wisdom to patients based on the particular disease they have contracted, favoring cancers that are associated with depression over those that are not.

No, when we persist in the belief that melancholy, pared down, is a special state, we are referring to run-of-the-mill depressions, the ones that arise in the predisposed when they are subjected (or subject themselves) to trauma and adversity. And even here there are distinctions.

We may have our doubts about whether melancholy, the source of awareness and self-awareness, refers to depression as it occurs in unconflicted straight shooters. Think of Margaret, the administrator in the insurance firm, when she encounters depression as an invading presence, an illness out of the blue. What enrages her is the suggestion that depression constitutes a royal road to truth about the self or the world. If she learns from her suffering, that learning does not arise from depression's special texture; for her, depression had the simple quality of any misfortune, any self-betrayal of mind and body. Many patients with strong familial patterns of depression are like Margaret, recurrently depressed without being "depressive" in personality style. They are dragged down without becoming contemplative. They never adopt pessimism; they remain optimists deprived of hope and health.

If we attribute special talent to "bad girls," who come to their depression through antisocial behavior and drug abuse—and I am not sure that we do—what we have in mind will be less the mood disorder than the rebelliousness. In a conformist society, we may admire marginality or discontent of any sort as an expression of individuality.

We are left to make our claims about melancholy with regard to a smaller group, depressives who seem emotionally attuned from the start, neurotic depressives. And even here, it is only certain stages of the illness that meet our standards. The small hippocampus and glia-deprived prefrontal cortex do not qualify; we have little interest in verbal memory loss and catastrophic responses to minor stress. When we say that melancholy confers depth, we may mean only in the initial steps of deterioration, the first two or three episodes, say, in a person who is not born a good distance down the common pathway of deterioration. Or—looking at Kierkegaard—is it a chronic state, between later episodes, that appeals?

And do we imagine that it is the *experience* of depression that counts? But then late-life depression should suffice. Silent strokes confer all the requisite symptoms. If late-life depression is not heroic melancholy, why are we drawn to younger depressions? The physiology of younger depressions—the diminished regional blood flow—resembles the effects of the silent strokes. It seems worrisome that the depth of modernity should reside in some highly delimited subspecies, say, depression in young, educated, pessimistic, middle-class neurotics.

Somewhere in this train of inquiry, our own nausea may set in. I reached my personal limit at a conference about depression in inner-city women. These are patients in our core category, women who have come to mood disorder through a combination of heredity, trauma, adversity, and unhappy choices. They were molested in early childhood, received substandard educations, became pregnant young, and married unwisely.

Researchers at the meeting were evaluating interventions meant to help prevent "intergenerational transmission" of mood disorder, mother to daughter. The background narrative accounts were as bleak as one might expect, tales of social and professional failure, broken families, abuse and neglect, apathy and despair.

I was wrestling with this question of melancholy—does it confer an exceptional worldview? I asked my colleagues whether they had noticed any hidden benefits of depression—creativity or profundity or exquisite empathy. Sitting with the depressed mothers, are you in the presence of special authenticity? Does a window open for you on our condition as modern men and women? I laid the ground for these questions, came to my subject slowly. Even so, the researchers have looked at me as if I had come from another planet. Perhaps it would be more exact to say, from another century.

230 * Against Depression

We may suppose that one way to save heroic melancholy is to make it metaphorical. The alienation a person feels in mental illness *resembles* the alienation a thoughtful person might feel in a corrupt society. The despair that is a symptom of depression *mimics* the despair that might accompany full awareness of the absurdity of our lives. But even this limited usage of heroic melancholy may come to sound strange. Why is depression, in particular, the fit metaphor? Schizophrenics are alienated—alienation, in the sense of distance from immediate experience, is a classic symptom of schizophrenia. Almost any critically ill person is likely to be despairing. If we recognize depression as a particular disease, we will no longer treat it as the all-purpose affliction, the stand-in for suffering in general.

As melancholy is whittled away, the discarded elements tend to lose their symbolic immediacy. There may be room, in the examined life, for a state that corresponds to drunkenness—blind self-satisfaction laced with camaraderie and tinged with impending sadness. But alcoholism is not the ecstatic intoxication of the modern soul. Panic disorder is not the existential angst of the twenty-first century. Post-traumatic stress disorder is not the universal injury that history imposes on us. Migraine is not weltschmertz; it is a specific sort of headache that in bad poetry might *stand for* spiritual pain. We just don't refer to well-defined neurological or psychiatric conditions in that way—or if we do, we understand that we are coining a metaphor in which the distance between the signifying illness and the idea signified is great. To my ear, phrases like *melancholy is the depth of modernity* have that tinny sound.

When I hear melancholy praised, or depression for that matter, often I find that what is intended is a statement about politics or the human condition. We believe, with Kierkegaard and the rest, that life is absurd, chaotic, and brief. We know that bourgeois contentment can be superficial. Complacency is a barrier to authenticity or self-fulfillment. The moral quest ennobles us. Discomfort or quirkiness or outsider status can be a spur to quest. But none of these homilies requires a claim about depression in particular. The pain of syphilis might have sufficed for Isak Dinesen. Until I took that walk at Rungstedlund, I assumed it had.

Melancholy is a sack that has been emptied. Melancholy is no more. And yet, and yet . . . one does not just jettison two thousand years of tradition. In our lives, depth seems so endangered and happiness so overblown, so commercial, so stupefying, that we may be inclined to cling to some version of melancholy, never mind what doctors say about depression.

Eighteen

❖

Art

PERHAPS THE MOST COMMON favorable belief about depression is that it inspires great creative efforts. Heroic melancholy may be dead, but the depressive artist is with us still, in imagination. That's why Prozac leads directly to van Gogh.

But it turns out that the evidence linking depression to creativity is shaky. And once we have found depression to be especially dangerous, we might demand quite solid evidence—might say that the bar has been raised, in terms of the proof that would satisfy us.

Part of the problem concerns melancholy, the empty sack. Early modern studies of madness and genius looked mostly at psychotic disorders, especially schizophrenia. More recently, the important work has focused on manic depression, also called bipolar affective disorder, and its variants. Most of the research that linked art and melancholy had only a tangential relationship to depression.

Until now, I have skirted the topic of bipolar disorder. It is the illness that comprises various sequences of depressive and manic episodes. Manic depression has its own vast scientific literature; to do the topic justice would require another book. But if we are to discuss genius, there is no avoiding a quick orientation.

Mania is characterized by racing thoughts, frenetic activity, impulsivity, irritability, and poor judgment. Manics can be euphoric, but sometimes the state is painful—tears and intense anxiety can be signs of mania. In their manic phase, manic-depressives are often delusional, grandiose, and paranoid. Despite points of overlap, manic depression appears to be a distinct disease from major depression, differing in its genetics, gender distribution, pattern of medication response, and biological markers. To give one example: when manic depression affects the hippocampus, the abnormalities appear to be in a different type of neuron than the ones most affected in depression. In bipolar patients, the hippocampus can be *hyper*active, with cells firing more than usual, albeit in disorganized fashion.

In the literature on creativity, a good deal of attention is paid to hypomania, an agitated state—it can occur also as a personality trait—that sits just shy of mania. Hypomanics are expansive, energetic, and pleased with themselves. Recent studies of creativity emphasize the importance of confidence and positive mood, along with a moderate willingness to question conventional wisdom. One current image of the creative thinker—and also of the business executive, salesman, preacher, or publicist—is the hypomanic.

Bipolar affective disorder, the full-blown disease, may have ties to literary production as well. The most-quoted, best-designed modern study of creativity and mental illness is a pilot project, conducted in the 1970s and '80s and never replicated. Nancy Andreasen, an eminent psychiatric researcher, looked at thirty members of the faculty of the Iowa Writers' Workshop, the program where Philip Roth, Kurt Vonnegut, and John Cheever once taught. She compared the thirty teachers to thirty control subjects matched for age and social class. The writers had a marked excess of mood disorder (now using the phrase broadly), especially manic depression and alcoholism.

Andreasen's findings were strong—faculty members were bipolar or alcoholic in numbers that were unlikely to be due to chance alone. The small study was influential in turning attention to mania as a writerly trait.

More widely read than Andreasen's research, which it cites, is Kay Redfield Jamison's book-length consideration of mood and creativity, *Touched with Fire*. The study is a labor of love, based on dozens of interviews conducted and hundreds of reference sources read. Jamison is herself bipolar; her book's bibliography alone would make a quiet argument for the benefits of a high level of energy. Jamison concludes that manic depression *is* the artistic temperament. Flights of fancy, mercurial moodiness, tempestuous brilliance, visionary imagination, brooding, morbidity, despair, sensuality, mutability—all are aspects of bipolarity. Jamison makes the claim most strongly for poets, notably British poets born in the eighteenth century. Blake, Wordsworth, Coleridge, Byron, Shelley, and Keats are in the group. In effect, Jamison's book considers the narrow version of heroic melancholy—that it leads to lyric verse—and centers the relevant pathology in bipolar affective disorder, not major depression.

In speaking with scientists about research on depression, I have also asked their opinion of the state of our knowledge about mood disorder and creativity. The responses have been reasonably uniform, that there is not enough good data on the heroic melancholy hypothesis in any of its versions—but that, as regards mania and poetry especially, there may well be something there.

The experts mention a number of technical problems. Biographical material may not yield precise diagnoses. (Do we count van Gogh as manic, or epileptic? How do we factor in Poe's alcoholism and epileptic symptoms?) Because artistic success depends on prevailing tastes, inclusion criteria become dicey; if a study looks at poets whose work is gathered in standard collections, the sequence of events that led to the choice of poems and authors comes into play. Do anthologists value depressive poems, or rely on the judgment of generations that did? It turns out to be hard to get outside the culture, influenced as it has been by centuries of fascination with heroic melancholy.

If the association between bipolarity and creativity is real, how it works remains unclear. Does manic depression constitute an original perspective? Is the disease associated with genes that produce compensatory talents? Or is it a matter of energy only? Or of inflated self-esteem? Because it includes vigor and confidence, hypomania, which can persist for long intervals in manic-depressive patients, seems helpful in any number of careers.

Jamison's research suggests as much. She finds connections between bipolarity and leadership in science, business, religion, politics, and military affairs. That is to say, she has also revived the broad theory of heroic melancholy, again centering it on bipolar affective disorder, not major depression.

If manic depression confers a benefit, it may be through increased productivity in general. Never mind the aching heart and drowsy numbness, if you are not reasonably busy and self-assured, you can't die young of tuberculosis, as Keats did, and leave a body of poems behind. Perhaps for a romantic poet, the combination is ideal—enough depression to create familiarity with the morbid themes that literary convention values, and then the manic flight that gets the work done. In contrast, the dense and steady depression of patients like Betty and Margaret and Mariana lacks compensatory "fire," the vigor and decisiveness and electrifying leaps of mind that characterize a certain sort of creative fertility.

In this field, psychobiography, the shift of interest away from unipolar depression has been especially striking. Recent research into the writing patterns of Emily Dickinson, once a standard example of the depressive poet, has revealed periods of intense production suggestive of bipolarity. In terms of presumptive diagnosis, an extraordinary number of writers and artists have moved in recent years from depressed or schizophrenic to bipolar. Jamison counts Edgar Allan Poe, Ezra Pound, and Virginia Woolf in this category. Regarding her own work, Jamison once told me, "I write when I'm manic and edit when I'm depressed," not a bad formula for an author.

Given this recentering of heroic and poetic melancholy, you might expect to find an extensive philosophical literature that debates the ethics of treating or preventing bipolar affective disorder or mania. There is not nearly the volume of writing that addresses depression. But then, even before evidence emerged, as it has recently, that bipolar disorder is associated with brain anomalies, we had come to accept that bipolarity constitutes pathology. Manic depression appears to be highly heritable. Manic episodes cause disruption out of proportion to any psychological cause. Mania ruins families quickly and brutally, through destructive acts that include suicide, violence, and the spending down of fortunes. Mania seems unnatural. To interrupt agitation is to restore normality.

Or perhaps it is that the metaphorical tradition is missing, mania as depth. It is true that the frenzy of Greek heroes for the most part sounds manic. Ajax slaughtered flocks of livestock—his colleagues' spoils of war—thinking they were his enemies; then he turned his sword on himself. But the romance of melancholy—Goethe, Keats, Carlyle—revolves around despair. Manic depression may produce poetry; it may even produce poetic souls whose life stories move us—think of Anne Sexton or Robert Lowell. But taken by itself, mania is likely to remind us of getting and spending. Hypomania is the affliction our society demands and induces. It is the disposition of traders and salesmen. The evidence of creative productivity notwithstanding, connotatively, mania is inauthenticity and surface.

I have often thought that this difference in connotation contributes to the contrast in our perceptions of medications for the different diseases. Lithium and the other mood-stabilizing drugs used in manic depression can be dangerous, in their secondary effects. And in principle, medicines that flatten mania—again, lithium is the best studied—should be suspect, as regards the squelching of creativity. In practice, bipolar patients often do complain that they are less imaginative on lithium. In one study of bipolar artists stabilized on lithium, a quarter said that the medication interfered with their creativity. (Half said it helped, because "lithium prevented their barren depressions and their overactive manias resulting in artistically valueless works.") But metaphorically, lithium prevents frenetic action and induces the serene, contemplative state valued by the ancient Greeks. And so there are few news stories about the side effects of antimanic compounds.

As depression achieves full status as a disease, apprehensions about treating it effectively should wane, as they have in the case of bipolar affective disorder. In any event, the objective evidence associating creativity with depression is weak. In the Andreasen study, depression appears twice as often in the Iowa writers as in the control group. But (as is not true for bipolarity) the numbers are too small to make the comparison meaningful. Also, there is just so much alcoholism in the sample—far more than among depressives in general—that it is hard to tell what role depression plays. Did alcoholic depressives invite one another into the academic department, creating a society tolerant of drinking? As for Jamison, she refers to depression, but for the most part, her research findings and her passion concern bipolarity. When we go back and look at studies we imagined made the link between creativity and depression, often we find that they deal with other diseases that were once grouped with depression in the catchall, melancholy.

Because objective evidence is lacking, we are left to consult our experience about the relationship between mood disorder and creativity. Certainly on a day-to-day basis, depression looks like a straightforward handicap. Patients tend to report that they did more and better work before they were depressed; and they do more and better work once they recover.

It is true that *difference* helps in the creative process, and depression is a form of difference. And of course, creative people make use of what life hands them. Some of the writers I have known, as friends and as patients, are odd enough. But the oddness is hardly all of one type.

A few writers have a minor variant of autism; they are awkward socially, and their conversation resembles lecture more than dialogue. Some writers struggle with a chronic sense of derealization; experience is distant from them, in a fashion that resembles the sensibility of certain epileptics, between seizures. Other writers live almost too insistently in the instant, the bon vivants and raconteurs. They are sprightly and funny, all glittering surface, in the manner of manics or even smooth-talking sociopaths. There are paranoid writers. Narcissism comes with the territory. Depression, yes—patients who are depressed and creative tend to seek me out, as a writer-doctor with an interest in mood disorder. But depression is one condition among many. Writing thrives on particularity, originality, distinctive voice and standpoint.

Mania, epilepsy, alcohol abuse—if we were to reconstruct the notion of the disturbed genius, we would need to replenish melancholy quite thoroughly. Don't some writers make their way via obsessionality, poring over the same patterns repeatedly? Although we may not be convinced that writers need to be eccentric; writers can be ordinary, to the extent that anyone is.

When I think of the relationship between depression and writing in particular, I prefer to imagine a complex process of mutual adaptation, between the disease and the medium. Think of the moment when the voyage of adventure becomes internal. Perhaps there are many such moments—in Bunyan, Shakespeare, Carlyle. Long before James Joyce reworks the *Odyssey* into interior monologue, the contemplative man styles himself the picaro, encountering demons and exploring strange territory without leaving his study.

If accounts of innerness constitute art, then the natural storytellers are those who have journeyed farthest and lived to tell the tale. Mania and depression are the antipodes. And perhaps depression has special standing. It is frightening, disorienting, and alarming, entailing as it does loss of faith in self. If self-consciousness is the subject of art, depressives are the ideal chroniclers.

Which is fortunate, since writing has long been held forth as a treatment for depression. If isolation begets melancholy, still, writing, so Renaissance authors say, is a specific against despair. Besides (in our time), writing is something that the depressed can do. Mustering the stamina for a regular job may be difficult, and conforming to the set hours, and composing the "game face" necessary to make a sale or inspire a team. Social intercourse may be painful. But paper is patient. It is available in the small hours, when insomnia rules. Writing can be set aside and then resumed. Words are subject to revision. Depressives, it is said, have little energy, but that little they apply doggedly. Perhaps this trait relates to the scrupulosity that German researchers note. It does not take much time to produce art, if one is good at it. Graham Greene set himself a goal and limit of 500 words a day. He would stop in midsentence.

Afternoons were spent indulging his ennui. Think how prolific Greene was. Later in life, he cut back to 300 words. Writing may have the same appeal for depressives that it has for stutterers, another well-represented group.

As for greatness, it seems a vexed concept. It has been some years since we have imagined, in nineteenth-century fashion, that the spirit of the times shows through in a single creative soul. Who is our great artist, after Picasso? What writers are replacing Updike, Bellow, and Roth? Did those men fill the shoes of Joyce, Woolf, and Faulkner, never mind Dickens and Tolstoy? Today, each of us is free to compose his own list, without reference to a canonical notion of the towering figure or to a universal image of the zeitgeist.

If we were comfortable with greatness, would depression, the illness, be a requirement? Our lack of conviction, regarding the linkage of art and depression, is evidenced by our long reach backward, to the nineteenth century, for examples. I have never been asked, "How will the availability of Prozac affect John Updike's work?"

"Not much" would be the answer—I mean, according to our imaginations. I have no way of knowing whether Updike has taken antidepressants. But our notion of melancholy no longer extends to embrace a man like Updike, a writer who seems, on the face of it, playful and affable, entranced by the pleasures and ironies of daily living.

I mention Updike in the spirit of memoir. Along with Saul Bellow, he represented contemporary art, the part of it I aspired to join, throughout my formative years. I particularly loved an early Updike short story, "The Alligators," about a fifth-grade boy who dreams of rescuing a new girl in the class, who is being teased by others. He reaches out to her, but too late: "It came to him that what he had taken for cruelty had been love, that far from hating her everybody had loved her from the beginning, and that even the stupidest knew it weeks before he did. That she was the queen of the class and might as well not exist, for all the good he would get out of it." The overtone of Kierkegaard in Updike's story, the wonderful confusion of altruism and selfishness, sympathy and self-pity, was right up my alley. The plot speaks to the injuries of daily life, humiliations universally endured—but without need of reference to depression.

Updike is the fictional diarist of a generation, the recorder of a time and place, postwar America. His predominance throughout the second half of the twentieth century reminds us of the appeal of art grounded neither in sadness nor in profound and determined alienation. In Updike, limitations of character take their toll, terrible events ensue, conventional perspectives prove shaky, until there is no fixed point to stand on—and yet, wonder at the world's riches is never absent. Even catastrophe is redeemed by faith and humor. Updike is one of many writers whose work suggests that heroic melancholy is more a matter of literary convention than medical reality.

Updike writes in the tradition without being of it. I am thinking particularly of his early work *The Centaur*. It was the novel assigned my freshman class the summer before our arrival at college—my first glimpse of what the university understood as literature. The book plays off the myth of Chiron, the centaur of the book's title. Chiron was the teacher of heroes: Jason, Achilles, and Hercules. Because he suffered from a never-healing wound, inflicted by one of Hercules' arrows, Chiron ceded his immortality to Prometheus, bringer of fire, who was then himself condemned to eternal pain. Both Chiron and Prometheus are icons of creativity.

Updike frames a contemporary novel around the classic myth. His Chiron is George Caldwell, a burnt-out schoolteacher struck in the foot by a student's arrow. An equally resonant wound is borne by George's fifteen-year-old son Peter, the Prometheus figure, who worries over the social consequences of his psoriasis. Work, aging, chance, and the inevitable failures of courage or of judgment—these suffice to wear away at a man. Grace, love, and sexual possibility provide compensations. The movement of the book is toward Peter's maturation, toward his awareness of the joys and burdens of creation. *The Centaur* is Updike's *Portrait of the Artist*. We understand that Updike's will be the art of the socially aware and socially integrated, art that can find inspiration in the modest victories of daily life.

Psoriasis, Updike later revealed in an autobiographical essay, is his own affliction. (He wrote of his stuttering, too, and his asthma; do we imagine that more is better?) On occasion, Updike will impose psoriasis on a fictional character, as an ongoing humiliating loss. "The name of the disease, spiritually speaking, is Humiliation," one Updike character concludes. He is a potter, and as his skin improves, the quality of his pots, and of his love life, declines. But wonder at nature's handiwork is never absent in Updike. In *The Centaur*, Peter Caldwell confesses: "The delight of feeling a large flake yield and part from the body under the insistence of a fingernail must be experienced to be forgiven."

Skin eruptions may once have constituted melancholy, but no longer. They do allow, in Updike's fiction, for adherence to narrative convention. We have the form of heroic melancholy, but with key elements muted. The template can stand on its own, shaping a story that involves neither mental abnormality nor (in the contemporary, human characters) grand genius.

There is, perhaps, room for embarrassment in confessing a devotion to Updike's work. By recent critical standards, he is precisely not melancholic enough; had Updike (so the rap on him goes) personally suffered more, his work might be deeper and he would evince broader sympathies. Cynthia Ozick complains that Updike's "fictive world is poor in the sorrows of history." Sorrow is the operative word. Political events and scientific discoveries serve as framework and metaphor in Updike's major novels. His writing is steeped in history. But the use is mutedly optimistic and American (consider the moon landing, as background in *Rabbit Redux*), rather than thoroughly bleak and European.

Not so the domain of that other hero of my youth, Saul Bellow. His best-known protagonist, Moses Herzog, inhabits the nightmare of history. He travels to Poland, is shaken by thoughts of the Holocaust. Most famously, he corresponds, in mind and on paper, with writers and philosophers long dead. His affinities are well placed: "Hegel understood the essence of human life to be derived from history. History, memory—that is what makes us human, that and our knowledge of death."

Though Herzog is in his forties, his fictional memoir adopts the arc of the youthful novel of self-formation. A romantic failure leads to despair, then the temptations of alienation, and finally a more or (as in

Herzog's case we suspect) less stable happiness rooted in acceptance of cultural norms.

Herzog announces his disorder in the first sentence: "If I'm out of my mind, it's all right with me." His quest is mostly internal and spiritual, but it has pronounced physical, geographic movement as well. He makes mad dashes from the Berkshires toward Martha's Vineyard, then to Manhattan and Chicago, and back to the Berkshires. Herzog is the frenzied melancholic, self-centered, self-righteous, voluble, irritable, impulsive, and enraged. As readers, we accept the convention; we accord Herzog his brilliance and (tattered) nobility. Traits on the manic spectrum serve well as indicators of heroism.

In James Atlas's recent biography of Bellow, the novelist appears to have a good deal in common with his protagonist. Bellow is self-absorbed, given to self-pity when abandoned, and occasionally hypochondriacal. He is energetic, seductive, vain, vengeful, and mistrusting. And he is a genius. Bellow is a melancholic malcontent, where that category stands apart from depression.

Because art comments on what has come before, because stories rely on and play off readers' expectations, because depression and recovery from depression inform our notion of the story line, heroic melancholy persists in art—even in the work of writers who are not themselves depressed. Perhaps the pairing will continue indefinitely; perhaps it will fade in the face of improvements in treatment. With the advent of antibiotics, infectious disease waned in importance as a source of plot and emotion. There was no second *Bohème*, no second *Magic Mountain*, until the era of *Rent* and *Angels in America*, responses to a new untreatable contagion, HIV-AIDS.

But then, depression is grander than tuberculosis, in its cultural effects. To write seriously is to comment on *Hamlet* and *Don Quixote*. Once a tradition is established, it draws the energies of writers of all stripes—a truth of which *Hamlet* and *Quixote* may themselves be examples.

I don't imagine that Shakespeare was depressed, nor Cervantes, for all that their great protagonists are melancholics. Cervantes was a military hero who lost the use of his left arm in one of the glorious battles of his era. Late in life, he imagined a reader addressing him as "the cripple who is sound, the great man, the jolly writer, and, in short, the joy of the Muses!" No one knows what Shakespeare and Cervantes were like. But we are free to imagine them vigorous, hearty, productive—resilient.

For the present, not only depressives, but all writers will want on occasion to don the mask of the wounded aesthete or the frenzied malcontent, as a narrator or protagonist. But in life, if suffering enriches art, it seems that any form will do: stuttering, asthma, hypochondriasis. No one would propose preserving bipolarity or alcoholism or epilepsy in order to maintain a supply of anguished artists of the sort Kierkegaard honored. Depression has a lesser claim, when it comes to creativity. Depression may relate to creativity only in the fashion of quite plebeian diseases and handicaps, like psoriasis or the narcissist's fragile ego.

Nineteen

❖

The Natural

A
ND STILL WE MAY FEEL PROTECTIVE toward depression, as a condition we would not want to see eradicated. One way to express this reluctance is to say that depression is natural. Scholars have been claiming as much for centuries. It is only natural in an unregulated (or overly regulated) political economy to feel depressed. It is natural to feel depressed in the face of loss or adversity.

Of course, once depression is securely ensconced in the realm of disease, the character of the natural changes. If you have a predisposing personality type (hostility and impatience now appear to be the key traits) and a familial tendency to high blood lipids, and if you live in a culture where stress and fatty foods are prevalent, it is natural that you should suffer a heart attack. That expectable consequence is what medicine addresses routinely, pathology whose causes we know something about. All diseases are natural, in this sense.

If we continue to speak favorably of depression as natural, we may mean that although it represents pathology, it is also adaptive, or was once. Adaptive functions can sometimes be discerned within devastating diseases. Sickle-cell anemia is the great example. An inherited defect in red blood cells (they take on a crescent shape), it causes pain, fatigue, infection, stroke, blindness, and widespread organ damage. A partial expression of the disease, sickle-cell trait, is protective against malaria. When sickling was limited to parts of the world where malaria was a common cause of death in children, the inherited trait was adaptive.

This example displays the practical limitations of information about adaptive value. If you are living in America, where malaria has been eradicated, and if your disease puts you at risk for blindness and stroke, you will not much care that a milder form of sickling serves a role in some other context. Your pain and disability suffice to shape a response. We would be happy to find an effective cure for sickle-cell anemia.

And it must be said that the case for depression, as a useful adaptation, is remarkably weak.

That *emotion* can be adaptive is beyond question. Fear is an inner signal that danger is at hand. Grief brings our attention to the rupture of precious social bonds. Emotion channels thought, and assigns priority, by signaling intensity and urgency. Emotion is a type of thought, an aspect of thought, thought's coloration.

Of course, emotion can mislead—we are all subject to groundless apprehension. Even in the absence of depression, we may suffer needlessly. And of course, we may also be prone to foolish optimism and inexplicable joy.

How to value emotion is a difficult matter. Like melancholy, emotion enjoys its vogues. These designations are inexact, but the "Age of Reason," as a label for the eighteenth century, refers to attempts to repress the (deceptive) passions, which then regain legitimacy in the nineteenth century's romantic era. To Freud, emotion's straightforward message is untrustworthy, but that deception points to unconscious truths. For the psychoanalyst and her patient, strong feeling is an X on the map—it says dig here. The *less* obviously explicable the affect, the more valuable the buried treasure.

The recent tendency has been to construe emotion not as a delusion or a mystery, but rather as an aspect or a variety of reason. Emotion is a way of reading the social world, so we can speak of emotional intelligence as a strength to be cultivated. Emotion is also a form of pleasure and a ticket to other pleasures, such as intimacy in private life and communal connections in the public sphere. Emotion is an aspect of liveliness. People who resemble calculating machines are missing something, in personal experience and in social judgment. Emotional perceptiveness enriches daily life and leads to good choices. On these points, popular writers and philosophers are in accord.

In this era, when emotion is accepted as an accurate mode of perception, it becomes a challenge to explain why mood disorder is beneficial. Sad mood, yes—we need to be aware of events that injure us or those we love. But not depression. Depression represents a loss of emotional responsiveness. If finely tuned affect constitutes intelligence, what good can we say about a mind that gets overwhelmed and loses touch with external stimuli? How do we make the case for a brain that responds now to challenges that occurred five months ago? Once we grant that the parts of the brain that integrate emotional input are subject to pathology, once we point to a basis for lost concentration and fixed negative mood, we might want to pull back from any claim that depression is an apt response to circumstance. In what sense is depression adaptive?

The most vigorous answers to this question have come from the young discipline of evolutionary psychology, the application of Darwinian principles to mood and behavior. Evolutionary psychologists make the case that depression contains a measure of accuracy after all—as a signal and as a coercive force, one that bullies the animal into passivity. Depression may make an animal withdraw from a losing effort and conserve its energy—say, to stop foraging in a time of drought. Depression can signal a need for submission in a failed fight for hierarchy dominance. And in both these cases, the external signs of depression may serve to elicit caring from others.

But these theories lose some of their force in the face of our new understanding of what depression is. For one thing, it is unclear that depression conserves energy. Yes, we can imagine a defeated animal sticking close to home. But depression is hardly a quiet state. The stress system is revved up, fight-or-flight hormones are produced in excess and responded to extravagantly, even relative to their rate of production. Anyone who has seen a depressed patient pace and wring his hands will doubt that depression saves on energy. And anyone who has seen a depressed patient obsess over a failing business plan or love affair will doubt that mood disorder is an effective way to make an animal change course in the face of a losing struggle. Besides, there are too many collateral costs to depression. For instance, the risk of infection and heart disease rises. Our calculation of energy conservation and survival enhancement needs to take those consequences into account, not to mention the possibility of suicide, the final form of entropy.

As for submission, its economic value (for primates) has proved hard to assess. Death is common among adolescent male monkeys driven out of the troop into which they were born. Dominance turns out to be extremely important for reproduction and the successful rearing of offspring, for mothers and fathers both. The hierarchy arrangement may benefit a troop. But most evolutionary theory concerns the survival and reproduction of individuals; for the individual primate, the benefits of prolonged submission are uncertain. What is at stake in depression is not an ordinary response to adversity but an enhanced one. How adaptive is it to be *especially* prone to submission? And then to be unable to terminate the response, once it begins? And to be at high risk for the internal harm humiliations cause? On the face of it, resilience might be preferable—certainly the ability, after withdrawal, to fight again.

Then there are the problems of early trauma and neglectful parenting. In all the animal models, harm in childhood leads to extreme stress responses in adulthood, including listlessness, social withdrawal, timidity in the face of novel stimuli, and difficulty with cognitive challenges, like maze tests. If trauma and neglect produced healthier, fitter monkeys, wouldn't all mothers make sure their offspring experienced them? If the depressive posture were valuable, wouldn't most monkeys behave like traumatized ones? They don't. When resources are scarce, most animals still forage. Altogether, the lack of uniformity of response is a perplexity for evolutionary psychology—leading Darwinians have admitted as much. The notion that animals who were injured early are more adaptive seems strange. Why isn't depression just what it looks like, a progressive impairment?

And what good can be said about uncaused depressions, the episodes that can arise in the absence of any environmental trigger? It's just hard to make a case that those catastrophes are adaptive. The schema has not been proposed that justifies the seriously stuck switch. Chronic and long-standing depressions merely create victims.

These considerations have caused a shift in focus among evolutionary psychologists. Perhaps, depression is adaptive less because it causes animals to abandon futile efforts than because it causes them to persevere. The preeminent evolutionary psychiatrist Randolph Nesse favors this speculation. Granted, depressive traits are "the exact opposite of the optimism, energy, and a willingness to make changes that would help a person get out of a bad situation." But pessimism, Nesse argues, prevents animals from changing direction too rapidly.

> The pursuit of large goals requires constructing expensive social enterprises that are difficult to replace—marriages, friendships, careers, reputation, status, and group memberships. Major setbacks in these enterprises precipitate life crises. In such situations, it is often useful to inhibit any tendency to shift quickly to a different endeavor. . . . [P]essimism, lack of energy, low self-esteem, lack of initiative, and fearfulness can prevent calamity even while they perpetuate misery.

This new account of depression is elegant—far from convincing animals to give up on projects, the syndrome forces them to persevere. As Nesse himself notes, this justification for the negative mind-set leaves theorists straddling a critical issue. Depression serves to encourage people both to stay the course and to change course. Sometimes, depression serves "both to decrease investment in the current unsatisfying life enterprise and also to prevent the premature pursuit of alternatives."

But even this nice resolution underplays the sorts of triggers that typically lead to depression, the human equivalents of ejection from a primate troop. We're fired, our spouse leaves, we're humiliated and cast out. Our major setbacks tend to be ones that endanger large investments, like career and marriage and group membership. We can't drop those and cling to something more basic—they're as basic as it gets.

Nor in the midst of a depression do people make especially prudent choices about where to hang on and where to let go. Depressives cling to failing romantic relationships; they persist in pursuing dead-end Ph.D. projects overseen by abusive advisors. Nesse notes that "failure to disengage can cause depression, and depression can make it harder to disengage." In practice, depressives make mistakes of every variety. They will impulsively drop a winning strategy just when it is at the verge of success, and then they will double up on losing bets.

I have said that I am uneasy with the Darwinian approach to psychology. Often, like Voltaire's relentless optimist, Dr. Pangloss, it praises whatever happens to be the case. A highly refined justification for a devastating disease strikes me as dicey. How would we ever know whether depression once caused men and women to make precisely the right choices in our hunter-gatherer phase?

The more we think about what depression is, the less likely we are to imagine that it is a condition that has been well designed to produce evolutionary fitness. If we grant, for the sake of argument, that a brief episode of depression in adolescence serves some function, what benefit do we see in a longer, more complex second episode in young adulthood? Shouldn't all episodes be about the same length—a given degree of food shortage or social rejection giving rise to a corresponding period of withdrawal? Overall, the chronic and recurrent nature of depression is worrisome. What is the point of depressions that begin in childhood and settle in to stay, even in times of plenty? If you were designing a disease intended to help you thread your way, in hostile environments, between enterprises that merit perseverance and those that should be abandoned, mightn't you build enhanced memory and sharpened concentration into the package? Why foster passivity that tends even in early episodes to last six or nine months? Having a switch makes sense, but why a stuck switch? Why should evolution favor a condition that has, broadly speaking, the same effects as small strokes in the parts of the brain that fine-tune emotions?

Like attempts to delimit stable subtypes of depression, efforts to define depression's adaptive benefits have proved frustrating. There is always a script on the table, but the floor is littered with discarded past efforts. Each time we learn more about depression, the prevailing theory needs to be revised.

Depression is so debilitating! Years ago, I was the psychiatric liaison to a surgical ward. The most common consultation request involved patients who would not follow routine instructions after an operation: walk, cough, eat, breathe deeply. Depressed patients just gave up. They had no strategy, not even obedience to those they trusted. Retreat to the cave to lick your wounds, fine—but get licking. In demanding circumstances, how often is it adaptive to lose the capacity for action altogether? I mean, in this fashion, where death seems preferable to effort, where the signals of a supportive community—nurses, friends, family—are ignored?

Seeing the depressed fail regularly, in the face of challenges that others meet, might dispose anyone to the alternative possibility, that depression confers no benefit. Some illnesses, and some normal traits, represent happenstance in evolution.

In a famous essay, the late Stephen Jay Gould compared such evolutionary accidents to "spandrels." Spandrels are triangular spaces below the domes of Gothic churches. (The correct term of art for such a space is *pendentive*, but *spandrel* remains the word used in the evolution debate.) Long assumed to be purposive—they hold images of the apostles—spandrels turn out to be not planned decorations but incidental forms that result from the limitations of medieval architectural methods. If you mount a dome on pairs of rounded arches, you're stuck with spandrels. The apostles are late additions—a use that was conceived centuries after the construction of the Cathedral of San Marco in Venice and others.

Spandrels are by-products; they represent limitations of engineering, an unintended consequence. It is the main project that is shaped and optimized by natural selection, not the spandrel, which comes along for the ride. Sometimes spandrels are later put to use, as in the addition of mosaic portraits of saints. Gould coined the word *exaptation* to cover this development, a late modification that manages to make the best of a spandrel. Depression may be a spandrel—natural without having contributed evolutionary advantage. And then there is no reason that depression would not be decorated exaptively—for instance, by attracting a mythology regarding its value, or through acquiring a role in song and story.

Of course, evolutionary processes are invisible. What looks destructive today may once have had its uses. But the room for evolutionary speculation about depression is limited.

The "medical depressions"—the ones stemming from strokes, hormone abnormalities, and cancers—are pretty clearly spandrels. It is hard to know why victims of pancreatic cancer should be adapted to maintain (or withdraw from) their customary activities any more than victims of lung cancer. To call the depression natural is only to say that nature can be cruel. Ordinary resilience would serve the patient as well.

The genetically predisposed, who start some distance down the slope to "uncaused" depression, seem strikingly disadvantaged. The early adversity that leads to poor education, poor social support, recurrent trauma, and divorce has little to recommend it. Coming to depression through drug abuse is a peculiarly human phenomenon; here it seems a matter of frying your brain in a way that other primates cannot. And within this mix, the routes to reproductive fitness are just too varied. The bad girls may get knocked up early, while shy and sensitive depressives enter the marital pool late. The results of depression documented by anthropology-minded researchers in our culture—fewer offspring, less living space, earlier death—hardly point in the direction of any clever response to circumstance.

And then there is the variety of symptoms within depression. Some depressives starve themselves, some overeat. Some suffer insomnia, some sleep too long. Some depressives become irritable, others turn docile. The symptom clusters vary in a fashion that seems unrelated to circumstance or history: a patient can starve herself in one depression and binge in the next. We can imagine a challenge, to monkeys or to hunter-gatherers, for which one subset of these responses would confer an adaptive advantage. But the symptom constellation associated with the next depression, in similar circumstances, would make matters worse.

Overall, the variety of depression suggests a failure in function. Depression is what you get when parts of the brain that integrate emotional input are overwhelmed. To put the matter in the terms favored by Robert Sapolsky, you have a system engineered to cope with acute stress—a zebra facing a lion—that meets its design limitation when stressors become chronic. Flight is the adaptation; depression is the spandrel.

The adaptive function of depression, if any, seems to me unknowable—in any case, unknown. If the formulations of evolutionary psychology tempted me at all in the years when I was focused on mood disorder, it was in my work with reasonably stable men attracted to depressed women. The coloration of the desire in those men—compulsion without overtones of perversion—made me think about instinctive drives.

Just hypothetically, imagine that depressed females were especially exact in matching energy expenditures to foraging opportunities on the savanna. Under adverse conditions, women with that proclivity would be more likely to survive, along with their young. Then it would be advantageous for a male to have mated with a depressive female. Males drawn to depressives would see their offspring live to adulthood, to reproduce and pass on a portion of the paternal genes. On a natural, evolutionary basis, depression would become sexually charming, as would early indicators of a propensity for depression.

A similar conclusion would arise from almost any explanation of depression's benefits. Traits (like broad hips, as indicators of an ample birth canal) that imply adaptive advantage are taken into account in sexual selection. Fitness becomes attractive.

This account, if we accept its premise, goes some distance toward explaining the favored status of depression in general—how protective we can feel toward it. If depression was adaptive in the era when our instincts were set, then the allure of depression should feel—and would be—natural. Other tendencies—romanticizing depression, in literature and art—would have invisible support as well.

Unfortunately for this flight of imagination, we don't have a clear reason for assuming that depression is anything but a spandrel. But we can retell the sexual selection story in a way that accepts depression, the disease, as defect merely.

There is a line of research that seeks to explain why women suffer a high rate of depression. As an illness, depression (once it is under way) behaves similarly across genders. After a first or second episode of depression, a man will encounter a second or third episode about as often as a woman will. The difference in liability has largely to do with the onset of a recurring condition. Women are more likely to get depressed at all—that is, to suffer a first episode.

Some of that difference may be genetic, related to broad differences in the way that men and women are constructed. For example, the hormonal variation in monthly cycling may confer incidental vulnerability to perturbations in stress hormones. But researchers looking into the social basis of depression also found a sex difference that relates to triggers for an initial encounter with depression.

It turns out that very serious adversity affects men and women similarly. If his wife dies or falls gravely ill or leaves, a man is about as likely to suffer depression as is a woman in parallel circumstances of loss. The same is true of disruptions involving a person's child or parent. But if you cast the net farther and ask about misfortunes befalling aunts and uncles, neighbors and friends, or more distant acquaintances of any stripe—then men and women no longer look the same.

Losing someone you care about can trigger depression; that part is universal. But "caring about" covers more territory for women. A wider network of attachments entails more losses. A portion of the difference in rates of depression can be attributed to differences in social investments. Studies suggest that it is not only major losses that matter; because of their multiple attachments, women also suffer more minor, daily stress than men. Within the genders, too—comparing men with men, or women with women—those individuals who care more broadly are more prone to depression.

Research of this sort has led to the "cost of caring" hypothesis. Depression is, in part, the downside of affiliation. Parenthetically, "cost of caring" studies throw into doubt the value of "social support networks" as buffers against stress. For women, these networks are also potential *sources* of stress. Weighing risk against benefit, it turns out that the additional support women draw on does not compensate for the additional exposure to grief.

So caring, which is a social good, turns out to be a risk factor for depression. This theory is compatible with the belief that depression is a disease, straightforwardly. Caring may be, or may have been, adaptive, in the sense that it helps you safely pass on your genes. Vulnerability to depression is still a spandrel, and depression is still a disease. You contract depression when injuries damage the stress-response system. But it happens that, for certain depressives, their increased liability to mood disorder is due in part to traits that on their own are useful and attractive, affiliation and caring.

Now, there are all sorts of depressives. This late in our deliberations, I do not want to undercut the important truth that the clueless and isolative, the heartless and the vicious fall prey to depression. "Caring" explains a very small percentage of the liability to mood disorder.

But the willingness to attach and nurture is a crucial trait in evolutionary terms. Even a modest, probabilistic link between depression and nurturance might have social consequences. Suppose from the viewpoint of onlookers that when you see depression, you can infer a propensity for social bonding. Maybe depression in a woman signals the capacity for fit and engaged mothering in particular. It's not that the depression does her or her offspring any good, but the fact of her depression indicates that, when healthy, she attaches strongly. In that case, the ability to detect and respond to that marker would be an evolutionary advantage for prospective mates. Young men attracted to depressive young women would be rewarded with trustworthy partners, and with offspring who are well attended to. The genes of those men would be selected for, which is to say that attraction to aspects of depression might become well established (culturally or, perhaps, genetically) in subsequent generations.

If depression and the vulnerability to depression carry appeal, it may be because they correlate, modestly, with traits that make a good spouse and parent. We are so aware (when we are) of depression's downside that we may find it hard to accept claims that the illness hints at evolutionary advantage. What of postpartum psychosis, where a mother kills her newborns? What of suicide? What of dense anhedonia, in which a mother neglects her young children? To the extent that those outcomes are rare, the probabilistic evolutionary cost will be slight. Depressives make bad parents. But that truth holds only for the intervals when the illness is active; many women who are moody during courtship will make fine wives and mothers.

And of course, the likelihood of various outcomes may have been different in the past. If life was short, if communities were supportive, if chronic stress was a less common aspect of daily life, who knows how often downstream episodes of depression came into play? This model does not require that depression do anyone any good. It can be deterioration simply. If you design for attachment, you happen to get excess disease. But the illness may come to carry some appeal, as a visible sign of good engineering elsewhere.

Of course, the depression has a terrible downside—all the consequences of disease. Often in nature, mimicry confers special advantages. Perhaps better than liability to depression would be the appearance of it, the simulacrum, in the absence of actual illness or even warm feeling. In this fantasy, apparent depressive symptoms (like Marlene Dietrich's on-screen) might to continue to seduce even where they lack any connection to the capacity for loyalty or nurturance.

Indeed, mimicry might succeed even when it is detected. Reaching for the perverse, Andre Codrescu writes: "In Venice women wear their grief with such grace that men are often overcome by lust just watching them in church." Codrescu is evoking Casanova. Sincere grief signals the capacity to attach; feigned grief signals playfulness and resilience. Both can be appealing. We will have no trouble imagining a host of complex ways in which mood disorder becomes woven into the fabric of desire.

Well, I can seen that I have gone too far, in my speculation. Depression may have no positive function, not even as an exaptation. But depression is widespread. It is common in the young, and often mild or short-lived in early episodes. It confers a marked perspective—a difference, especially at an age (late adolescence) where wrestling with difference is a developmental task. It resists treatment. Perhaps any disease with these characteristics will be attributed worth.

Think again of tuberculosis. TB confers no advantage. But at its peak, it had an extraordinary prevalence. Its symptoms wax and wane. The torpor and excitation that tuberculosis variously engenders mimic normal personality states. In its mild phases, and even beyond, tuberculosis is compatible with creative production. Chopin was tubercular for the whole of his adult life and was famously prolific in his thirties, when the disease was most apparent. Anton Chekhov was likely afflicted for twenty-two years; he wrote his most famous works—*The Cherry Orchard, The Three Sisters*, "The Lady with the Dog"—in the seven years that his tuberculosis was under active treatment. If tuberculosis was romantic, if tuberculosis had its adherents, why not depression?

My own observation is that the attractions of depression can be muted by shifts in our beliefs—a sign, perhaps, that our susceptibility to its charms is not firmly encoded.

I practice in a city that hosts half a dozen colleges. My office has always been on or near College Hill.

It is hard to overestimate the prevalence of depressive symptoms on campus. One survey has found that 90 percent of adolescents report having experienced periods of marked sad feelings. Most of these students are not and never will be depressed. Even so, dealing with low mood is a requirement of social functioning on campus. Students will often find a touch of depression reassuring in a prospective partner. You can understand, be there, offer a shoulder to cry on. In the dating game, catching someone on the rebound is a skill, one rooted in sensitivity to depressive states. Young men and women with no other social advantage may become specialists in spotting and tending to disordered mood.

You would think that if the pull of depression were natural, the campus is the spot where that effect would be most evident. But my sense is that the attraction of depression, for college students, is on the wane.

Naming the disorder has been enough to taint it. When I was an undergraduate, thirty or forty years ago, students had only the dimmest awareness of depression. Certainly then, young men looked right past mood instability in the case of women who were pretty or warm or clever. Twenty years ago, when I began practicing in Providence, students were still blithely oblivious. For this narrow population, college students, public health efforts to destigmatize depression have had a paradoxical effect. Today, students recognize depression and consider it an illness.

Whether public awareness campaigns have resulted in increased use of mental health services is hard to say. My impression is that visits peaked in the 1960s, when psychotherapy was in vogue; at selective colleges, about half of undergraduates visited "psych services." Then interest waned, and therapists were dropped from the clinics. Now, the infirmaries are overwhelmed in the face of new treatments for, and new anxiety over, a range of mental illnesses. (At selective colleges, by the time of graduation about a quarter of students will have been prescribed an antidepressant at the on-campus clinic; this figure omits those who receive medications from a doctor at home.) So the direct result of "destigmatization" may be the intended one, more treatment of mood disorders.

The campaigns may have succeeded in this sense as well: most students would agree that a person is not morally responsible for his depression, any more than for juvenile-onset arthritis. But ailments hardly lend appeal. No one wants to marry into depression. In fact, parents might (and do) advise against it: "She's very sweet, but she strikes your father as depressive."

In a culture that values minute consistency in child rearing, and one in which children are born to older parents, depression now signals the future risk of relative unfitness. We know that depression spells trouble that worsens over time. The result is to turn depressive traits into social impediments, or at least to dim their (natural or historic) luster. Depression has lost its social stigma, but only insofar as it has gained reasonably accurate medical stigma. It is like alcoholism in this regard.

Not that the social stigma of depression was very marked on campus. For forty years, there has been virtue in "growing up absurd"—alienated, beat, foot-dragging, rebellious, slackerly, different. The melancholic malcontent did not go out of fashion. I have memories from my own college years of feeling jealous admiration of men and women who lived lives of intense emotional drama, a category that extended to conditions requiring hospitalization.

To destigmatize depression is to rob it of romance. My impression is that on campus today depressed students are the least attractive that they have been in decades. If this observation has any validity—and it is based only on my impression of the difficulties of patients in my small practice—then the allure of depression is plastic, responsive to social pressures and perceptions.

In the short run, as someone who tends to the depressed, I find restigmatization hurtful. I don't want my depressed patients to encounter objectivity. I am pleased when they find devoted partners, never mind the illusions (or evolved instincts) that help along the way. But I do understand that in the long run, there something to be said for clearsightedness, a rapprochement between *what it is* and *what it is to us*.

Less and less do I see hidden benefit in depression. Medicine knows any number of "stuck switch" illnesses, where the immune system, say, attacks a pathogen and then continues to function in high gear long after the enemy has been driven from the field. Multiple sclerosis is probably like that, and tertiary syphilis, and the autoimmune diseases, lupus and scleroderma and others. A mechanism that ordinarily protects ends in destroying the body's own cells. That the disease occurs in a necessary, adaptive system says nothing in its favor. Disease is system failure. Interpersonal sensitivity and loyal attachment are admirable; acute stress responses are apt defenses to certain threats. But mood disorder is what the name implies, dysfunction—of the very systems we value when we call emotion adaptive.

The question, I suppose, is whether we can make distinctions—whether we can value caring and still combat depression. If you think about the lines of research in depression treatment and prevention, they are all in accord with that project. Whether modulating cytokines or stress hormones, working with genes or drugs, attempting to prevent cell death or encourage cell growth, the intent is to interrupt deterioration and catalyze repair—to protect the brain from the consequences of disappointment and adversity.

One way to envisage resilience is as a force that makes the world safe for caring. Given more resilience, those exposed, through attachment, to the risk of loss would no longer suffer deterioration. Make your social network as extensive as you please. If those you love suffer harm, you may experience intense and nuanced sadness, informed by memory. But your prefrontal cortex cells will not be stripped of protection, your hippocampal cells will not die, your neural connections will stay intact, new nerve cell pathways will be formed. The switch will not stick. You will be at no greater risk for future depression than you were before the loss. At the least, your progress down the pathway to intractable mood disorder will be no faster than that of someone born with more capacity for recovery or subject to less childhood trauma. Your natural, adaptive functions, whatever they are, will remain intact. In a society that could reliably offer neuroresilience, early depression would carry no stigma, because downstream depressions would be rare; depression would be stopped in its tracks.

The great goal of psychotherapy is the capacity to feel what we feel; the great impediment to emotional awareness is the fear of being overwhelmed, so that our identity splinters. Psychotherapy intends for us to remember past wounds, but without their automatically distorting attachments now. Insurance against depression would free us to know ourselves, frankly, radically, without risk of decompensation. We could bear affect. Robert Frost writes that "Happiness Makes Up in Height for What It Lacks in Length." Something comparable would be true of sadness; we could plumb the deeps, knowing we would resurface.

That is one fantasy anyway, one utopia. It presumes that to attenuate depression is to honor emotion. If sensitivity and affiliation are the evolved traits and depression is a spandrel, then to respect adaptation is to favor some substantial level of emotional resilience in those who feel intensely and attach strongly.

Twenty

❖

Alienation

PERHAPS THERE IS SOMETHING TOO NEAT, too sanitary, in
this utopian fantasy, the eradication of depression the disease
only. Yes, we can imagine it—protecting the brain against harm,
without otherwise dampening moods or emotions. But would it ever
work that way? Isn't this talk about pathology really a foot in the door
for the great American campaign of self-improvement, consumerism,
and bland happiness?

In the aftermath of *Listening to Prozac*, I faced that sort of question
repeatedly, particularly in my encounters with medical ethicists. One
philosopher wrote: "[S]uppose you are a psychiatrist and you have a
patient . . . say, an accountant living in Downers Grove, Illinois, who
comes to himself one day and says, Jesus Christ, is this it? A Snapper
lawn mower and a house in the suburbs? Should you, his psychiatrist,
try to rid him of his alienation by prescribing Prozac?"

This challenge was pretty obviously directed at me, although in a
sense it only restated what I had said in my book. I had worried about

"cosmetic psychopharmacology" and, with it, the possibility that in developing medications to treat depression, we might create implicit social pressures to alter personality styles that are not sufficiently upbeat.

Now, imagining the newly dislocated accountant, I found myself leaning the other way, to this extent: my first response was, tell me more. Has the accountant noticed other changes—in sleep, in appetite, in the capacity to enjoy what he usually enjoys? Does he have a history of depression, or a family history? Has he suffered recent losses? Were there early ones as well? These automatic doctorly questions would not be in the service of any particular intervention; I would be open to trying psychotherapy if treatment was called for. But I would not want to overlook a depressive episode, if one was brewing.

What sort of sensation was the accountant referring to? What does it mean that he "comes to himself one day"? Did the dislocation seem to arise out of the blue? He might have been experiencing a change in taste merely; perhaps he liked his neighborhood less well, but he remained an optimist, a planner and a doer, a man who would set about bringing his life into conformity with his new ideals. Still, it didn't sound that way—not if he was a psychiatric patient considering medication. I suspected that the alienation might be of a particular sort: depressive alienation. Perhaps the word *alienation* was being used loosely, so that, in this context, alienation meant depression. Now, immersed in depression, my first concern was not to miss a mood disorder.

It was Carl Elliott who had asked about the Illinois accountant. Elliott is a leading student of the ethics of enhancement. He a gentle, funny young man, with a quiet Southern accent. Elliott trained as a doctor, then veered off into philosophy. We hit it off immediately when we met. He and I shared a love of the novelist Walker Percy. Percy had encouraged each of us, early in our careers. But it was around Percy's ideas that we came into conflict.

Percy's heroes tend to be courteous, middle-aged men who feel a bit wrong in their skin. Percy says that they are right to do so, since alienation is a self-aware response to our place in this commercial culture and God's cosmos. Elliott wrote that the patients I describe in *Listening to Prozac* "sound strikingly like the alienated Southern heroes in Walker Percy's novels." Elliott pointed to protests that the patients make, before treatment: "The whole world seems to be in on something that I just don't get," and "I don't know who I am." If they examine themselves, these confused outsiders will discover that for them, as for Percy's protagonists, the nearest diagnosis is "existential alienation," a justifiable sense of not being at home in the world.

To appreciate my response to Elliott's critiques, you have to understand that I had in practice prescribed medication only ever for patients who met standard criteria for treatment. The patients whose outcries Elliott identified as indicative of existential alienation were, in fact, actively depressed.

Hillary is the name I gave to the woman who complained that she seemed not to get something that the whole world did. A series of doctors had diagnosed Hillary as depressed and prescribed conventional medications, along with psychotherapy. When she approached me for treatment, Hillary's prominent symptom was the inability to enjoy or look forward to anything at all. She also complained of sad mood, poor concentration, and constant sleepiness. Hillary's psychiatrists disagreed about what condition was primary; one doctor had identified a possible sleep disorder. But no one doubted that Hillary suffered recurrent depression.

Hillary's complaint was that her mood state was inexplicable. It persisted in the face of manageable life circumstances. When, briefly, the anhedonia remitted, Hillary was relieved. When it returned, she found herself in terrible shape. Having for a few months experienced ordinary pleasure, Hillary retained a fresh cognitive awareness of what others were able to enjoy. That personal knowledge—of vital feelings from which she was again cut off—made her inner emptiness yet more frustrating. Her complaint was not that our society is alienating, but rather that she lacked the capacity to feel with immediacy, even in the face of what should have been compelling experiences.

Sally is the patient who worried about her identity, saying, "I don't know who I am." Sally, too, was depressed. As a child, she had been a victim of sexual molestation. In adulthood, Sally suffered exhaustion, tearfulness, and poor concentration, accompanied by a sense of impending disaster. She was temperamentally shy, and when her depression lifted, her diffidence diminished as well.

Let me be clear, Elliott's commentary was hardly outrageous; for the most part, it was a refinement of what I myself had written. I had used Hillary's and Sally's response to antidepressants in order to pose a hypothetical question: In the case of someone who was not and had never been depressed, would we (or should a doctor) feel comfortable giving medication to ameliorate temperamental shyness or to enhance a person's ability to experience pleasure?

Elliott had brushed aside the issue of temperament and identified the proper worry as being over a person's existential status. Hillary and Sally were not anhedonic or shy; they were alienated. And here, Elliott was not fabricating a Snapper-mowing suburbanite but commenting on these very women, my patients.

To me, his understanding just seemed wrong. Neither Hillary nor Sally had any complaint about the culture, other than that her depression or her personality had prevented her from entering into it with gusto. Neither I nor my patients had ever believed that their despairing outcries should be heard as signals of women's distance from self, society, or cosmos. For me, Elliott's remarks had an unintended effect. They demonstrated that seemingly "existential" complaints—ones so typical and convincing as to be illustrative of the category—often arise as mere symptoms in the course of painful mental disorders.

It occurred to me that Elliott's commentary was a translation into life of the literary tradition of the melancholic malcontent. If you think about it, most of the literary figures who inform our image of alienation are mentally ill, and in actively destructive ways. Camus's Meursault, emotionally anesthetized in the face of his mother's death, bursts into unmotivated violence against strangers. J. D. Salinger's Holden Caulfield, Ken Kesey's Randle McMurphy, and Jack Kerouac's Dean Moriarty are drawn to suicide. Virtually every Walker Percy protagonist has an actual illness, psychiatric or neurological, diagnosed (in the text of the novel) by a physician.

• •

Of course, mental illness can be used metaphorically in fiction; the suicidality of the depressed drug abuser can serve as a dramatic metaphor for the despair and sense of social disconnection that any healthy citizen might, and perhaps should, feel on any given day. But then we would not want to confound the two conditions in daily life.

For Walker Percy, this problem—confusing existential alienation with mental illness—did not exist. Percy valued disease. He had contracted tuberculosis during his medical internship and called it the best thing that had ever happened to him. The enforced rest turned him into a philosopher and novelist. In his fiction, Percy writes of characters who suffer epilepsy and overt psychosis. In each case, the ailment is an indication of special standing. (As regards epilepsy, one might say special falling—Percy makes plays on physical collapse and Adam's moral fall.) To Percy, symptoms are divine mysteries, to be savored. Yes, Percy objects to the medicalization of personality traits, like obsessionality; but he is already further down the road. In effect, he questions the medicalization of standard medical conditions, like epilepsy and tuberculosis. First and foremost, suffering constitutes spiritual news.

This position is perfectly tenable. We can attribute divine meaning to disease. Psychiatrists are reasonably content for depression to be in the same boat as epilepsy and tuberculosis, whatever boat that is. But Percy's position blurs distinctions we might want to make. It overstates the case only slightly to say that for Percy, there is no difference between treating epilepsy and treating alienation. Both are best approached via faith and revelation, not technology.

For Elliott, disease does exist as a distinct entity. He writes, "I do not want to call into question the use of serotonin reuptake inhibitors for major depression." Still, Elliott says, in the case of the accountant, to approach his alienation as a symptom, rather than an indicator of a predicament, is to make a category mistake. He quips that seeing alienation as a psychiatric issue is like seeing Holy Communion as a dietary issue.

But of course, alienation sometimes is a psychiatric issue, or an indicator of one. In my years of immersion, I was obsessed with category mistakes from the other direction. I had seen too many patients who came in complaining of a sudden loss of interest in marriage or career, but who, upon evaluation, turned out to be in the midst of a depressive episode. Category mistakes are generally in that direction—study after study shows that most depression goes undiagnosed.

And then, in the case of the man from Downers Grove, there was the matter of the many identifiers—Midwest, accountant, suburb, lawn mower. They seemed to signal aspects of the culture we are meant to scorn—conformity, pollution, consumerism. I was reminded of the contempt for Carl Rogers. Do we assume that Illinois accountants are mostly blind to the emptiness of their lives, until they are rescued by sudden and intense discomfort?

The Illinois accountant struck me as a figure from existentialist fiction, a literary creation—and so many of those are suicide-bound. It was hardly reassuring that Elliott had begun by selecting patients with diagnosable illness, Sally and Hillary, as exemplars of the alienated. In the case of the Downers Grove accountant, I found I did want assurance that his new disenchantment was not a psychiatric issue.

Speaking in public alongside Elliott, as I did once or twice in those years, I learned something about myself and the medical model. It is true, when you embrace depression as disease altogether, you become more suspicious of alienation. Not contemplative alienation, not joyous alienation, not alienation that leads to vigorous political action, but the anxious or depressive variety, the type that brings a person to a psychiatrist.

This attitude, I know, will make me seem hostile to a trait that is an element in any thoughtful life. To counteract, or at least moderate, this suspicion, I want to change course for a moment and present my bona fides as a person who can appreciate alienation, both the social and existential varieties. This project involves a foray into memoir. I will try to keep the detour brief—just long enough, I hope, to clarify my personal relationship to alienated states.

❖ ❖ ❖ ❖

I was born in New York City just after World War II and grew up in the shadow of the Holocaust. All my relatives were German Jews. Those few who had managed to get out—they included my parents, my grandparents, and one great-grandmother—had done so at the last possible moment. Most other family members were killed or died of medical neglect.

Both sides of the family began poor. My father's father (my Opa) was the son of a landless peasant; when Opa's father died, his mother had so few resources that she turned her remaining children over to an orphanage. My mother's father (my other Opa) was the twelfth of thirteen children; he left school at age twelve to support himself. Both grandfathers fought in World War I and suffered in the final months, as the army retreated on short rations. Then came Germany's economic collapse, and then the rise of Nazism, followed by emigration, immigration, and, of course, the next war.

While in the army here, my father contracted tuberculosis. In my first four years of life, he was hospitalized twice for extended periods. My mother essentially became a single parent, and I was by all accounts a difficult child. She and I moved into the small apartment where her parents lived with her father's mother, my Grossmutti. All my relatives coped well, but I spent my early years among people under strain.

My father rejoined the family, and when I was five, my parents and I moved to the suburbs. By then, my sensibility was thoroughly European. I viewed the routine of American childhood from the outside. I went to summer camp. In high school (to leap ahead), I played varsity sports. But I was intensely intellectual, in a way that continued to keep me on the margins. My junior year, the school sent me out of class three days a week to work independently in the library, in mathematics, English, and French.

That summer, at a National Science Foundation program at Cornell, I made friends with a boy who was a good deal like me. David, it turned out, was also in the NSF weekend program I attended during the school year at Columbia University. I took to spending Saturday nights with him and his family in Manhattan.

What neither of us knew was that just after David's birth, his mother had been diagnosed with Hodgkin's lymphoma. (She is the woman whose secrecy I referred to previously, as something out of Kierkegaard.) So David, too, had experienced a separation from a parent early in life.

He, too, spent his childhood in the shadow of death—though all unknowingly. David favored Mozart, as one who understood the wistfulness that tinctures joy.

David and I were both admitted to Harvard, and we applied to room together. At the start of our sophomore year, David's mother suffered a recurrence of her lymphoma. David first learned of the illness when she was in the terminal phase. It will seem odd that this should be so, but when David's mother died, there was no special response from any adult. David grieved alone, in our dorm room. We became further immersed in literature about absurdity, alienation, and existential angst. I had no distance from this material. It described life as I experienced it.

I was a European born in America. In its acquisitiveness and superficiality, in its apparent blindness to life's dangers, my native land was foreign to me. And yet I was estranged from Europe, as hostile—the site of the Holocaust.

I was a Jew, but I had never been to temple, except to attend other children's bar mitzvahs. I did not believe in God. Perhaps atheism should appear as a separate item on this list. I felt distant from believers and belief. If an omnipotent spirit existed, he had a lot to answer for.

I had moved into a teenage position of conflict with my parents.

I was the first boy from my school to attend Harvard. I had not met prep school kids before. They seemed to constitute an alien culture amid which I was consigned to live.

My politics were anomalous. I opposed the Vietnam War early, in 1966. But a fledgling antiwar organization I helped found had its budget absorbed by the SDS, in a democratic coup. I resigned. I fretted over methods.

I found camaraderie on the student newspaper, but I was too delicate in my radicalism, too grateful to the university. I became the token moderate, tapped to write reports on rioting in the streets when a trustworthy voice was required. I abandoned the newsroom and filed stories from the dorm.

David and I listened to the classical music we could afford, on the Nonesuch label. Mozart was still a staple, and the grimmer Schubert *lieder.* We studied the least-loved aspects of English literature: medieval domestic correspondence, Milton's early writings, eighteenth-century essays, the poetry of Jonathan Swift.

Warrior politicians and their businessman allies, inflexible college administrators, politically unengaged teachers, the mass of gung ho classmates, and our parents—all were suspect to us in their different ways. We adopted eccentrics as friends. We had no truck with popularity.

I was aware of death, as a constant possibility. Life's arbitrariness was no theoretical construct. Family history testified to it, as bedrock reality. So did David's loss of his mother. And the Vietnam War.

Senior year, I spent hours alone in my room, sitting in an armchair upholstered in faded green velvet, an item rescued from an outgoing student's discard heap. I wrote my senior thesis on death in the work of Charles Dickens.

Don't talk to me about alienation. I lived where it flourished, at Harvard in the sixties, and even there I was a brooding outsider.

When I write about social estrangement, it is from a position of sympathy. But I think it is fair to say that my identification with opposition and resistance only ever went so far. If alienation was a value for me, it was also a problem. I was intent on making America my home. If I took pride in my outsider status, it was also a condition I hoped to overcome.

I was not depressed. In the dining hall, I ate third and fourth helpings. I could sleep at any hour. I dated every weekend; I adored my girlfriends, somewhat indiscriminately. I was ever hopeful. But adults worried about me. In my senior year, the house senior tutor took me aside. He suggested that if I continued to be this way, I might consider seeing a therapist.

What way was that? I scarcely knew what he meant.

Although it was true: I had spent hours in that green armchair.

Certainly I envied friends, men and women alike, who lived close to the edge. They seemed brave, in touch with the world as it was. I feared that I was too logical, too companionable, too appreciative of each new day to be a writer. Alienation notwithstanding, I could be crudely happy, the cockeyed optimist.

I admired one freshman classmate who came from a wealthy family and could afford to fail. He wrote short stories about a young Russian nobleman, a nihilist wandering Harvard Square, committing absurd acts. In our sophomore year, this classmate hanged himself. Philosophical suicide, I thought. Later, it emerged that he had had been addicted to heroin and killed himself when in withdrawal. That news disappointed me, but it came as a relief as well. The killing-yourself part had never made sense to me. Life is so good.

As my tutor had recommended, I sought therapy. After college, on a postgraduate scholarship in London, I entered psychoanalysis. My analyst mistrusted my caution, my warding off the evil eye through self-effacement, my holding back from those around me. In my contempt for popular culture, he saw prissiness. He thought that I could afford to pursue pleasure straight on. He feared I had the potential for depression, and he wanted none of it. The part of me that could enjoy my own successes, that was the part he hoped to nurture.

When I announced that I wanted to enter medical school and become a psychiatrist, my analyst did not discourage me. He had never seen me (this was how I had envisaged my future) as a melancholic, isolated writer. But my early, unsettled years had been a constant topic in the therapy. My analyst wanted me to understand that the wish, from childhood, to protect my relatives—the need to ward off depression and to conquer disease—was shaping my career choice. He was right, of course—and it would be right to make a similar comment about this book. I have written elsewhere that most psychological theory is veiled autobiography; I do not deny that my attitudes toward mood disorder have deep roots.

In the course of the analysis, I began writing. I began to take pleasure in the easy entertainments the culture offers, popular film and sports. I enrolled in the science courses that would prepare me for medical school. I was coming in from the cold.

For me, the passage of time has not diminished alienation's appeal. America is such a curious nation, in its political makeup and in its mass culture. During the years of my dialogue with Carl Elliott, I wrote a novel about a good husband and father who blows up trophy homes, out of loyalty to a French model of radicalism that was popular in the 1960s. I make full claim to my standing as a member of my generation.

But as I aged, the alienation I experienced was stripped of some of its pain. Absurdity confronts all humans, as the condition of our lives. We are alone in an uncaring universe; how to respond to that reality is the puzzle we will never solve. But surely alienation, social or existential, is less a trait than a challenge—one best approached with flexibility, energy, and a sense of humor, the capacities so often absent in depression.

As for that, I consider myself a depressive manqué. I have a potential for depression, one that was probably greatest in my college years and just after. I remain grateful to my analyst for directing me away from the abyss, to higher, safer ground. That might be the theme of my progress, up from melancholy.

As for the notion that I might have been more creative if more depressed—having seen depression in action, I do not buy it. I began work on my first book only after I was married; I finished it when my wife and I had our first child. Leaving a job I disliked seemed useful— I wrote better when I did not sit within an oppressive hierarchy. I loved patient care. The full life seemed to suit me. We had two more children. I wrote at home, mornings, amid the babies.

Robert Coles once told me of a conversation he had with Walker Percy, after Percy had been diagnosed with terminal cancer. Percy's father and grandfather had committed suicide, and Percy wondered whether his mother, who died in a car accident, had also killed herself intentionally. To live long enough to die of cancer, Percy had said, that is a victory.

Similarly, to avoid depression through midlife, as I have done, seems to me a good outcome, if one that has required no bravery. It has been generations since any member of my family has been as blessed as I, living a private life uninterrupted by war, famine, disease, poverty, exile, or persecution.

As for wondering, *Is this it?*—I don't think that anyone who has ever asked that question stops asking it. Bland, uncritical husbands dragged into couple therapy by their unfulfilled wives do "get it." The men say, Well, if you think that divorcing me will solve *that* . . . Short of ecstatic and delusional states, there is no condition psychiatry sees—including good health—in which the existential concerns are absent. Accountants living in the suburbs worry over the meaning of their lives, even on good days; at least the New England ones seem to, in their conversations with me. I expect to see alienation. But I want to know what is at stake when a person's relationship to his condition changes suddenly for the worse—when ruminations become paralyzing, and the horizon turns black. I do not want to miss a chance to fulfill a function psychiatrists serve, identifying illness early and interrupting it.

❖ ❖ ❖ ❖

This line is the one I draw. I admire alienation, but I demand that it prove its own bona fides, as a state that is separate from depression. And not alienation alone. Certain sorts of interpersonal sensitivity— like the type where small rejections send you into a tailspin—are suspect. Excesses of guilt, insecurity, and self-doubt all bear looking into.

Audiences, when they questioned me, and philosophers, when they wrote about my work, would challenge my tendency to see these apparent signs of refinement first as symptoms. In dissecting a case vignette, they would point to a trauma in a patient's past and say, Isn't the hypersensitivity *justified*? Which meant that since it was rooted in history, the trait, however burdensome, was an authentic part of the person, to be altered only through self-understanding.

I understood the objection. The favored trait (self-doubt, emotional sensitivity) was always the type we are comfortable around, a form of pain that makes us feel protective, pain that is bearable in others. Like alienation, the trait under discussion might be one I admire. But that was part of the problem. When you work with depression, charming states become suspect.

I would retell the case vignette to the questioner—troubled childhood, adult adversity. Only, now I would have us imagine that the symptom at issue is a different one: irritability, rage, and low-level violence toward family members. Do we say that the bad temper is justified? It is, in the sense that it has historical roots; we might hope that the sufferer will come to understand those sources. But it is also unjustified—disproportionate, in extent and duration.

Well, so is the sensitivity, if it is the sort doctors worry over, unending vulnerability to small disappointments. Nor is sensitivity innocuous. A mother who falls into a deep funk in response to small setbacks may not be able to give her child the parenting he needs. That child will watch his step, just as might a child whose parent has a quick temper. The hypersensitive mother's erratic moods and behaviors may put her child at risk, for heightened feelings of guilt and insecurity, and for episodes of depression.

Which may be what the sensitive or ill-tempered mother is suffering as well. If the exaggerated trait persists, despite a reasonable effort at understanding, then we will become yet more uneasy. There may be about the response a suggestion of the stuck switch—the phenomenon psychiatrists call "functional autonomy," when a behavior pattern outlives its causes. We will wonder whether what is at issue is a prodromal or residual symptom of a mood disorder, particularly if there are other reasons for that belief.

See enough depression, and you cast a jaundiced eye on extremes of otherwise arguably attractive traits: apathy, anhedonia, ambivalence, scrupulosity, and the rest.

This suspicious outlook is not a necessary consequence of embracing *what it is*. But depression and its symptoms are so value-laden, and our investment in them is so ingrained, that it would seem disingenuous to suggest that the new evidence about mood disorder would have no wider ripples.

Valuation of the emotions does vary over time. I wonder if we are not in any event entering a period of change. Philip Fisher, an influential critic, has recently contributed a book, *The Vehement Passions*, that makes a case for feelings that are less ambivalent than those favored by modern intellectuals. He focuses most on outward-facing emotions: anger, obstinacy, desire, jealousy, and wonder. The Greeks favored these passions—when they were not warning against them as part of the campaign for equanimity. Anger in particular once had a noble cast. Aristotle held that to fail in anger, in response to slights, is to be a slave. Good citizenship, love, and friendship depend on spiritedness and the capacity for rage; we need to respond with fierceness when we receive a slight at a friend's hands.

For centuries, philosophers have railed against irony and double-mindedness and only succeeded in making them more attractive. Quite unlikely partisans, like Walter Benjamin, call for less ambivalence, less indecision, less paralysis, and more straightforward assumption of responsibility. If we could mitigate depression, perhaps we could be wholehearted in our adoption of that ideal. We may already value full, bold emotion more than we once did.

Fisher presents even grief as a potentially vigorous emotion, one often laced with anger. Today, many people think of grief as a corollary of depression. Of course, it can be. The standard psychiatric nomenclature separates grief from depression; but in his genetics research, Ken Kendler counts episodes of grief as episodes of mood disorder, if the symptoms of depression arise. His logic is unassailable. If upon the death of your husband, you are afflicted with more than two weeks of sadness, guilt, low self-esteem, insomnia, and suicidality, how it that different from a comparable response when your husband is imprisoned? An event is a stressor for us if it affects us that way, in the manner of nonshared experience.

In practice, the elements of grief often differ from those of depression. Careful observers have found that the slowing of thought and action that constitutes a symptom of depression—"psychomotor retardation"—is almost entirely absent in bereavement. Suicidal thoughts, hopelessness, feelings of worthlessness, loss of interest in friends, and early-morning wakening are much more common in depression than in grief. (As if to signal the distinction between sadness and mood disorder, crying is more frequent in grief than in even quite severe depression, where emotion tends to be blunted.) Guilt in grief tends to be the guilt of omission—what one might have done—rather than guilt for wrong behavior. In other words, grief often contains hints of resilience, a sense finally of competence, despite the terrible pain of loss. And grief is not narrowly syndromal; symptoms of anxiety disorders are present almost as often as symptoms of depression. Reactions to loss vary.

Freud wrote that it is the ambivalent—those whose devotion is alloyed with hatred—who are most susceptible to depression in the face of loss. More straightforward love allows for grief that is not tinged with psychiatric pathology. I do not subscribe to Freud's view. I have seen bereavement produce depression in cases where, so far as I could tell, the lost relative was loved straightforwardly, without any substantial admixture of antagonism. I suspect that part of what Freud observed is the statistical association, determined in part by genes, that ties neurotic tendencies to risk of depression. But the distinction Freud makes remains interesting; the most direct and wholehearted forms of mourning may not resemble depression.

Often, the depressed complain that they cannot grieve. The blankness of depression extends to the pain of loss, muting it, so that the depressed feel very little altogether. If we think of mourning as a process of integrating memories and coming to terms with death, then in a real sense, those who become depressed may not mourn.

Part of what allows us to give ourselves over to mourning generously is the sense, subtle though it may be, that we will finally emerge. The resilient pull themselves together and rededicate themselves to causes they had shared with the loved one. Paralysis is not the only or the most admirable reaction to loss.

Fisher reminds us of this truth. Grief rouses to action, for Electra, for Antigone, for Achilles setting out to battle Hector. To Aristotle, Fisher informs us, despite any consideration of norms or moderation, the ideal of grief would "embrace a strongly felt, active, dominating experience of mourning." Even if that state results in no bold behavior, if it has no connection to anger, if it is only the private sensation and exploration of pain, still it stands at a distance from the emptiness and confusion of depression.

This ancient model has its appeal today. Understanding mood disorder differently, we may find that we expect and admire a different sort of grieving.

• •

So, in response to the accusation that depression is a stalking horse, that to take depression as illness altogether is to pull away from much we hold dear—alienation and passivity and sensitivity: Not directly, no. We call depression a disease because we find it to be one. But it may nonetheless be true that change in the way we receive depression will lead to change in the way we experience emotion. Once we accept depression as pathology, we may come to value ambivalence less and passion more.

Twenty-one

❖

After Depression

G IVEN WHAT DEPRESSION IS, what will it be? What future are we free to envisage?

Eradication is one answer. Not soon. The brain is inconceivably complex. Its major functions are sustained by multiple interacting systems that counterbalance one another. Inducing stable changes in the brain has proved difficult. As for genetic engineering, it is in its infancy. Our model of mood disorder remains tentative and incomplete. And still, once depression becomes disease altogether, we can imagine victory over it.

We may be waging that campaign already, though imperfectly and indirectly. Our medications, and probably our psychotherapies, moderate the effects of an overactive stress-response system. The dream of neuroresilience is hidden in projects that are routine in the practice of medicine, like preventing seizures and heart attacks. Efforts to protect children from abuse may also shield their adrenal glands and brains.

Perhaps advances against depression will continue in this piecemeal fashion. Scientists will identify a form of a gene that creates a strong vulnerability to depression; later, they will devise a cure, so that certain high-risk families will now have the same liability to depression as their neighbors. This process will then be repeated—more genetic variants, more families. Better antidepressants will end episodes of depression more quickly and more reliably. Biological markers will be discovered that help match drug to patient. Scientists will create medications that block the brain effects of trauma. These interventions will be used first in cases of rape, but then more widely. "Medical" depressions will be picked off one by one. Prevention of mood disorder will become a standard element in the treatment of cancer, stroke, and parkinsonism. And so forth. Each intervention will be refined and then applied to broader populations. Progress will occur in stages.

But the goal of resilience allows for more dramatic visions. I have mentioned my fascination with Robert Sapolsky's efforts at genetic engineering to contain the effects of stroke. I have imagined similar techniques applied to the prevention of depression. A gene is inserted into the brain. It allows people to remain as they are. It does not create synthetic happiness. It does not turn sourness into glibness. It does not interfere with passing feelings of isolation and despair, nor even with extended ones, so long as they pose no risk to the brain.

The medications we use today, and certainly our psychotherapies, tend to intrude on daily life, even between episodes of depression. While they treat or prevent mood disorder, antidepressants may also make us more confident and decisive, less anxious and compulsive— they cause us to behave in ways that the culture rewards. A genetic intervention might prove cleaner, if it addresses depression merely.

Only in the face of severe and protracted stress would the inserted gene come into play, and even then, only after an interval of time. It is when brain cells are imminently at risk that the gene acts, protecting them from harm and allowing for new growth and new learning. We can even imagine a variation where the inserted gene terminates a stress response only when we tell it to, say, by taking a medication that signals the gene to turn on.

Given the power to prevent mood disorder, might we once more look benignly upon brooding and obsessionality, knowing that they will cause no biological harm? How much alienation and anomie ought we to retain? I have alluded to a possible cultural shift, away from melancholy. But it is possible to imagine that, where depression is no longer a risk, the self-conscious, pessimistic states might regain their charm. The fantasy of exact control over depression, the disease, allows us to specify what we should continue to value in the emotions that cluster around mood disorder.

But taken in isolation, this approach does not correspond to my own imaginings about how substantial progress against depression might take place. In the family of medicine, psychiatry is the poor relation. Even when mental illnesses appear at the top of epidemiologists' lists in terms of the harm they do, other diseases get priority.

No matter. Improved neuroresilience is a quite general goal of health care. We hope to shield the brain from the effects of infections, seizures, blood flow disorders, and environmental toxins. Neuroprotection will be an element of any campaign against heart disease. If we as a society are interested in graceful aging, if we are concerned with learning early in life, if we set our scientists the task of sustaining and even enhancing the pedestrian cognitive functions of mind and brain, then neuroplasticity and neurogenesis will be at the top of the medical agenda. The prevention of depression might arise as a side effect of those efforts, so that depression is taken incidentally, in passing.

Imagine a future obstetrician, pediatrician, or geneticist. She is advising a couple whose family history contains instances, in childhood, of learning disorders and, in adulthood, of premature memory loss. Genetic screening confirms the risk of these outcomes. The counselor believes it advisable, in this couple's child, to tweak the brain's production of a factor that will encourage nerve cell growth, from early on, and to insert inducible genes to enhance neuroprotection. An incidental effect (will the parents be concerned that their child's depth or authenticity is at stake?) is a markedly decreased probability of depression.

If this conversation sounds unlikely, it is (among other reasons) because we know that this sort of general medical success would change our understanding of depression decisively. If tools to prevent dementia or reverse learning disorders give us a handle on depression, then we will be all the more inclined to believe that depression is a spandrel and not an adaptation. A condition that resembles Alzheimer's disease, in terms of its course and cure, is bound to be taken as a progressive failure of health maintenance in the brain.

And so our imagined counselor would not after all make an excuse for emotional resilience as a side effect of brain resilience. She would propose a package of interventions to help ensure the sound development and functioning of the mind. The effort—we are free to imagine—might be more general yet, extending to the competency of the immune or endocrine systems, to cellular resilience in some general sense. In such a system, the notion of disease might fade into the background, as medicine attended ever more to the preconditions for health. Depression would disappear by the way.

The question for us, looking forward, is what we make of this eventuality—depression approached as malfunction merely, depression made to disappear incidentally, in the wake of a general campaign of neuronal and bodily health. Is the fantasy utopian or dystopian?

At the first level, the question answers itself. Our premise begins with a series of medical successes. People live longer. Heart attacks are avoided. The management of infections and cancers is simplified, as mood-related side effects no longer come into play. Certain people are spared dementia as they age. Without depression, other illnesses go easier for the afflicted, so that now asthma, arthritis, and diabetes, when they occur, are less burdensome. These benefits are poignant, because of the histories of some of those who enjoy them. Adults who were molested in childhood no longer contract heart disease prematurely. Those who lost a parent young are spared osteoporosis and bone fractures in later life. And of course, now other mental illnesses are no longer triggered or complicated by depression—which means that there is less alcoholism, less anorexia, slightly less pain in the course of schizophrenia.

Then there are the gains that come when we are spared the havoc depression wreaks on daily life. Parenting becomes easier, for those depressives who would otherwise have been overwhelmed. Young children no longer need to watch their step to protect fragile mothers. Older children no longer need to grow up prematurely to take on family responsibilities. This good alone, rescuing childhoods, would justify our efforts.

There are also days of employment gained, both by the vulnerable and by those who would have taken time out to care for them—billions of dollars in benefit to the economy. Years of creativity that would have been lost become available to artists, scholars, inventors, and entrepreneurs. The years are good ones, not hampered by the impaired memory, the insomnia, the timidity, and the fear of recurrence that blight even the time between episodes in the depressed. Continuity is maintained at work, stability in the home.

All this without mentioning the experience of depression, the dank joylessness, the murky distractedness, the horror so overwhelming as to be quite beyond expression. How extraordinary it is to imagine a society relieved, not of all suffering, but of that particular excruciating sort.

Against these extraordinary gains, what loss?

There are quite general objections to the scenario I have painted. We may mistrust genetic engineering, as opposed to the workings of nature. We may ask about the distribution of resources—health for whom?—or about side-effect disasters. We may worry over the role of drug companies or doctors or the government, depending where our mistrust lies. We may dislike the notion of a culture so focused on health. We may favor decay, decadence, some rebellious ideal. Or we may prefer health earned through meditation and exercise over health achieved via technology.

Of course, psychiatry is always happy to face concerns that apply to the whole of medicine. Count us in, we say. Worry about those issues, please, so long as you start with pneumonia and Crohn's disease and thyroiditis. We simply do live our lives in a culture that emphasizes health, distributes resources unevenly, and relies on capitalism for scientific progress. If the future I have summoned up makes us uneasy, it is not clear that the blame lies with progress against depression.

The most conventional objections to combating depression begin with concern about excessive happiness, or happiness attained mechanically, superficial happiness. Much discussion of antidepressants in particular is framed in these terms. In its report on biotechnology, the (largely conservative) President's Council on Bioethics includes an essay with the ironic title "Happy Souls." The critique worries that the public does not understand that happiness is striving, not satisfaction.

I hope that my account of depression and my evocation of a future undercut the happiness objection. For all that depression has shaped our tastes and opinions, only 16 or 17 percent of Americans ever experience major depression. Expanding the definition to more minor conditions might raise the proportion to a quarter. Not all of those cases involve the biology of depression, the stuck switch, with the consequences for the brain that our imagined intervention prevents. Even if our utopian preventative were universal, the vast majority of people would never see the relevant gene activated. They would be euphoric or despondent, calm or anxious, according to personality and circumstance, as their forebears are now. Their happiness, when they are blessed with it, would be vacant or rich, random or justified. Under the terms of our thought experiment, even the artificially resilient would experience pain, sadness, and emptiness at their usual level, up to the point of the onset of a depressive episode.

At the least, this imagined course of events moves the ethical objection back a few steps. *Must happiness be earned?* becomes *Must resilience be earned?* And here we will want to look at the many pathways to the loss of resilience: genetic happenstance, the random flux of molecules *in utero*, maternal stress, sexual trauma in childhood, the loss of a parent followed by the loss of educational opportunities. Where in this chain of misfortune would we be reluctant, if given the chance, to protect the developing brain? At which point are we content for the child to incur the many liabilities, to heart disease and the rest? Preventing depression seems especially moral, especially just—a way to avoid further punishing the victim.

The eradication of depression does not hand us contentment on a silver platter, any more than the eradication of anorexia or panic anxiety would, or kidney disease for that matter. Protected from depression, we are free to be quirky, free to be neurotic, free to care. We have desires, including the wish to be competent and successful. We need to strive, as much as humans do need to strive—although I must say that this emphasis on effort as the proper means to happiness seems to favor one sort of human over another, the worker over the lover, the Puritan over the hedonist, the twice-born over the once-born. Perhaps the ideal—to strive—hides and reveals prejudice over temperament, in which melancholy is valued more than sanguinity.

The other objection to resilience is that at some level it constitutes forgetting. But in my fantasized future, we maintain sharp recollections of our own past. Our imagined intervention does not block the intense emotions that burn experience into memory. To the contrary, heading off depression preserves memories, by averting the confusion and loss of concentration that come with mood disorder, and the obsessive, stereotyped self-flagellation that interferes with a free assessment of our own history. And of course, the vulnerable will avoid the arbitrary, "uncaused" depressions that simply distort the interior account of the self.

I would add one private consideration to this list of benefits. We—all of us, and not only those most at risk—would no longer be braced against depression. For a group that extends far beyond the minority who go on to suffer the syndrome, depression is the disease that stands in the wings. Many of us, and here I include myself, spend much our lives fending off depression, in those we care about, but also in ourselves. There are chances we do not take; they would be favorable and prudent gambles, if only we could bear for them to fail. That strategy has ancient roots, in the Greek practice of ataraxia—muted feeling, limited attachment—as a prophylactic against the horrors of loss. How much freer we would be to live life, knowing ourselves to be reliably resilient.

Not fearing depression, we might love more generously. Indirectly, the mind and brain may translate immunity from depression into a bodily awareness that carries a message of cognitive therapy or transactional analysis—I'm okay, solid enough to risk what we say that people should risk: openness and commitment and intimacy. In a society free of depression, our old account of passion might look strange, tied up as it is with operatic responses to loss. We might come to identify passion with an inner sense of security—with confidence.

If we consider emotion a human good, and if we consider emotion a way of reading the world, we will stand against depression.

In my years of immersion, I wondered—alongside my *what if* questioners—about the ways a successful campaign against depression might change the arts. Wouldn't van Gogh's painting have been different, had he been given Prozac? But of course, in a society that has effective remedies for depression, it is not only artists who would have access to treatment. It is not only van Gogh (if we consider him depressive) who has the safety net beneath him, but also his viewers.

At the least, in such a culture, art would be relieved of one of its burdens—I mean, protecting us from the risk of mood disorder. A. E. Housman, a classicist as well as a poet, wrote a conversational poem on the subject, "Terence, This Is Stupid Stuff." Here poetry fulfills the role of ancient Greek philosophy, instilling a low level of sadness to fortify reader and author alike against more serious decompensation.

In "Terence," the poet's companions tease him about his sour verse. Why not drink and be merry? the friends ask. "[M]alt does more than Milton can / To justify God's ways to man."

In reply, the poet retells the story of an ancient king who took poison in increasing doses, so that when enemies put arsenic and strychnine in his meat, he was unaffected. "Mithridates, he died old," is the conclusion. Use melancholic poetry to acclimate yourself to sadness, and the real ills of the world will not overwhelm you. Sour verse steels us against the embittered hour. Melancholic poetry induces serenity, equanimity—ataraxia.

If the medical profession can handle depression, painting and poetry may lose one of their therapeutic functions. A society shielded from depression might demand poetry with a wide sweep of subjects and story lines—less moodiness, if not more malt. If high culture illuminates the challenges and contradictions of its time, then different ages need different art.

We should have little difficulty conjuring up a less sentimental aesthetic. It is with us already, in the judgment of certain critics. I am especially fond of the writing of Gabriel Josipovici, a British novelist and essayist. Josipovici evaluates the melancholy strain in poetry and the novel, via a fictional character who speaks for him:

> Much as I love English literature, he said, I have to admit that a strain of sentimentality and unfocussed emotion runs through it. It is not confined to the Victorians. Think of the Monk's Tale of Ugolino eating his children in the locked tower. Think how much more austere Dante's original is than Chaucer's retelling. Think of the murder of MacDuff's children, we are not all that far here from the death of Little Nell. Much as I love English literature, he said, I cannot help feeling that this is a weakness to which it is all too prone. Today, of course, he said, there is nothing but that, cynicism and sentimentality, sentimentality and cynicism, two facets of the same thing.

In addition to Dante, Josipovici's literary beacons include Rabelais, Sterne, and Wallace Stevens. Josipovici writes, half jokingly, of wet and dry authors. Aristophanes is dry, as are John Donne, Jonathan Swift, Jane Austen, and Ivy Compton-Burnett. Above all, Josipovici praises the spareness of Homer. Odysseus' loyal dog Argos dies, in a single line, and we never hear tell of him again. It is calm in the evocation of grave loss that pleases Josipovici. "Compared to Homer, *all* writing is sentimental."

In my years of immersion, Josipovici seemed a kindred spirit. Nor is he alone in his judgments. There is an Eastern European strain of thought, one that I encountered first in the writing of Milan Kundera, that reserves special praise for the rough-and-ready literary narratives that precede the development of the coming-of-age novel. Kundera brings to our attention works in which moral judgment is suspended, and the reader smiles as bad things happen to good people. Rabelais's *Gargantua and Pantagruel* is the paradigmatic example, but Kundera has favorable things to say about the more heartless aspects of Cervantes, Diderot, Sterne, Thomas Mann, and Salman Rushdie. Kundera is echoing the writing of the critic Mikhail Bakhtin, about a special sort of humor (in Rabelais) attached to the upsetting of social structures, as feudalism loses power and the common man comes into his own.

This line of thought addresses any inclination we might have to defend sentimental literature, like the novel or memoir of depression, on the grounds that it is implicitly political, celebrating difference, promoting exploration. All genres can be political. The Eastern Europeans love Rabelais because mirth is subversive; tyrants cannot bear the people's hearty laughter.

Perhaps this pulling back from sentiment is apparent in mainstream American literary taste as well. Harold Bloom, the best-known critic writing today, judges Shakespeare's Falstaff to be Hamlet's equal as a complexly developed character. That choice seems to signal an abandonment of the standard that gives the sole place of honor to the melancholic malcontent.

In my years of immersion, I found myself drawn to the dry writers. I took to reading their biographies; they point to an earlier image of the artist or writer, very different from the examples of van Gogh, Kierkegaard, Nietzsche, and Poe.

I developed a particular fascination with stories about Miguel de Cervantes. His military career ended with his capture by the Moors, and then a series of daring escape attempts. Later, he became a commissary officer, a sort of roving tax collector. Because Spain was teetering between feudalism and modernity, the job required great political astuteness— knowing which authority structure applied where. Cervantes dabbled in theater. He pursued a religious vocation. He fathered a child with one woman and married another. Whatever the reality, by legend Cervantes personified the writer as Figaro, a vigorous jack-of-all-trades.

Nor was Cervantes alone. Rabelais studied law, took holy orders, and practiced medicine. At the dawn of the novel and of the nation-state, this hero was plausible, the warrior-*bricoleur*-litterateur. An earlier dry writer, Dante, was a soldier and a politician, and not tentatively, but with determination. Where Cervantes suffered imprisonment, Dante endured endless exile from his beloved Florence. Were these writers happy? Surely not in the trivial sense. They seem to have been resilient. They were not interior adventurers only, but men of grand experience in the world.

Toward the start of his career Karl Marx wrote of the ideal life, unconstrained by the division of labor, in which a man can choose to hunt in the morning, fish in the afternoon, rear cattle in the evening, and write essays after dinner. This looking forward was also a sort of nostalgia, as is my own here. There once were polymaths who wrote great books. We are free to imagine that making inroads against depression would lead not to the marginalization of literature but to a golden age. We can be as utopian as we please.

Although perhaps it is simpler to say how much more art there would be, how much more of every creation we value, were it not for depression.

If we could treat depression reliably, we would have different artists, different subjects, different stories, different needs, different tastes. The details—what sort of art and artists—are matters for science fiction. Which is what the whole of this speculation amounts to—fantasy intended finally to provide a perspective on the present. I mean mainly to ask why we would not let go of melancholy, and trust ourselves with responsive minds and resilient brains.

If this fantasy, substituting resilience for depression, remains eerie, it may be because the terms of the discussion retain their complex connotations. We persist in asking: Seeing cruelty, suffering, and death, shouldn't a person be depressed? There are circumstances, like the Holocaust, in which depression might seem *justified* universally, for every participant or observer. Awareness of the ubiquity of horror—awareness of inhumanity as an aspect of humanity—is the modern condition, our condition. Picasso's painting *Tragedy* seems to express that truth.

But of course, depression is not ubiquitous, even in terrible times. I have said that patients' abrupt recoveries are utterly convincing, for doctors, in framing depression as pathology. A second, similarly striking phenomenon arises in work with people who have survived war or terror or comparable horrors arising from political repression. I have treated a number of these patients. They come to depression years after enduring extreme privation. Typically, such a person will say: "I don't understand it. I went through—." And here he will name one of the shameful events of our time. "I lived through *that*, and in all those months, I never felt *this*." *This* refers to the relentless bleakness of depression, the hopelessness, the emptiness, the self as hollow shell.

To see the worst things a person can see is one experience; to suffer depression is another. There is nothing eerie about these accounts of survival, nothing that points to unawareness or an incompleteness of self. All of the patients I have debriefed about political terror and widespread death have seemed to me fully human—and not less so when their episode of depression has ended. In all cases, their resilience, in the years before mood disorder caught up with them, seemed (to me) fortunate and admirable. It was a capacity I hoped to restore to them and might wish for others.

We know also that trauma can cause psychic injuries, such as flashbacks and phobias and impulsive rage, and yet not elicit this distinctive pathology, depression. If over many years I held depression to be disease, if I considered it inevitable that the biological research would confirm that belief, it is in part because depression is a specific, and not a universal, response to the unspeakable.

In *Listening to Prozac*, I referred to what was then known about the death of the great Italian writer Primo Levi. To readers of his accounts of imprisonment and survival in the Holocaust, Levi stood out as a man who retained humane judgment and emotional subtlety in unspeakable surroundings. Though prone to mood disorder, Levi had endured Auschwitz without falling prey to depression. Afterwards he succumbed, and at age sixty-seven in a recurrence, he (almost certainly, though there are those who understand the events differently) committed suicide. The news was particularly demoralizing because the suicide seemed to represent defeat in a man who had faced horror and remained vital and complex.

I had discussed Levi's depression in the course of a consideration of kindling, asking about the effects of accumulated stress on the aging brain. Whatever the truth about Levi, there is nothing unnatural in the man as we perceive him through his Holocaust memoirs. In the face of great evil, a person can be wise, observant, and disillusioned, and yet not depressed. We should have no trouble imagining resilience that contains as much depth as any ever attributed to depression.

In the course of my clinical work, I have the privilege of observing many modest, individual victories over depression. As I was winding down the writing of this book, I was privy to one such instance of resilience. The event may at first seem unremarkable. A woman's house burned down, and she did well enough. I can tell you that I found that result deeply moving, as affecting as any number of more dramatic medical successes.

The patient had come to depression through a series of crushing losses, including the deaths, in rapid succession, of her sister and husband. An antidepressant had been helpful to my patient at first. It seemed to return her to life. But she did not stay on medication for long.

Instead, she and I embarked on a psychotherapy that lasted years. Often it looked to childhood traumas that made the losses in adult life especially hard to bear. Often it remained in the present, constituting a kind of coaching in the management of risk. I observed any number of setbacks—seemingly minor disappointments made my patient lose ground. As are a surprising number of depressives, she was a natural optimist, prone to investing her affections unwisely. We examined self-destructive habits of mind, mixed motivations in relationships, experiences of shame and humiliation; endlessly, we discussed loss. With time, my patient's depressive traits diminished, and with them an aura of vulnerability. Once she was better—really, very much better—we stopped our weekly sessions. But my patient continued to consult me regularly, at longer intervals. She said that she was filling a toolbox with implements that helped her solve problems that, unmanaged, might leave her exposed to danger.

Her house burned to the ground. With it went irreplaceable objects, mementos of loved ones. Few people do well in the face of these shocking losses. The fire displaces you, to strange living quarters. It makes you deal daily with strangers whose interests are not your own—inspectors, adjusters, contractors. Work stresses do not stop. Those who count on you continue to make demands. Life is too wide open. Your goals and values come into question. Why am I here at all?

What happened was—my patient took the loss in stride. Not immediately, not perfectly. There were shaky days. But quickly, ten or twelve weeks down the road, she declared herself out of the woods. "I don't know that you ever stop missing what you lose," she said. "But you know how I used to stick with men too long? It was that way with the house. The neighborhood had changed—it wasn't right for me. The fire is the push I needed."

That resolution to a minor crisis might serve as well as any other, as an example of resilience in daily life. My guess, my assumption, my fantasy, is that the psychological resilience reflects some better arrangement in the brain, a lessened liability to a protracted stress response, a capacity in the face of crisis to form new neural connections. Perhaps it was the exposure to medication that mattered most. The antidepressant seemed to allow my patient to become unstuck, so that new learning could begin. Perhaps some healing took place in the many good months during the course of therapy. Perhaps, as my patient believes, it was a matter of having certain tools to hand, new ways of dealing with difficult emotions. It would be good to know.

When I refer to resilience, I am not pointing to my patient's optimism. That trait was one she seemed to own temperamentally, when she was not bowed down by mood disorder. My interest is in a simpler outcome, the relapse that was avoided.

A patient who has experienced depression in the past now faces a challenge; she does not decompensate. These minor victories justify the psychiatrist's career. There is no fretting, of this you can be sure, over the imagined benefits of the depressive episode that might have been. No, these small successes are cause for relief, for quiet satisfaction, for rejoicing. They are beyond the reach of ambivalence.

We are, I hope I have said as much, far from conquering depression. In practical terms, the professions have been treading water for ten years—perhaps longer, depending on what one counts as progress. But a breakthrough could occur at any time.

The new research tools are extraordinary. Until brain imaging ma-chines achieved a sufficient level of resolution, no one thought of implicating the hippocampus in depression. Most old medications were discovered by serendipity, or through coarse biological models; now pharmacology researchers clone receptors, depict them three-dimensionally, and match chemicals to them. Scientists can construct a genetically altered mouse, to help refine theories of injury and recovery. They can attach genes to a viral vector and see them function in the brain.

We have new models of mood disorder; new concepts allow for new solutions. Only for the last ten or fifteen years have psychiatric re-searchers been focused on medications meant to interrupt the effects of stress hormones on neurons. Work on neuroresilience factors is not far past its infancy; work on neurogenesis is yet younger. Genetic engineer-ing applied to psychiatric disease has barely begun, in rodent models. But these efforts and many others are under way. If it is hard to believe that we will make very substantial progress against depression, in some ways it is harder to believe that we will not.

From a psychiatrist's point of view, we must. The many worries that accompany our efforts are understandable, each in its way. But I think it is important, in assessing them, to remember how deeply ingrained depression is in human consciousness.

There is an old Southern joke in which a man buys an ill-fitting suit off the rack and after many visits back to the salesman for advice, ends up walking down the street with one shoulder hiked up, the opposite arm stretched forward, and so forth. The punch line involves two ladies who see him limping along. One says, "Ain't it terrible the way Buck has the arthuritis." The other replies, "Yes, but don't that suit fit him fine!" After millennia of accommodation, depression fits us in that way; to be rid of it would be to discover new customs, a new way of walking. I think we are ready. Even now, our attachment to melancholic forms of literature feels confining. A willful quirkiness is evident in our elevation of joyless alienation as an ideal. It seems perverse to appeal to the natu-ral as regards a condition that eats away at the brain. At the least, some retailoring is in order.

I do not find it at all strange to hope for a future in which the vulnerable are granted a measure of resilience—resilience in the brain and throughout the body—so that they are not punished repeatedly for their misfortunes. That prospect, too, is beyond the reach of ambivalence. How glorious it will be to free ourselves from depression.

Notes

ONE: THE FINAL MEMOIR

4 **experienced a dramatic response:** In *Listening to Prozac* (New York: Viking, 1993), I wrote that these transformations are infrequent. A suggestion that they may be more common than I had believed comes from an unexpected quarter. When researching negative effects, David Healy, a vocal critic of antidepressants and drug companies, also found a good number of these marked positive outcomes. David Healy, personal communication, and R. Tranter et al., "Functional Effects of Agents Differentially Selective to Noradrenergic or Serotonergic Systems," *Psychological Medicine* 32 (2002): 517–24. See also D. Healy, "The Case for an Individual Approach to the Treatment of Depression," *Journal of Clinical Psychiatry* 61 (suppl. 6) (2000): 18–23.

4 **alter personality traits:** This claim, likewise, was speculative when I made it in 1993. That the new antidepressants have effects on personality, even in those who have never been depressed, was confirmed, in preliminary fashion, in B. Knutson et al., "Selective Alteration of Personality and Social Behavior by Serotonergic Intervention," *American Journal of Psychiatry* 155 (1998): 373–79.

5 **depressives:** Some mental health advocates object to the use of nouns like *schizophrenics* that refer to people by the disease they suffer. But doctors have long spoken of consumptives, asthmatics, and even "cardiac cripples." If substantives referring to the mentally ill are stigmatizing, the

reason has to do with the way the culture responds to the disease. By *depressives*, I mean people who suffer chronic or recurrent depression.

5 **autopathography:** The word *pathography*, meaning biography from a medical and psychological viewpoint, dates to the writings of the nineteenth-century German psychiatrist Paul Julius Möbius. See J. A. Schioldann, "What Is Pathography?" [letter], *Medical Journal of Australia* 178 (2003): 303. Freud used the word to cover psychoanalytic speculations about historical figures. In the 1980s, it was revived to describe accounts of exposure to or participation in deviant behavior, especially sexual abuse. I first used *autopathography*—the coinage may be my own—in this broad fashion (in "Autopathography," *Psychiatric Times*, June 1995, 3ff). Here (as in "The Anatomy of Melancholy," *The New York Times Book Review*, April 7, 1996, 27), I am reverting to a narrow sense, memoir that emphasizes the impact of illness.

9 **"optimizing" a patient's level of discomfort:** This method is associated with older, Freudian schools of psychoanalysis. P. D. Kramer, "Empathic Immersion," in *Empathy and the Practice of Medicine: Beyond Pills and Scalpel*, ed. Howard Spiro et al. (New Haven: Yale University Press, 1993).

11 **tuberculosis ... signifies refinement:** Susan Sontag, *Illness as Metaphor* (New York: Farrar Straus Giroux, 1978), discussed in chapter 3 below.

TWO: RETURN

19 **no apparent reason:** In the surveys by Kenneth S. Kendler (see chapter 11), about 40 percent of episodes of depression arise in the absence of a stressful life event. In a given patient's life, later episodes are more likely than early ones to be "uncaused."

21 **face of depression less often:** There is no data on this topic. Seeking an informal test of my impression, I turned to E. Fuller Torrey, a psychiatrist known for his contention that major mental illness is on the increase. (See his book *The Invisible Plague: The Rise of Mental Illness from 1750 to the Present* [New Brunswick, NJ: Rutgers University Press, 2002].) In correspondence, Torrey agreed that widely available modern treatments have mitigated the course of depression. E. Fuller Torrey, personal communication, 2002.

25 **Philip Roth novel:** *I Married a Communist* (Boston: Houghton Mifflin, 1998).

26 **attributed too much meaning:** Of course, one can never prove that meaning is absent. A Freudian might say that a given episode or symptom of depression has a cause that is unknown to patient and doctor, or to their conscious minds. From the same viewpoint, one might take at face value

the acknowledgments of guilt that the patient makes while depressed. This choice has epistemological problems of its own.

It is not only Freudians who can read meaning into symptoms. Margaret's discomfort can be understood as a critique of power imbalances: between parent and child, teacher and student, man and woman, boss and worker, or stultifying culture and autonomous individual. I came to wonder whether my concern over those sorts of social problems had contributed to my willingness to empathize with feelings that Margaret would later disown. For a thoughtful critique of contemporary efforts to link episodes and concrete causes, see the comments on "de-subjectivation" in Herman M. van Praag, Ron de Kloet, and Jim van Os, *Stress, the Brain, and Depression* (Cambridge: Cambridge University Press, 2004).

THREE: WHAT IF

31 **probably high-dose digitalis:** See T. C. Lee, "Van Gogh's Vision: Digitalis Intoxication?," *Journal of the American Medical Association* 245 (1981): 727–29, and the references in the note for "van Gogh was understood" below.

32 **art and neurosis:** See Edmund Wilson, "Philoctetes: The Wound and the Bow," in *The Wound and the Bow: Seven Studies in Literature* (Cambridge, Mass.: Riverside Press, 1941), 272–95, and Lionel Trilling, "Art and Neurosis," in *The Liberal Imagination: Essays on Literature and Society* (New York: Viking, 1950), 160–80. I discuss this debate in *Listening to Prozac.*

34 **Kierkegaard's diaries:** See Alastair Hannay's selections of the *Papers and Journals* (London: Penguin, 1996) and Hannay's later rendering of these same passages in *Kierkegaard: A Biography* (Cambridge: Cambridge University Press, 2001). The standard citations are: *Papierer* IX A 70 and II A 495 and 509.

37 **famous essay:** Sontag, *Illness as Metaphor.*

37 **Sand . . . Chopin:** See Benita Eisler, *Chopin's Funeral* (New York: Knopf, 2003).

37 **Tuberculosis became repulsive:** With reports of multiple-drug-resistant TB and a concentration of illness among the poor, the disease may have regained its "repulsive" status. Regarding the less usual case, disease that elicits positive emotional responses, see chapters 6 through 8.

38 **Dinesen and her medical condition:** Linda Donelson, *Out of Isak Dinesen* (Iowa City: Coulsong, 1998). See also Judith Thurman's *Isak Dinesen* (New York: St. Martin's Press, 1982) and Isak Dinesen, *Letters from Africa,*

1914–1931, ed. F. Lasson, trans. A. Born (Chicago: University of Chicago Press, 1982).

38 **Poe refers:** "The Fall of the House of Usher."

39 **Dostoevsky . . . Dante:** Alice Flaherty, *The Midnight Disease* (Boston: Houghton Mifflin, 2004).

40 **epileptologist updated:** C. W. Bazil, "Seizures in the Life and Works of Edgar Allan Poe," *Archives of Neurology* 56 (1999): 740–43.

40 **van Gogh was understood:** Flaherty, *Midnight Disease*. The leading diagnostic theory today combines epilepsy and bipolar affective disorder. See D. Blumer, "The Illness of Vincent van Gogh," *American Journal of Psychiatry* 159 (2002): 519–26; W. W. Meissner, "The Artist in the Hospital: The van Gogh Case," *Bulletin of the Menninger Clinic* 58 (1994): 283–306; J. C. Morrant, "The Wing of Madness: The Illness of Vincent van Gogh," *Canadian Journal of Psychiatry* 38 (1993): 480–84; P. H. Voskuil, "Vincent van Gogh's Malady: A Test Case for the Relationship Between Temporal Lobe Dysfunction and Epilepsy?," *Journal of the History of the Neurosciences* 1 (1992): 155–62.

FOUR: AMBIVALENCE

42 **Residual symptoms predict relapse:** See, for example, M. B. Keller, "Past, Present, and Future Directions for Defining Optimal Treatment Outcome in Depression," *Journal of the American Medical Association* 289 (2003): 3152–60; L. L. Judd et al., "Major Depressive Disorder: A Prospective Study of Residual Subthreshold Depressive Symptoms as Predictor of Rapid Relapse," *Journal of Affective Disorders* 50 (1998): 97–108; L. L. Judd et al., "A Prospective Twelve-Year Study of Subsyndromal and Syndromal Depressive Symptoms in Unipolar Major Depressive Disorders," *Archives of General Psychiatry* 55 (1998): 694–700; and M. B. Keller and R. J. Boland, "Implications of Failing to Achieve Successful Long-Term Maintenance Treatment of Recurrent Unipolar Major Depression," *Biological Psychiatry* 44 (1998): 348–60.

44 **contradictory beliefs:** Consider this additional scrap from my collection: At its annual meeting in 2001, the American Psychosomatic Society debated the resolution "Psychosocial Interventions Can Improve Clinical Outcomes in Organic Disease." The affirmative and negative teams assessed the legitimacy of twenty-three research studies that demonstrate the utility of psychotherapy in the treatment of everything from cancer to the common cold. Everything, that is, except depression.

Depression was not ignored. The doctors argued whether psychotherapy for depression prevents heart attacks or shortens the duration of infections. The monographs under consideration discussed the deleterious effects of mood disorder on the integrity of the circulatory, hormonal, and immune systems—some of the very evidence that had helped to establish depression's standing as medical pathology. The audience included scientists who had conducted the studies. No one suggested the need to debate whether—or concede that—psychotherapy treats depression, *which is itself an organic disease.* Even experts in the interface of mind and body are capable of forgetting—en masse—*what depression is.* The debate is transcribed in five articles in *Psychosomatic Medicine* 64 (2002): 549–70.

46 *faute de mieux:* The phenomenon bears an obvious relationship to Leon Festinger's concept, *cognitive dissonance,* elaborated in *A Theory of Cognitive Dissonance* (Stanford, Calif.: Stanford University Press, 1957). I mean for *"faute de mieux"* to stand for a specific outcome—the attribution of value to a disease (or symptoms of a disease) for which we have no treatment, or ineffectual ones. Often, with regard to depression, people seem to be able to bear or ignore dissonance, valuing and devaluing simultaneously.

46 **symptoms . . . as virtues:** Beyond being viewed as vice or virtue, symptoms of depression are sometimes construed as clues to particular past traumata or current unexamined inner conflicts—loss of appetite as unwillingness to "swallow" a given idea, etc. At the height of Freudian predominance, this theory applied to many diseases, so that a gastric ulcer might signify anger directed inward, while infertility might signify unresolved rage at a parent. (See Georg Groddeck's *Book of the It* [1923; reprint, New York: Random House, 1949].) It may give us pause to think how misguided these highly specific attributions appear in retrospect.

FIVE: ALTOGETHER

49 **Szasz . . . assertion:** T. S. Szasz, "The Myth of Mental Illness," *American Psychologist* 15 (1960): 113–18; see also his slew of books and monographs in the subsequent forty years.

50 **television debate:** "Is Depression a Disease?" *Debatesdebates* (Warren Steibel, producer), March 31, 1998.

51 **"biological markers":** In Szasz's heyday, the philosopher Hilary Putnam tried to draw a bright line between diseases whose presence can be confirmed by laboratory tests and diseases known only syndromally. See

H. Putnam, "Brains and Behavior," in *Analytical Philosophy Second Series*, ed. R. Butler (Oxford: Basil Blackwell & Mott, 1963). The case might be made for an intermediate category composed of disease (for example, Pick's dementia) whose physical pathology is apparent postmortem. My contention, sketched in this chapter, is that depression has moved beyond syndrome-only status. A Wesleyan College undergraduate, Kathryn Schoendorf, brought the Putnam essay to my attention.

51 **"priority communication":** G. Rajkowska et al., "Morphometric Evidence for Neuronal and Glial Prefrontal Cell Pathology in Major Depression," *Biological Psychiatry* 45 (1999): 1085–98. See also J. J. Miguel-Hidalgo et al., "Glial Fibrillary Acidic Protein Immunoreactivity in the Prefrontal Cortex Distinguishes Younger from Older Adults in Major Depressive Disorder," *Biological Psychiatry* 48 (2000): 861–73. I have supplemented published material with interviews and correspondence with Drs. Rajkowska and Stockmeier. The Rajkowska findings have been confirmed and expanded in subsequent research; the deficits in major depression appear to be characteristic and not shared with bipolar affective disorder or other mental illnesses: D. Cotter et al., "Reduced Glial Cell Density and Neuronal Size in the Anterior Cingulate Cortex in Major Depressive Disorder," *Archives of General Psychiatry* 58 (2001): 545–53.

56 **"Maybe serotonin is the police":** *Listening to Prozac*, 134.

57 **provocative research:** Y. I. Sheline et al., "Depression Duration but Not Age Predicts Hippocampal Volume Loss in Medically Healthy Women with Recurrent Major Depression," *Journal of Neuroscience* 19 (1999): 5034–43.

57 **the hippocampus . . . is sometimes smaller:** For an overview, see C. Campbell et al., "Lower Hippocampal Volume in Patients Suffering from Depression: A Meta-Analysis," *American Journal of Psychiatry* 161 (2004): 598–607, and J. D. Bremner et al., "Hippocampal Volume Reduction in Major Depression," *American Journal of Psychiatry* 157 (2001): 115–17. For an alternative view to Sheline's, one in which a small hippocampus predicts chronicity of depression, see T. Frodl et al., "Hippocampal and Amygdala Changes in Patients with Major Depressive Disorder and Healthy Controls During a One-Year Follow-up," *Journal of Clinical Psychiatry* 65 (2004): 492–99.

58 **verbal memory:** See also J. D. Bremner et al., "Deficits in Hippocampal and Anterior Cingulate Functioning During Verbal Declarative Memory Encoding in Midlife Major Depression," *American Journal of Psychiatry* 161 (2004): 637–45.

59 **"There may be mechanisms . . .":** *Listening to Prozac*, 135.

59 **Gage's article:** P.S. Eriksson et al., "Neurogenesis in the Adult Human Hippocampus," *Nature Medicine* 11 (1998): 1313–17.

60 **neurogenesis might be impossible:** P. Rakic, "Limits of Neurogenesis in Primates," *Science* 227 (1985): 1054–56.

60 neurogenesis . . . prefrontal cortex: E. Gould et al., "Neurogenesis in the Neocortex of Adult Primates," *Science* 286 (1999): 548–52.

61 **Sheline's and Rajkowska's . . . previewed:** G. Rajkowska, "Morphometric Methods for Studying the Prefrontal Cortex in Suicide Victims and Psychiatric Patients," *Annals of the New York Academy of Sciences* 836 (1997): 253–68; Y. I. Sheline et al., "Hippocampal Atrophy in Recurrent Major Depression," *Proceedings of the National Academy of Sciences* 93 (1996): 3908–13.

61 **contradictory findings:** See the note on hippocampal size above, and the note on "messy data" in chapter 10.

SIX: CHARM

66 **Emotionality . . . is a risk factor:** See the discussions of neuroticism, in chapter 11, and of the cost of caring, in chapter 17.

68 **earliest English-language memoirs:** See P. D. Kramer, "The Anatomy of Melancholy." Cowper was probably bipolar.

70 **"scarce is there . . .":** Robert Burton, *The Anatomy of Melancholy* (1621), first partition, section 3, member 1, subsection 2, "Symptoms or Signs in the Mind." The passage is one selected in Jennifer Radden, ed., *The Nature of Melancholy* (Oxford: Oxford University Press, 2000). The readings in this anthology are especially well chosen; for *anomalies of the will*, see the excerpt therein (pages 225–29) from Wilhelm Griesinger's 1867 text *Mental Pathology and Therapeutics*.

72 **standard definition:** *Diagnostic and Statistical Manual of Mental Disorders: DSM-IV* (Washington, D.C.: American Psychiatric Press, 1994); similarly for *DSM-IV-TR* (text revision, 2000). See also chapter 13.

72 **German . . . scrupulosity:** See Hubertus Tellenbach, *Melancholy: History of the Problem, Endogeneity, Typology, Pathogenesis, Clinical Considerations*, trans. E. Eng (Pittsburgh: Duquesne University Press, 1980). Here, "orderliness" is the central trait of the "typus melancholicus": "We have said that the melancholic type is especially exacting, orderly, painfully scrupulous, and conscientious. . . . The melancholic shows a *more than usual sensitivity* in matters of conscience as far as relations with persons and things are concerned" (89–90).

SEVEN: MORE CHARM

77 **William Styron's** *Darkness Visible*: New York: Random House, 1990. See also P. D. Kramer, "Darkness Obscured," *Psychiatric Times*, January 1991, and Kramer, "The Anatomy of Melancholy."

78 **Words fail:** It can be argued that to style it ineffable is equally to make depression more and less than an illness. Gabriel Josipovici, the British novelist and critic, refers to "the hallmark of the Romantic sensibility, the assertion that *words fail him*" (*Moo Pak* [Manchester: Carcanet, 1994], 48). The pain of neuritis and the aura of epilepsy may be no easier to convey than the emptiness of depression; it is only that, with depression, we need to be reminded of the degree of difference from the everyday.

79 **"I should jump now . . .":** A. L. Kennedy, *On Bullfighting* (New York: Anchor, 1999).

80 **suicides . . . where depression was the primary diagnosis:** About half of patients who commit suicide carry a diagnosis of depression. See N. E. Barklage, "Evaluation and Management of the Suicidal Patient," *Emergency Care Quarterly* 7 (1991): 9–17, cited in A. M. Gruenberg and R. D. Goldstein, "Depressive Disorders," in *Psychiatry*, ed. Allan Tasman, Jerald Kay, and Jeffrey Lieberman (Philadelphia: W.B. Saunders, 1997).

80 **suicide rates:** M. Olfson et al., "Relationship Between Antidepressant Medication Treatment and Suicide in Adolescents," *Archives of General Psychiatry* 60 (2003): 978–82; C. B. Kelly et al., "Antidepressant Prescribing and Suicide Rate in Northern Ireland," *European Psychiatry* 18 (2003): 325–28; D. Gunnell et al., "Why Are Suicide Rates Rising in Young Men but Falling in the Elderly? A Time-Series Analysis of Trends in England and Wales, 1950–1998," *Social Science and Medicine* 57 (2003): 595–611; M. S. Gould et al., "Youth Suicide Risk and Preventive Interventions: A Review of the Past Ten Years," *Evidence-Based Mental Health* 6 (2003): 121; A. Carlsten, M. Waern, and J. Ranstarn, "Antidepressant Medication and Suicide in Sweden," *Pharmacoepidemiology and Drug Safety* 10 (2001): 525–30; G. Isacsson, "Suicide Prevention—A Medical Breakthrough?," *Acta Psychiatrica Scandinavica* 102 (2000): 113–17; W. D. Hall et al., "Association Between Antidepressant Prescribing and Suicide in Australia, 1991–2000: Trend Analysis," *British Medical Journal* 326 (2003): 1008; and C. Barbui et al., "Antidepressant Drug Use in Italy Since the Introduction of SSRIs: National Trends, Regional Differences, and Impact on Suicide Rates," *Social Psychiatry and Psychiatric Epidemiology* 34 (1999): 152–56. The thrust of these studies is that when antidepressants are introduced or become more widely used, suicide rates

decrease, even while alternative indicators of stress, like alcoholism, remain constant.

80 **suicidal thoughts and impulses:** In *Listening to Prozac*, I suggested that the suicidality might not be due merely to increased activation or agitation in people already inclined to suicide but that medication might, on an idiosyncratic biological basis (perhaps by impairing serotonin-based neurotransmission), actually stimulate new suicidal inclinations.

Recent overviews, based partly on previously unpublished research conducted (and then concealed) by drug companies, confirm that antidepressants can arouse suicidality, but the research findings are less specific than I had anticipated. An analysis indicates that *all* antidepressants, old and new, are associated with suicide attempts in the first weeks that the drugs are administered. It had long been known that medications, if they affect energy before they alter mood, can activate depressed patients, with dangerous results. Though I am inclined to stick with my earlier reading of the risks, it is possible that the newer antidepressants do not present the specific danger I had feared. The overall findings speak to the need to monitor patients when they are first prescribed an antidepressant.

In a widely discussed study of suicidal thought and behavior in children and adolescents, the clearest excess risk was not in depressives, but in patients with anxiety disorders. The complete study is available from the Food and Drug Administration, at www.fda.gov/ohrms/dockets/ac/04/briefing/2004-4065b1-10-TAB08-Hammads-Review.pdf. Regarding antidepressant efficacy in adolescents, see the notes to chapter 16.

For a thoughtful overview of the entire topic, see L. Culpepper et al., "Suicidality as a Possible Side Effect of Antidepressant Treatment," *Journal of Clinical Psychiatry* 65 (2004): 742–49.

80 ***Should You Leave?:*** New York: Scribner, 1997; see chapters 12, 14, and 16.

82 **husbands or wives . . . are twice as likely:** J. Hippisley-Cox et al., "Married Couples' Risk of Same Disease: Cross Sectional Study," *BMJ* 325 (2002): 636–40. The fact that similarities in levels of distress are apparent within the first two years of marriage points to choice (assortative mating) as an important factor: G. Galbaud du Fort, V. Kovess, and J. F. Boivin, "Spouse Similarity for Psychological Distress and Well-Being: A Population Study," *Psychological Medicine* 24 (1994): 431–47.

82 **most studies conclude:** C. A. Mathews and V. I. Reus, "Assortative Mating in the Affective Disorders: A Systematic Review and Meta-Analysis," *Comprehensive Psychiatry* 42 (2001): 257–62. In this overview, integrating the major research to date, the risk of depression in the spouse of a depressive is well over two times the risk for controls.

83 **mechanical emotionally:** There has been research interest in this other sort of assortative mating, especially in the courtship years, between depressive young women and distant, unsupportive young men. The pattern seems to hold, but the reason is unclear: moody women may choose overly stable men, or depression in a woman may cause a man to pull back. See S. E. Daley and C. M. Hammen, "Depressive Symptoms and Close Relationships During the Transition to Adulthood: Perspectives from Dysphoric Women, Their Best Friends, and Their Romantic Partners," *Journal of Consulting and Clinical Psychology* 70 (2002): 129–41.

EIGHT: EROS

92 **devotion to partners:** C. S. Lewis, *A Grief Observed* (New York: Seabury Press, 1961); John Bayley, *Elegy for Iris* (New York: St. Martin's Press, 1999).

NINE: OBVIOUS CONFUSION: THREE VIGNETTES

96 **show's catalogue:** Marilyn McCully, ed., *Picasso: The Early Years, 1892–1906* (Washington, D.C.: National Gallery of Art, 1997); for an analysis of Picasso's use of the face and habitus of depression, see also Jeffrey Weiss, ed., *Picasso: The Cubist Portraits of Fernande Olivier* (Washington, D.C.: National Gallery of Art, 2004). Regarding the early erotica, see Jean Clair, ed., *Picasso Érotique* (Munich: Prestel, 2001).

98 **Borges story:** Jorge Luis Borges, "Funes the Memorious," in *Labyrinths*, ed. Donald A. Yates and James E. Irby (New York: New Directions, 1962).

99 **classic version of tragedy:** David Gullette, professor of English at Simmons College, kindly shared with me his notes on the uses of the word *tragedy.*

100 **Carl Rogers's classic:** *On Becoming a Person* (1961; reprint, Boston: Houghton Mifflin, 1995); a portion of this chapter is a reworking of my introduction to that edition.

103 **"... an alienated Sisyphus ...":** C. Elliott, "Pursued by Happiness and Beaten Senseless: Prozac and the American Dream" *Hastings Center Report* 30, no. 2 (2000): 7–12, anthologized in Carl Elliot and Tad Chambers, eds., *Prozac as a Way of Life* (Chapel Hill: University of North Carolina Press, 2004). The Camus quotations are from the English translation of *The Myth of Sisyphus and Other Essays* (New York: Vintage, 1955).

104 **on the poster:** I am referring to Camus's Sisyphus, Sisyphus the most pru-

dent and the most passionate of mortals, Sisyphus the rebel-hero, punished for stealing the wisdom of the gods. There are versions of the myth in which Sisyphus is a highwayman and murderer.

105 **melancholy . . . confer worth:** As a further example from my collection of scraps, I offer this passage from a *New York Times* listing for a Whitney Museum exhibition of works by Joan Mitchell: "Abstract paintings this suave and sure-footed must be glib and manipulative, you may be excused for telling yourself. Distrust your distrust. Lush, opulent fields of colors, seemingly all paradisiacal, contain shades of melancholy that reveal themselves to you after your eyes adjust to their light." It is the overlay of melancholy that saves and justifies the whole and makes the exhibit worth a visit.

106 **a contrast William James discussed:** *The Varieties of Religious Experience*, especially lectures 4 and 5, "The Religions of Healthy-Mindedness," and 6 and 7, "The Sick Soul."

107 **"Proximate to the point . . .":** Sarah Whitfield, ed., *Bonnard* (London: Tate Gallery Publishing, 1998).

108 **"Though the public . . .":** From a summary introduction to S. Meisler, "Pierre Bonnard," *Smithsonian*, July 1998, 33ff; the text of the essay contains almost identical language.

109 **How had the obvious come to be:** This topic has long fascinated me. *Should You Leave?* deals with the construction of the obvious in psychotherapy, and then considers the consequences of resisting the obvious, when making decisions in relationships.

TEN: ALTOGETHER AGAIN

115 **form a circuit:** J. D. Bremner, "Structural Changes in the Brain in Depression and Relationship to Symptom Recurrence," *CNS Spectrums* 7 (2002): 129–39. Bremner hypothesizes that disruptions to a circuit including the amygdala, hippocampus, caudate, thalamus, and prefrontal cortex underlie symptoms of depression. Antidepressants like Prozac appear to work via altering levels of activation throughout this circuit, particularly in the prefrontal cortex: H. S. Mayberg et al., "Regional Metabolic Effects of Fluoxetine in Major Depression: Serial Changes and Relationship to Clinical Response," *Biological Psychiatry* 48 (2000): 830–43; C.H.Y. Fu et al., "Attenuation of the Neural Response to Sad Faces in Major Depression by Antidepressant Treatment: A Prospective, Event-Related Functional Magnetic Imaging Study," *Archives of General Psychiatry* 61 (2004): 877–89.

116 **Robert Sapolsky:** Here, I have tried to summarize the rich material in *Stress, the Aging Brain, and the Mechanisms of Neuron Death* (Cambridge, Mass.: MIT Press, 1992). I have relied also on conversations with Sapolsky and on numerous monographs. For those interested in connections be-tween mental illness and this corner of the stress literature, good places to begin include: A. L. Lee, W. O. Ogle, and R. M. Sapolsky, "Stress and De-pression: Possible Links to Neuron Death in the Hippocampus," *Bipolar Disorders* 4 (2002): 117–28; R. M. Sapolsky, "The Possibility of Neurotoxi-city in the Hippocampus in Major Depression: A Primer on Neuron Death," *Biological Psychiatry* 48 (2000): 755–65; R. M. Sapolsky, "Gluco-corticoids and Hippocampal Atrophy in Neuropsychiatric Disorders," *Archives of General Psychiatry* 57 (2000): 925–35; R. M. Sapolsky, "Gluco-corticoids, Stress, and Their Adverse Neurological Effects: Relevance to Aging," *Experimental Gerontology* 34 (1999): 721–32; R. M. Sapolsky, "Cellular Defenses Against Excitotoxic Insults," *Journal of Neurochemistry* 76 (2001): 1601–11; B. S. McEwen, "Protective and Damaging Effects of Stress Mediators," *New England Journal of Medicine* 338 (1998): 171–79; and R. M. Sapolsky, "Why Stress Is Bad for Your Brain," *Science* 273 (1996): 749–50.

117 **stress hormones:** This term is shorthand for ones common in the older lit-erature, "stress-response hormones" and "stress-responsive hormones."

117 **aging . . . exposure to stress hormones:** The correspondences are more substantial than I have indicated in the text. The injuries are of the same sort, in the same parts of the hippocampus.

117 **neurons lose connective wiring:** These losses, in otherwise apparently healthy rats, can be enormous. A fifth of hippocampal cells will be missing but fully half of the receptors for stress hormones will have disappeared.

118 **The damaged hippocampus is . . . stuck switch:** J. P. Herman, "Neurocir-cuitry of Stress: Central Control of the Hypothalamo-Pituitary-Adrenocortidal Axis," *Trends in Neurosciences* 20 (1997): 78–84; D. M. Lyons et al., "Early Life Stress and Inherited Variation in Monkey Hip-pocampal Volumes," *Archives of General Psychiatry* 58 (2001): 1145–51.

118 **enlarged adrenal glands:** C. B. Nemeroff et al., "Adrenal Gland Enlarge-ment in Major Depression: A Computed Tomographic Study," *Archives of General Psychiatry* 49 (1992): 384–87. Depressed patients may also have enlarged pituitary glands—for reasons of space, I have omitted considera-tion of the role of the pituitary in depression and in Cushing's disease.

118 **overactive hormonal responses:** Scientists have also begun to find correla-tions between liability to depression and genetic variations in humans' capacity to *handle* stress hormones. See S. Claes et al., "The Corticotropin-

Releasing Hormone Binding Protein Is Associated with Major Depression in a Population from Northern Sweden," *Biological Psychiatry* 54 (2003): 867–72.

119 **bone densities:** D. Michelson et al., "Bone Mineral Density in Women with Depression," *New England Journal of Medicine* 335 (1996): 1176–81. The stress hormone measured is cortisol.

119 **dendrites grow:** Although in discussing depression I will focus on failures in arborization, it bears noting that not all neuronal connections are in the service of mental health; anxiety disorders appear to be characterized by the excessive formation of connections in parts of the brain associated with fear.

120 **brain-derived neurotrophic factor, or BDNF:** For summaries of the BDNF evidence, see a series of overview papers by Ronald Duman, including: R. S. Duman, "Structural Alterations in Depression: Cellular Mechanisms Underlying Pathology and Treatment of Mood Disorders," *CNS Spectrums* 7 (2002): 140–47; Y. Shirayama et al., "Brain-Derived Neurotrophic Factor Produces Antidepressant Effects in Behavioral Models of Depression," *Journal of Neuroscience* 22 (2002): 3251–61; R. S. Duman, S. Nakagawa, and J. Malberg, "Regulation of Adult Neurogenesis by Antidepressant Treatment," *Neuropsychopharmacology* 25 (2001): 836–44; R. S. Duman, J. Malberg, and S. Nakagawa, "Regulation of Adult Neurogenesis by Psychotropic Drugs and Stress," *Journal of Pharmacology and Experimental Therapeutics* 299 (2001): 401–7; V. A. Vaidya and R. S. Duman, "Depression—Emerging Insights from Neurobiology," *British Medical Bulletin* 57 (2001): 61–79; J. E. Malberg et al., "Chronic Antidepressant Treatment Increases Neurogenesis in Adult Rat Hippocampus," *Journal of Neuroscience* 20 (2000): 9104–10; R. S. Duman et al., "Neuronal Plasticity and Survival in Mood Disorders," *Biological Psychiatry* 48 (2000): 732–39; R. S. Duman, J. Malberg, and Johannes Thome, "Neural Plasticity to Stress and Antidepressant Treatment," *Biological Psychiatry* 46 (1999): 1181–91; R. S. Duman, "Novel Therapeutic Approaches Beyond the Serotonin Receptor," *Biological Psychiatry* 44 (1998): 324–35; and R. S. Duman, G. R. Heninger, and E. J. Nestler, "A Molecular and Cellular Theory of Depression," *Archives of General Psychiatry* 54 (1997): 597–606. Regarding loss of antidepressant efficacy, see the work of Lisa Monteggia referenced below. The research on BDNF and neurogenesis began with a paper cited earlier, Gould et al., "Neurogenesis in the Neocortex."

For reasons of space, I am omitting reference to a line of research involving the role of glutamate and gamma-aminobutyric acid. In brief, a developing theory holds that one result of a glial defect in depression is dysregulation of brain energy metabolism, leading to the inhibition of genes that produce BDNF. In effect, this research proposes a specific link between anatomical observations (of abnormalities in glial cells) and failures of neurogenesis and neuroresilience. Gerard Sanacora is a leader in this area.

120 **Depleting an animal of BDNF:** L. M. Monteggia et al., "Essential Role of Brain-Derived Neurotrophic Factor in Adult Hippocampal Function," *Proceedings of the National Academy of Sciences* 101 (2004): 10827–32.

120 **Rajkowska . . . deficit in BDNF:** Personal communication, 2002. For an overview of the relationship of her own work to neuroresilience theory, see G. Rajkowska, "Postmortem Studies in Mood Disorders Indicate Altered Numbers of Neurons and Glial Cells," *Biological Psychiatry* 48 (2000): 766–77, and H. K. Manji et al., "Neuroplasticity and Cellular Resilience in Mood Disorders," *Molecular Psychiatry* 5 (2000): 578–93.

121 **meshes well with older research:** See Duman references above. Serotonin and norepinephrine changes can cause, and be caused by, changes in stress hormones: van Praag et al., *Stress, the Brain, and Depression*, pp. 189–96, and G. E. Tafet, "Correlation Between Cortisol Level and Serotonin Uptake in Patients with Chronic Stress and Depression," *Cognitive, Affective, and Behavioral Neuroscience* 1 (2001): 388–93.

121 **in the face of messy data:** G. M. MacQueen et al., "Course of Illness, Hippocampal Function, and Hippocampal Volume in Major Depression," *Proceedings of the National Academy of Sciences* 100 (2003): 1387–92; T. Frodl et al., "Hippocampal Changes in Patients with a First Episode of Major Depression," *American Journal of Psychiatry* 159 (2002): 1112–18; M. Vythilingam et al., "Childhood Trauma Associated with Smaller Hippocampal Volume in Women with Major Depression," *American Journal of Psychiatry* 159 (2002): 2072–80. Christine Heim and Charles Nemeroff have assembled a substantial body of research on early trauma as a source of anatomical damage; see K. M. Penza, C. Heim, and C. Nemeroff, "Neurobiological Effects of Childhood Abuse: Implications for the Pathophysiology of Depression and Anxiety," *Archives of Women's Mental Health* 6 (2003): 15–22.

122 **Multiple sclerosis:** D. C. Mohr et al., "Association Between Stressful Life Events and Exacerbation in Multiple Sclerosis: A Meta-Analysis," *British Medical Journal* 328 (2004): 731–35; and D. Buljevac et al., "Self Reported Stressful Life Events and Exacerbations in Multiple Sclerosis: Prospective Study," *British Medical Journal* 327 (2003): 646–70.

122 **resemblance to . . . dementias:** See Miguel-Hidalgo et al., "Glial Fibrillary Acidic Protein."

122 **"how the body . . .":** Burton, *The Anatomy of Melancholy*, first partition, section 2, member 5, subsection 1, "Continent, Inward, Antecedent, Next Causes, and How the Body Works on the Mind."

ELEVEN: GETTING THERE

124 **work of . . . Kenneth Kendler:** In this chapter, I have relied on our regular conversations and my reading, over years, of Ken's published results. For an overview, see K. S. Kendler, C. O. Gardner, and C. A. Prescott, "Toward a Comprehensive Developmental Model for Major Depression in Women," *American Journal of Psychiatry* 159 (2002): 1133–45. See also: K. S. Kendler, J. Kuhn, and C. A. Prescott, "The Interrelationship of Neuroticism, Sex, and Stressful Life Events in the Prediction of Episodes of Major Depression," *American Journal of Psychiatry* 161 (2004): 631–36; K. S. Kendler et al., "Life Event Dimensions of Loss, Humiliation, Entrapment, and Danger in the Prediction of Onsets of Major Depression and Generalized Anxiety," *Archives of General Psychiatry* 60 (2003): 789–96; K. S. Kendler, L. M. Thornton, and C. A. Prescott, "Gender Differences in the Rates of Exposure to Stressful Life Events and Sensitivity to Their Depressogenic Effects," *American Journal of Psychiatry* 158 (2001): 587–93; K. S. Kendler and C. A. Prescott, "A Population-Based Twin Study of Lifetime Major Depression in Men and Women," *Archives of General Psychiatry* 56 (1999): 39–54; K. S. Kendler et al., "Stressful Life Events, Genetic Liability, and Onset of Episodes of Major Depression in Women," *American Journal of Psychiatry* 152 (1995): 833–42; and K. S. Kendler et al., "A Longitudinal Twin Study of One-Year Prevalence of Major Depression in Women," *Archives of General Psychiatry* 50 (1993): 843–52. Extensive though it is, this list omits numerous important monographs; some more are listed below.

126 **The one factor that raises the level:** Because of potential inaccuracy in diagnoses made at one moment in time, current estimates may understate the heritability of depression. As one paper puts it: "Major depression . . . may be a rather highly heritable disorder of moderate reliability rather than a moderately heritable disorder of high reliability" (K. S. Kendler and M. C. Neale, "The Lifetime History of Major Depression in Women: Reliability of Diagnosis and Heritability," *Archives of General Psychiatry* 50 [1993]: 863–70).

128 **As one reviewer on the research on worms noted:** S. Austad, "Development: Varied Fates from Similar States," *Science* 290 (2000): 944 (a review of C. E. Finch and T. B. L. Kirkwood, *Chance, Development, and Aging* [New York: Oxford University Press, 2000]).

128 **prenatal stress:** C. L. Coe et al., "Prenatal Stress Diminishes Neurogenesis in the Dentate Gyrus of Juvenile Rhesus Monkeys," *Biological Psychiatry* 54 (2003): 1025–34; E. Gould, "Experience-dependent Effects on Structural Plasticity in Limbic and Cortical Structures Involved in Emotion Regulation" (presentation, American Psychiatric Association Annual Meeting, New York, N.Y., May 4, 2004). The stress involves exposing the pregnant monkey to startling noises; the inhibition of neurogenesis is apparent years later in the offspring.

128 **childbirth complications:** T. G. Van Erp et al, "Contributions of Genetic Risk and Fetal Hypoxia to Hippocampal Volume in Patients with Schizophrenia or Schizoaffective Disorder, Their Unaffected Siblings, and Healthy Unrelated Volunteers," *American Journal of Psychiatry* 159 (2002): 1514–20.

129 **nature of the interaction:** A. Fanous et al., "Neuroticism, Major Depression, and Gender: A Population-Based Twin Study," *Psychological Medicine* 32 (2002): 719–28; K. S. Kendler et al., "A Longitudinal Twin Study of Personality and Major Depression in Women," *Archives of General Psychiatry* 50 (1993): 853–62. See also S. B. Roberts and K. S. Kendler, "Neuroticism and Self-Esteem as Indices of the Vulnerability to Major Depression in Women," *Psychological Medicine* 9 (1999): 1101–9.

130 **serotonin transporter gene:** K. P. Lesch et al., "Association of Anxiety-Related Traits with a Polymorphism in the Serotonin Transporter Gene Regulatory Region," *Science* 274 (1996): 1527–31. See also D. A. Collier et al., "A Novel Functional Polymorphism Within the Promoter of the Serotonin Transporter Gene: Possible Role in Susceptibility to Affective Disorders," *Molecular Psychiatry* 1 (1996): 4453–60; A. D. Ogilvie et al., "Polymorphism in Serotonin Transporter Gene Associated with Susceptibility to Major Depression," *Lancet* 347 (1966): 731–33; D. L. Murphy et al., "Genetic Perspectives on the Serotonin Transporter," *Brain Research Bulletin* 56 (2001): 487–94. For good popular overviews of research on genes, transporters, anxiety, and depression, including both the serotonin and dopamine hypotheses, see D. Hamer and P. Copeland, *Living with Our Genes* (New York: Doubleday, 1998); S. H. Barondes, *Mood Genes* (New York: W. H. Freeman, 1998); and S. H. Barondes, *Better than Prozac* (New York: Oxford University Press, 2003).

There is one striking oddity to the 5-HTT story. The transporter is involved in serotonin reuptake, the pulling back of serotonin into transmitter cells. (The transporter is the site where Prozac and similar medications act.) Extra 5-HTT should *lower* cells' access to serotonin. The theories that explain the beneficial effects of the long variants of the gene sometimes posit the induction of compensatory mechanisms early in life, in response to high production of the transporter.

130 **other genes that might cause:** For example, a gene called DRD4 codes for a protein involved with cells' handling of dopamine, another neurotransmitter implicated in mood maintenance. One form of the gene seems to predispose to risk taking. Thrill seekers have diminished rates of depression—and they are not worriers. Lacking the risk-seeker variant of the DRD4 gene, a person is statistically slightly more liable to neurosis and depression both. This correlation, too, accounts for only a small effect; and even that finding is controversial. See the Hamer and Copeland book and the Barondes books above.

130 **second look at 5-HTT:** A. Caspi et al., "Influence of Life Stress on Depression: Moderation by a Polymorphism in the 5-HTT Gene," *Science* 301 (2003): 386–89.

132 **"... a flea-biting to one ...":** Burton, *Anatomy of Melancholy*, first partition, section 1, member 1, subsection 5, "Melancholy in Disposition, Improperly So Called, Equivocations."

134 **environment that matters ... is nonshared:** D. L. Foley, M. C. Neale, and K. S. Kendler, "Reliability of a Lifetime History of Major Depression: Implications for Heritability and Co-Morbidity," *Psychological Medicine* 28 (1998): 857–70.

135 **groups ... have replicated:** See, for example; T. C. Eley and J. Stevenson, "Using Genetic Analyses to Clarify the Distinction Between Depressive and Anxious Symptoms in Children," *Journal of Abnormal Child Psychology* 27 (1999): 105–14.

135 **when depression runs in families:** P. F. Sullivan, M. C. Neale, and K. S. Kendler, "Genetic Epidemiology of Major Depression: Review and Meta-Analysis," *American Journal of Psychiatry* 157 (2000): 1552–62.

135 **a minor finding:** K. S. Kendler and C. O. Gardner, "Monozygotic Twins Discordant for Major Depression: A Preliminary Exploration of the Role of Environmental Experiences in the Aetiology and Course of Illness," *Psychological Medicine* 31 (2001): 411–13.

137 **genetic predisposition to addiction:** J. M. Hettema, L. A. Corey, and K. S. Kendler, "A Multivariate Genetic Analysis of the Use of Tobacco, Alcohol, and Caffeine in a Population Based Sample of Male and Female Twins," *Drug and Alcohol Dependence* 57 (1999): 69–78; K. S. Kendler et al., "A Population-Based Twin Study in Women of Smoking Initiation and Nicotine Dependence," *Psychological Medicine* 29 (1999): 299–308.

139 **"select themselves into high-risk environments":** K. S. Kendler, L. M. Karkowski, and C. A. Prescott, "Causal Relationship Between Stressful

Life Events and the Onset of Major Depression," *American Journal of Psychiatry* 156 (1999): 837–41. The data also show that the genes for depression act partly through increasing (probably via temperament) the likelihood of stressful life events (K. S. Kendler and L. M. Karkowski-Shuman, "Stressful Life Events and Genetic Liability to Major Depression: Genetic Control of Exposure to the Environment?," *Psychological Medicine* 27 [1999]: 539–47).

140 **overarching statistical analysis:** In Kendler, Gardner, and Prescott, "Toward a Comprehensive Developmental Model." If depression is more heritable than current estimates suggest—if diagnostic inaccuracy has led to an underestimation of the role of genes—then the environmental part of the model is astonishingly complete in its reach, and reasonably "coarse" life events are the ones that matter for the initiation of depressive episodes.

140 **Freud . . . lingering grief:** In "Mourning and Melancholia" (1917).

141 **"upstream" causes:** That is to say, Kendler found that although these four factors may cause one another (as when a child's genetics lead to family disruption), nothing downstream causes them (so that, for example, a child's anxiety, insofar as it is on an environmental basis, does not lead to child abuse).

143 **circumstances are benign:** Kendler's team assessed the family environment through repeated estimates, by both twins and parents, of parental warmth and family tone, and by specific inquiries about arguments, hitting, mutual support, and so on.

144 **depressed alcoholics . . . glial loss:** Rajkowska, personal communication. See also J. J. Miguel-Hidalgo and G. Rajkowska, "Comparison of Prefrontal Cell Pathology Between Depression and Alcohol Dependence," *Journal of Psychiatric Research* 37 (2003): 411–20. The two disorders appear to have distinct destructive effects on the prefrontal cortex, as well as differing effects on the hippocampus; the combination of depression and alcoholism results in especially extensive precortical glial loss.

144 **"kindled" illness:** The concept of kindling comes from animal models of epilepsy. Small currents applied to a mouse brain may cause no apparent response—until finally, a current of the same magnitude triggers a seizure. Thereafter, quite minor stimuli may give rise to a seizure. In time, the animal will seize spontaneously. Many diseases have the opposite pattern: if you contract chicken pox, you may become immune to subsequent exposures to the varicella-zoster virus. The kindling theory of depression is largely the work of Robert Post of the NIMH. I discuss this research in *Listening to Prozac*.

145 **Risk and experience:** K. S. Kendler, L. M. Thorton, and C. O. Gardner, "Genetic Risk, Number of Previous Depressive Episodes, and Stressful

Life Events in Predicting Onset of Major Depression," *American Journal of Psychiatry* 158 (2001): 582–86.

145 **genes affect the kindling:** K. S. Kendler, L. M. Thorton, and C. O. Gardner, "Stressful Life Events and Previous Episodes in the Etiology of Major Depression in Women: An Evaluation of the 'Kindling' Hypothesis," *American Journal of Psychiatry* 157 (2000): 1243–51.

147 **markers . . . modestly predictive:** See this discussion of "atypical depression" in *Listening to Prozac*. Research on this topic by Donald Klein's group at Columbia University includes J. W. Stewart et al., "Atypical Features and Treatment Response in the National Institute of Mental Health Treatment of Depression Collaborative Research Program," *Journal of Clinical Psychopharmacology* 18 (1998): 429–34; M. R. Liebowitz et al., "Antidepressant Specificity in Atypical Depression," *Archives of General Psychiatry* 45 (1988): 129–37; and many other articles.

147 **valedictory monograph:** G. Winokur, "All Roads Lead to Depression: Clinically Homogeneous, Etiologically Heterogeneous," *Journal of Affective Disorder* 45 (1997): 5–17.

TWELVE: MAGNITUDE

151 **burden of disease:** The bulk of the data in this chapter is culled from the monumental works edited by Christopher J. L. Murray and Alan D. Lopez: *The Global Burden of Disease: A Comprehensive Assessment of Mortality and Disability from Diseases, Injuries, and Risk Factors in 1990 and Projected to 2020* and *Global Health Statistics: A Compendium of Incidence, Prevalence, and Mortality Estimates for over 200 Conditions.* Both were published in 1996 by the Harvard School of Public Health on behalf of the World Health Organization and the World Bank and distributed by Harvard University Press. The findings were summarized in a series of monographs in the *Lancet*, including C. J. L. Murray and A. D. Lopez, "Global Mortality, Disability, and the Contribution of Risk Factors: Global Burden of Disease Study," *Lancet* 349 (1997): 1436–42.

151 **young adulthood is valued:** This weighting arises from preferences that people express in surveys: Which year would you rather give up to disability? How much would you pay to add a year of life at a given age? The value of a year of life peaks in the early twenties. The summary graph is on p. 60 of the first volume, *Global Burden.*

152 **Not AIDS, not breast cancer:** In the *Global Burden of Disease* studies, HIV-AIDS ranked twenty-eighth in the 1990 data, when major depression

ranked fourth; in the projected 2020 data, depression moves into the number 2 spot and AIDS leaps to number 10. For developing regions, HIV remains in the number 10 spot, but depression moves to number 1. In developed regions, depression is expected to move to third, behind ischemic heart disease (like most heart attacks) and cerebrovascular disease (like most strokes), but HIV drops below the top 10 again. Cancers appear low on the lists. The exception is respiratory cancers in developed countries in the 2020 projections.

152 **diarrhea:** A study conducted in rural Pakistan found maternal depression to be a potent risk factor for infantile diarrhea—so some of the burden of the diarrheal illness may be properly attributed to depression: A. Rahman et al., "Impact of Maternal Depression on Infant Nutritional Status and Illness: A Cohort Study," *Archives of General Psychiatry* 61 (2004): 946–52.

153 **seven categories of severity:** For the disability classes, see *Global Burden*, p. 40.

153 **ongoing study is updating:** WHO World Mental Health Survey Consortium, "Prevalence, Severity, and Unmet Need for Treatment of Mental Disorders in the World Health Organization World Mental Health Surveys," *Journal of the American Medical Association* 291 (2004): 2581–90.

153 **indirect measures support:** See, for example, P. S. Wang et al., "Effects of Major Depression on Moment-in-Time Work Performance," *American Journal of Psychiatry* 161 (2004): 1885–91; W. F. Stewart et al., "Cost of Lost Productive Work Time Among U.S. Workers with Depression," *Journal of the American Medical Association* 289 (2003): 3135–44; R. C. Kessler et al., "The Effects of Chronic Medical Conditions on Work Loss and Work Cutback," *Journal of Occupational and Environmental Medicine* 43 (2001): 218–25; G. E. Simon et al., "Depression and Work Productivity: The Comparative Costs of Treatment Versus Nontreatment," *Journal of Occupational and Environmental Medicine* 43 (2001): 2–9; R. C. Kessler et al., "The Association Between Chronic Medical Conditions and Work Impairment," in *Caring and Doing for Others*, ed. Alice S. Rossi (Chicago: University of Chicago Press, 2001); E. R. Berndt et al., "Lost Human Capital from Early-Onset Chronic Depression," *American Journal of Psychiatry* 157 (2000): 940–47; R. C. Kessler et al., "Depression in the Workplace: Effects on Short-Term Disability," *Health Affairs* 18 (1999): 163–71; and E. R. Berndt et al., "Workplace Performance Effects from Chronic Depression and Its Treatment," *Journal of Health Economics* 17 (1998): 511–35.

154 **over 16 percent:** R. C. Kessler et al., "The Epidemiology of Major Depres-

sive Disorder: Results from the National Comorbidity Survey Replication (NCS-R)," *Journal of the American Medical Association* 289 (2003): 3095–105. The diabetes data is from Centers for Disease Control surveys.

154 **A recent study:** D. G. Kilpatrick et al., "Violence and Risk of PTSD, Major Depression, Substance Abuse/Dependence, and Comorbidity: Results from the National Survey of Adolescents," *Journal of Consulting and Clinical Psychology* 71 (2003): 692–700. As a point of reference, the prevalence before age twenty of another common chronic and disabling illness, diabetes, is 0.25 percent, according to the CDC.

On a related issue: it is often said that depression is epidemic—rising fast over the past twenty-five years, especially among the young. For reasons that have little to do with science, and more to do with my clinical practice and my reading of novels from the past three centuries, I have long believed to the contrary that depression has always been highly prevalent and that the recent increase resulted from more careful questioning and more honest reporting of pathology. (I see the willingness to believe in an epidemic as resulting in part from a *Gemeinschaft-Gesellschaft* fallacy that demonizes industrial or post-industrial society and romanticizes the supportive nature of communities in prior eras. For a poignant account of the tendency to ignore and deny frank depression in a communal society, see Nancy Scheper-Hughes, *Saints, Scholars, and Schizophrenics: Mental Illness in Rural Ireland*, 3d ed. [Berkeley: University of California Press, 2001].) I was therefore interested to encounter a lone monograph—an element in the famous Stirling County Study—that finds depression rates to have been reasonably constant from 1952 to 1992. The same paper references the contrasting research that shows depression to be on the rise: J. M. Murphy et al., "A Forty-Year Perspective on the Prevalence of Depression: The Stirling County Study," *Archives of General Psychiatry* 57 (2000): 209–15.

154 **third leading cause of death:** ages 15–19 and ages 20–24; for ages 25–34 it is the second cause; for 35–44, the fourth: *National Vital Statistics Report* 50 (September 16, 2002). Regarding the relationship of suicide to depression, see also Barklage, "Evaluation and Management." Since causes of suicide that arise in late life—terminal illness or chronic pain—are less frequent in adolescence, it is likely that more than half of adolescent suicides involve depression. It is hard to gauge the accuracy of estimates because most diagnoses are made postmortem. Suicide attempts (as opposed to completed suicides) often involve teenagers who are less ill; still, the leading study found that over 37 percent of attempters had been depressed: M. S. Gould et al., "Psychopathology Associated with Suicidal

Ideation and Attempts Among Children and Adolescents," *Journal of the American Academy of Child and Adolescent Psychiatry* 37 (1998): 915–23.

155 **every aspect:** These findings come from the work of Ronald Kessler.

155 **almost 8 percent:** M. W. Weissman et al., "Depressed Adolescents Grown Up," *Journal of the American Medical Association* 281 (1999): 1707–13.

155 **single diagnosis of depression:** Alexander Glassman, personal communication, 2003.

155 **dramatic claim:** A. Solomon, "A Bitter Pill," *The New York Times*, March 29, 2004. The actual figure may be closer to 6 percent. The estimates come from the work of John Greden, cited in Andrew Solomon, *The Noonday Demon* (New York: Scribner, 2001).

156 **death and depression in the elderly:** R. Schulz et al., "Association Between Depression and Mortality in Older Adults: The Cardiovascular Health Study," *Archives of Internal Medicine* 160 (2000): 1761–68. If anything, the study underestimates the harm major depression does; the criteria used included subjects in mild depressive states, which are presumably less lethal. And some of the variables eliminated are not independent—depression can lead to a slide in social class. The true contribution of (minor and major) depression to mortality in late life is somewhere between 24 and 40 percent; major depression alone almost certainly confers a yet higher risk. The relationship between cigarette smoking and depression is tricky; it had long been thought that depression led to smoking, but it may be that genetic and familial factors predispose in parallel to both problems: K. S. Kendler et al., "Smoking and Major Depression: A Causal Analysis," *Archives of General Psychiatry* 50 (1993): 36–43.

156 **Less well constructed studies:** Reviewed in L. R. Wulsin, G. E. Vaillant, and V. E. Wells, "A Systematic Review of the Mortality of Depression," *Psychosomatic Medicine* 61 (1999): 6–17; see also L. R. Wulsin, "Does Depression Kill?," *Archives of Internal Medicine* 160 (2000): 1731–32.

156 **Adult-onset diabetes:** D. L. Musselman et al., "Relationship of Depression to Diabetes Types 1 and 2: Epidemiology, Biology, and Treatment," *Biological Psychiatry* 54 (2003): 317–29.

156 **tumors may grow faster:** D. Spiegel and J. Giese-Davis, "Depression and Cancer: Mechanisms and Disease Progression," *Biological Psychiatry* 54 (2003): 269–82; M. Watson et al., "Influence of Psychological Response on Survival in Breast Cancer: A Population-Based Cohort Study," *Lancet* 354 (1999): 1331–36.

THIRTEEN: EXTENT

159 **The standard definition of depression:** *Diagnostic and Statistical Manual of Mental Disorders: DSM-IV* (Washington, D.C.: American Psychiatric Press, 1994): similarly for DSM-IV-TR (Text Revision, 2000).

159 **uncomplicated bereavement:** See the extended comment on grief and depression in the notes to chapter 20.

161 **"depression" applies prognostically:** R. Kendell and A. Jablensky, "Distinguishing Between the Validity and Utility of Psychiatric Diagnoses," *American Journal of Psychiatry* 160 (2003): 4–12.

162 **One such study:** National Institute of Mental Health Collaborative Program on the Psychobiology of Depression, reported on, for example, in: M. B. Keller and R. J. Boland, "Implications of Failing to Achieve Successful Long-Term Maintenance Treatment of Recurrent Unipolar Major Depression," *Biological Psychiatry* 44 (1998): 348–60; L. L. Judd et al., "Psychosocial Disability During the Long-Term Course of Unipolar Major Depressive Disorder," *Archives of General Psychiatry* 57 (2000): 375–80; T. I. Mueller et al., "Recurrence After Recovery from Major Depressive Disorder During Fifteen Years of Observational Follow-up," *American Journal of Psychiatry* 156 (1999): 1000–1006; T. I. Mueller et al., "Recovery After Five Years of Unremitted Major Depressive Disorder," *Archives of General Psychiatry* 53 (1996): 794–99; M. B. Keller et al., "Time to Recovery, Chronicity, and Levels of Psychopathology in Major Depression: A - Five-Year Prospective Follow-up of 431 Subjects," *Archives of General Psychiatry* 49 (1992): 809–16. See also Keller, "Past, Present, and Future Directions."

163 **Diagnosis is prognosis:** See Kendell and Jablensky, "Distinguishing Between the Validity and Utility"; and Robert A. Woodruff, Donald W. Goodwin, and Samuel B. Guze, *Psychiatric Diagnosis* (New York: Oxford University Press, 1974).

164 **patients with residual symptoms:** See the first note to chapter 4, p. 296.

165 **criteria for major depression:** K. S. Kendler and C. O. Gardner, "Boundaries of Major Depression: An Evaluation of DSM-IV Criteria," *American Journal of Psychiatry* 155 (1998): 172–77.

165 **suicidal thoughts . . . serious outcomes:** The same results apply to estimates of heritability; patients with more marked or persistent symptoms are only slightly more likely to have first-degree relatives who are at risk.

166 **criteria for less severe disorders:** *Dysthymia* is characterized by extensive low mood. So: sadness for more days than not, for two years, in which no two months are symptom-free; and two or more additional symptoms, such

as problems with sleep or excessive guilt or suicidal thoughts. The dysthymic must not experience a full-blown episode in the first two years of the low-level mood disorder. *Minor depression* is just like major depression but with less intensity: two weeks of moderate depressed mood or anhedonia, but only one or a few additional symptoms. *Recurrent brief depression* involves full intensity (five symptoms, including sadness or anhedonia) but briefer duration. Episodes last less than two weeks, but they recur monthly for a year. *Subsyndromal symptomatic depression* is defined in the chapter text.

See N. Sadek and J. Bona, "Subsyndromal Symptomatic Depression: A New Concept," *Depression and Anxiety* 12 (2000): 30–39; L. Pezawas et al., "Recurrent Brief Depression—Past and Future," *Progress in Neuropsychopharmacology and Biological Psychiatry* 27 (2003): 75–83; M. H. Rapaport et al., "A Descriptive Analysis of Minor Depression," *American Journal of Psychiatry* 159 (2002): 637–43; L. L. Judd, P. J. Schettler, and H. S. Akiskal, "The Prevalence, Clinical Relevance, and Public Health Significance of Subthreshold Depressions," *Psychiatric Clinics of North America* 25 (2000): 685–98; L. L. Judd et al., "Psychosocial Disability During the Long-Term Course of Unipolar Major Depression," *Archives of General Psychiatry* 57 (2000): 375–80; L. L. Judd et al., "A Prospective Twelve-Year Study of Subsyndromal and Syndromal Depressive Symptoms in Unipolar Major Depressive Disorders," *Archives of General Psychiatry* 5 (1998): 694–700; H. S. Akiskal et al., "Subthreshold Depressions: Clinical and Polysomnographic Validation of Dysthymic, Residual and Masked Forms," *Journal of Affective Disorders* 45 (1997): 53–63; L. L. Judd et al., "Socioeconomic Burden of Subsyndromal Depressive Symptoms and Major Depression in a Sample of the General Population," *American Journal of Psychiatry* 153 (1996): 1411–17; and L. L. Judd et al., "Subsyndromal Symptomatic Depression: A New Mood Disorder?," *Journal of Clinical Psychiatry* 55 (4, suppl.) (1994): 18–28.

168 **incidence of the depressions:** L. L. Judd, H. S. Akiskal, and M. P. Paulus, "The Role and Clinical Significance of Subsyndromal Depressive Symptoms (SSD) in Unipolar Major Depressive Disorder," *Journal of Affective Disorders* 45 (1997): 5–17.

169 **legitimating a range of "depressions":** The skeptical literature, opposing medical diagnosis on grounds that relate to its commercial effects, is now vast. One early example to stand for many is Lynn Payer, *Disease-mongers : How Doctors, Drug Companies, and Insurers Are Making You Feel Sick* (New York: John Wiley, 1992).

FOURTEEN: CONVERGENCE

172 **K. Ranga Rama Krishnan:** Much of the material in this chapter comes from conversations and correspondence with Ranga Krishnan. See S. H. Lee et al., "Subcortical Lesion Severity and Orbitofrontal Cortex Volume in Geriatric Depression," *Biological Psychiatry* 54 (2003): 529–33; L. A. Tupler et al., "Anatomic Location and Laterality of MRI Signal Hyperintensities in Late-Life Depression," *Journal of Psychosomatic Research* 53 (2002): 665–76; D. C. Steffens et al., "Cerebrovascular Disease and Depression Symptoms in the Cardiovascular Health Study," *Stroke* 30 (1999): 2159–66; D. C. Steffens and K. R. R. Krishnan, "Structural Neuroimaging and Mood Disorders: Recent Findings, Implications for Classification, and Future Directions," *Biological Psychiatry* 43 (1998): 705–12; K. R. R. Krishnan et al., "Depression and Social Support in Elderly Patients with Cardiac Disease," *American Heart Journal* 36 (1998): 491–95; K. R. R. Krishnan et al., "MRI-Defined Vascular Depression," *American Journal of Psychiatry* 154 (1997): 497–501; B. S. Greenwald et al., "MRI Signal Hyperintensities in Geriatric Depression," *American Journal of Psychiatry* 153 (1996): 1212–15; K. R. R. Krishnan and W. M. McDonald, "Arteriosclerotic Depression," *Medical Hypotheses* 44 (1995): 111–15; K. R. R. Krishnan et al., "Leukoencephalopathy in Patients Diagnosed as Major Depressive," *Biological Psychiatry* 23 (1988): 519–22.

173 **over 2 inches:** Krishnan has shared with me a slide of an 80-cubic-centimeter lesion that caused no problems in motor function or sensory perception but did result in a mood disorder. The empty space wanders, gerrymanderlike, in three dimensions throughout the brain. K. R. R. Krishnan, personal communication, 2004.

174 **Anatomically, vascular depression:** The same regions are implicated in the depressions associated with Alzheimer's, Huntington's, and Parkinson's diseases; in general, the evidence from neurology supports the hypothesis that depression is a coherent condition with reasonably uniform representation in the brain.

175 **"trail-making" test:** D. C. Steffens et al., "Performance Feedback Deficit in Geriatric Depression," *Biological Psychiatry* 50 (2001): 358–63.

178 **increase the risk of stroke:** K. R. R. Krishnan "Depression as a Contributing Factor in Cerebrovascular Disease," *American Heart Journal* 140 (2000): S70–S76; E. M. Simonsick et al., "Depressive Symptomatology and Hypertension-Associated Morbidity and Mortality in Older Adults," *Psychosomatic Medicine* 57 (1995): 427–35. It may be that in depression, the blood vessels in the brain respond less flexibly than they should to changes in

blood flow and blood pressure: P. Neu et al., "Cerebrovascular Reactivity in Major Depression: A Pilot Study," *Psychosomatic Medicine* 66 (2004): 6–8.

178 **link to poor heart health:** S. Wassertheil-Smoller et al., "Depression and Cardiovascular Sequelae in Postmenopausal Women," *Archives of Internal Medicine* 164 (2004): 289–98; L. R. Wulsin and B. M. Singal, "Do Depressive Symptoms Increase the Risk for the Onset of Coronary Disease? A Systematic Quantitative Review," *Psychosomatic Medicine* 65 (2003): 201–10; N. Frasure-Smith and F. Lespérance, "Depression—A Cardiac Risk Factor in Search of a Treatment," *Journal of the American Medical Association* 289 (2003): 3171–73; W. Jiang et al., "Patients with CHF and Depression Have Greater Risk of Mortality and Morbidity Than Patients Without Depression," *Journal of the American College of Cardiology* 39 (2002): 919–21; W. Jiang et al., "Relationship of Depression to Increased Risk of Mortality and Rehospitalization in Patients with Congestive Heart Failure," *Archives of Internal Medicine* 161 (2001): 1849–56; D. E. Bush et al., "Even Minimal Symptoms of Depression Increase Mortality Risk After Acute Myocardial Infarction," *American Journal of Cardiology* 88 (2001): 337–41; I. Connerney et al., "Relation Between Depression After Coronary Artery Bypass Surgery and Twelve-Month Outcome: A Prospective Study," *Lancet* 358 (2001): 1766–71; F. Lespérance et al., "Depression and One-Year Prognosis in Unstable Angina," *Archives of Internal Medicine* 160 (2000): 1354–60; H. D. Sesso et al., "Depression and the Risk of Coronary Heart Disease in the Normative Aging Study," *American Journal of Cardiology* 82 (1998): 851–6; and N. Frasure-Smith, F. Lespérance, and M. Talajic, "Depression and Eighteen-Month Prognosis After Myocardial Infarction," *Circulation* 91 (1995): 999–1005.

178 **largest study of psychotherapy:** ENRICHD Investigators, "Effects of Treating Depression and Low Perceived Social Support on Clinical Events After Myocardial Infarction: The Enhancing Recovery in Coronary Heart Disease Patients (ENRICHD) Randomized Trial," *Journal of the American Medical Association* 289 (2003): 3106–16 (the endnotes provide references for prior elements of the study).

179 **By contrast, the influential:** M. T. Shea et al., "Course of Depressive Symptoms over Follow-up: Findings from the National Institute of Mental Health Treatment of Depression Collaborative Research Program," *Archives of General Psychiatry* 49 (1992): 782–78.

179 **study of enriched nursing:** N. Frasure-Smith et al., "Randomised Trial of Home-Based Psychosocial Nursing Intervention for Patients Recovering from Myocardial Infarction," *Lancet* 350 (1997): 473–79; N. Frasure-Smith et al., "Long-Term Survival Differences Among Low-Anxious, High-Anxious and Repressive Copers Enrolled in the Montreal Heart Attack

---

Readjustment Trial," *Psychosomatic Medicine* 64 (2002): 571–79. Although the extra nursing care was sometimes harmful, lowering the depression rate did matter in these cardiac patients; those whose mood disorder remitted needed fewer hospital readmissions for heart disease.

180 **pilot study conducted at Columbia:** Alexander Glassman, personal communication, 2003, and A. H. Glassman et al., "Sertraline Treatment of Major Depression in Patients with Acute MI or Unstable Angina," *Journal of the American Medical Association* 288 (2002): 701–09.

180 **a 30 or 40 percent reduction:** This effect held up even when a variety of risk factors was controlled for. ENRICHD Investigators, "Effects of Treating Depression."

181 **depressed exercise less:** See for example H. C. Siegler et al., "Personality Factors Differentially Predict Exercise Behavior in Men and Women," *Women's Health* 3 (1997): 61–70.

181 blood platelet abnormalities: C. B. Nemeroff and D. L. Musselman, "Are Platelets the Link Between Depression and Ischemic Heart Disease?," *American Heart Journal* 140 (4, suppl.) (2000): 57–62; D. L. Musselman et al., "Platelet Reactivity in Depressed Patients Treated with Paroxetine," *Archives of General Psychiatry* 57 (2000): 875–82; D. L. Musselman et al., "Exaggerated Platelet Reactivity in Major Depression," *American Journal of Psychiatry* 153 (1996): 1313–17; V. L. Serebruany, P. A. Gurbel, and C. M. O'Connor, "Platelet Inhibition by Sertraline and N-Desmethylsertraline: A Possible Missing Link Between Depression, Coronary Events, and Mortality Benefits of Selective Serotonin Reuptake Inhibitors," *Pharmacological Research* 43 (2001): 453–62. SSRIs can even cause bleeding as a side effect: E. E. Welmoed et al., "Association of Risk of Abnormal Bleeding with Degree of Serotonin Reuptake Inhibition by Antidepressants," *Archives of Internal Medicine* 164 (2004): 2367–70.

182 **"invariant heart rate":** 16 percent of the depressed patients in the ENRICHD trial had heart rate invariability at a level that increases the risk of cardiac death by almost five times over thirty months: see R. M. Carney et al., "Depression, Heart Rate Variability, and Acute Myocardial Infarction," *Circulation* 104 (2001): 2024–28. See also M. W. Agelink et al., "Relationship Between Major Depression and Heart Rate Variability: Clinical Consequences and Implications for Antidepressive Treatment," *Psychiatry Research* 113 (2002): 139–49. Regarding effects of serotonin reuptake inhibitors, see Y. Khaykin et al., "Autonomic Correlates of Antidepressant Treatment Using Heart Rate Variability Analysis," *Canadian Journal of Psychiatry*. There is even evidence that psychotherapy may improve heart rate variability: R. M. Carney et al., "Change in Heart Rate and Heart Rate

Variability During Treatment for Depression in Patients with Coronary Heart Disease," *Psychosomatic Medicine* 62 (2000): 639–47.

183 **survey of smokers:** W. H. Sauer, J. A. Berlin, and S. E. Kimmel, "Selective Serotonin Reuptake Inhibitors and Myocardial Infarction," *Circulation* 104 (2001): 1894–98. The serotonergic antidepressants reduced the risk of heart attack by two thirds. The study was intended to investigate other outcomes; for measuring the effects of antidepressants on heart health, its design was not ideal.

183 **Stroke victims also benefit:** A. Rasmussen et al, "A Double-Blind, Placebo-Controlled Study of Sertraline in the Prevention of Depression in Stroke Patients," *Psychosomatics* 44 (2003): 216–21; for poststroke depression and prognosis, see L. S. Williams, S. S. Ghose, and R. Swindle, "Depression and Other Mental Health Diagnoses Increase Mortality Risk After Ischemic Strokes," *American Journal of Psychiatry* 161 (2004): 1090–95.

183 **Iowa and Argentina:** The research was conducted by Robert Robertson, the great American authority on stroke and depression. The medications studied were Prozac and an older (tricyclic) antidepressant, nortriptyline: R. E. Jorge et al., "Mortality and Poststroke Depression: A Placebo-Controlled Trial of Antidepressants," *American Journal of Psychiatry* 160 (2003): 1823–29; and K. Narushima and R. G. Robinson, "The Effect of Early Versus Late Antidepressant Treatment on Physical Impairment Associated with Poststroke Depression: Is There a Time-Related Therapeutic Window?," *Journal of Nervous and Mental Disease* 191 (2003): 645–52.

184 **Interferon-induced depression:** L. Capuron et al., "An Exaggerated HPA Axis Response to the Initial Injection of Interferon-Alpha Is Associated with Depression During Interferon Alpha Therapy," *American Journal of Psychiatry* 160 (2003): 1342–45; L. Capuron et al., "Neurobehavioral Effects of Interferon-Alpha in Cancer Patients: Phenomenology and Paroxetine Responsiveness of Symptom Dimensions," *Neuropsychopharmacology* 26 (2002): 643–52; M. Schaefer et al., "Interferon Alpha and Psychiatric Syndromes: A Review," *Progress in Neuropsychopharmacology and Biological Psychiatry* 26 (2002): 731–46; D. L. Musselman et al., "Paroxetine for the Prevention of Depression Induced by High-dose Interferon Alfa," *New England Journal of Medicine* 344 (2001): 961–66; F. D. Juengling et al., "Prefrontal Cortical Hypometabolism During Low-Dose Interferon Alpha Treatment," *Psychopharmacology* 152 (2000): 383–89. I have relied also on presentations at the symposium "Interferon-Induced Neuropsychiatric Side Effects: New Data and Treatments," annual meeting of the American Psychiatric Association, San Francisco, May 19, 2003.

185 **80/80 rule:** K. Steven and S. K. Herrine, "Approach to the Patient with

Chronic Hepatitis C Virus Infection," *Annals of Internal Medicine* 136 (2002): 747–57.

186 **Cytokines are signaling molecules:** There are two main classes of cytokines, inflammatory and anti-inflammatory. Here and throughout, I am referring to inflammatory cytokines.

186 **the presumed route:** Some psychiatrists have argued that all depression arises directly from elevated levels of cytokines. Cytokines cause the "malaise" of certain illnesses. According to the malaise-cytokine theory, depression is not a brain illness and sadness is not the central symptom; the core elements of depression are bodily pain and a feeling of sickness. It so happens that certain antidepressants (all-purpose drugs!) lower the circulating levels of inflammatory cytokines.

The experience with Paxil and interferon undercuts the cytokine/malaise theory. The antidepressant appears to work through altering serotonin transmission, stress hormone levels, blood flow to the prefrontal cortex, and neurogenesis—all while cytokine levels (the interferon administered to combat infection of cancer) remain high. On interferon, both successfully medicated and naturally resilient patients continue to feel the "sickness" symptoms of cytokines, such as fatigue, but are spared the sadness and anhedonia. These results suggest that malaise is distinct from mood disorder and that when cytokines cause depression, they do so through standard stress and neurotransmitter pathways.

For the maverick theory, see Bruce Charlton, *Psychiatry and the Human Condition* (Abingdon, U.K.: Radcliffe Medical Press, 2000); see also H. Anisman and Z. Merali, "Cytokines, Stress and Depressive Illness: Brain-Immune Interactions," *Annals of Medicine* 35 (2003): 2–11; and H. Anisman and Z. Merali, "Cytokines, Stress, and Depressive Illness," *Brain, Behavior, and Immunity* 16 (2002): 513–24.

Regarding the effects of antidepressants, see L. Capuron et al., "Treatment of Cytokine-Induced Depression," *Brain, Behavior, and Immunity* 16 (2002): 575–80; N. Castanon et al., "Effects of Antidepressants on Cytokine Production and Actions," *Brain, Behavior, and Immunity* 16 (2002): 569–74; B.J. Jacobs, "Adult Brain Neurogenesis and Depression," *Brain, Behavior, and Immunity* 16 (2002): 602–9; and C.A. Meyers et al., "Reversible Neurotoxicity of Interleukin-2 and Tumor Necrosis Factor: Correlation of SPECT with Neuropsychological Testing," *Journal of Neuropsychiatry and Clinical Neuroscience* 6 (1994): 285–88.

187 **high plasma cytokine levels:** D.L. Musselman et al., "Higher than Normal Plasma Interleukin-6 Concentrations in Cancer Patients with Depression: Preliminary Findings," *American Journal of Psychiatry* 158 (2001): 1252–57;

L. Capuron et al., "Neurobehavioral Effects of Interferon-Alpha in Cancer Patients: Phenomenology and Paroxetine Responsiveness of Symptom Dimensions," *Neuropsychopharmacology* 26 (2002): 643–52; C. L. Raison and A. H. Miller, "Cancer and Depression: New Developments Regarding Diagnosis and Treatment," *Biological Psychiatry* 54 (2003): 283–94; A. H. Miller, "Cytokines and Sickness Behavior: Implications for Cancer Care and Control," *Brain, Behavior and Immunity* 17 (2003): S132–34.

FIFTEEN: RESILIENCE

189 **Programs that target:** To choose one example: In the child foster care system in Oregon, researchers looked at an outreach program that taught parenting skills. The children under study had experienced abuse or neglect early in their development. As the foster parents' strategies changed, the preschoolers' stress hormone levels improved, as did the children's behavioral adjustment (Philip A. Fisher, personal communication). See also P. A. Fisher et al., "Preventative Intervention for Maltreated Preschoolers: Impact on Children's Behavior, Neuroendocrine Activity, and Foster Parent Functioning," *Journal of the American Academy of Child and Adolescent Psychiatry* 39 (2000): 1356–64.

190 **early antidepressants . . . are as effective:** This fact has been known from the time the new medications were first tested. In *Listening to Prozac*, I wrote (p. 126) that Prozac was less effective than earlier antidepressants in treating major depression. I thought that Prozac's special target would be low-level and early-stage mood disorder.

190 **antiglucocorticoids:** For an overview, see O. M. Wolkowitz and V. I. Reus, "Treatment of Depression with Antiglucocorticoid Drugs," *Psychosomatic Medicine* 61 (1999): 698–711; B. E. Murphy, "Antiglucocorticoid Therapies in Major Depression: A Review," *Psychoneuroendocrinology* 22 (1997): S125–32; and A. M. Ghadirian et al., "The Psychotropic Effects of Inhibitors of Steroid Biosynthesis in Depressed Patients Refractory to Treatment," *Biological Psychiatry* 37 (1995): 369–75.

192 **blockade of the brain effects:** One promising line of research involves the abortion pill, RU-486, which at high doses interferes with responses not only to sex hormones but also to stress hormones. Patients with psychotic depression, a vicious mood disorder whose nearest neighbors may be bipolar disorder and schizophrenia, sometimes respond to RU-486. This approach arose from a clinical observation: a patient with Cushing's disease was treated with RU-486 and her psychotic depression resolved. See J. K. Belanoff et al., "An

Open Label Trial of C-1073 (Mifepristone) for Psychotic Major Depression," *Biological Psychiatry* 52 (2002): 386–92; J. K. Belanoff et al., "Rapid Reversal of Psychotic Depression Using Mifepristone," *Journal of Clinical Psychopharmacology* 21 (2001): 516–21; B. E. Murphy, D. Filipini, and A. M. Ghadirian, "Possible Use of Glucocorticoid Receptor Antagonists in the Treatment of Major Depression: Preliminary Results Using RU 486," *Journal of Psychiatry and Neuroscience* 18 (1993): 209–13; K. R. Krishnan and D. Reed, "RU 486 in Depression," *Progress in Neuropsychopharmacology and Biological Psychiatry* 16, no. 6 (1992): 913–20; L. K. Nieman et al., "Successful Treatment of Cushing's Syndrome with the Glucocorticoid Antagonist RU 486," *Journal of Clinical Endocrinology and Metabolism* 61 (1985): 536–40.

192 **Corticotropin releasing factor:** C. Heim and C. Nemeroff, "Neurobiology of Early Life Stress: Clinical Studies," *Seminars in Clinical Neuropsychiatry* 7 (2002): 147–59; L. Arborelius et al., "The Role of Corticotropin-Releasing Factor in Depression and Anxiety Disorders," *Journal of Endocrinology* 160 (1999): 1–12; C. B. Nemeroff, "The Corticotropin-Releasing Factor (CRF) Hypothesis of Depression: New Findings and New Directions," *Molecular Psychiatry* 1 (1996): 336–42.

192 **In rodents, the stress model:** D. A. Gutman and C. Nemeroff, "Neurobiology of Early Life Stress: Rodent Studies," *Seminars in Clinical Neuropsychiatry* 7 (2002): 89–95; C. O. Ladd et al., "Long-Term Behavioral and Neuroendocrine Adaptations to Adverse Early Experience," in *Progress in Brain Research: The Biological Basis for Mind-Body Interactions*, vol. 122, ed. Emeran A. Mayer and Clifford B. Saper (Amsterdam: Elsevier, 2000); and P. M. Plotsky and M. J. Meaney, "Early, Postnatal Experience Alters Hypothalamic Corticotropin-Releasing Factor (CRF) mRNA, Median Eminence CRF Content and Stress-Induced Release in Adult Rats," *Molecular Brain Research (Brain Research)* 18 (1993): 195–200. Also, Paul Plotsky, personal communication, 2003. Regarding the hippocampus as the stuck switch, see notes to chapter 10.

193 **"antagonists" ... specific CRF receptor:** F. Holsboer, "The Rationale for Corticotropin-Releasing Hormone Receptor (CRH-R) Antagonists to Treat Depression and Anxiety," *Journal of Psychiatric Research* 33 (1999): 181–214; M. J. Owens and C. B. Nemeroff, "Corticotropin-Releasing Factor Antagonists: Therapeutic Potential in the Treatment of Affective Disorders," *CNS Drugs* 12 (1999): 85–92.

194 **"proof of concept" experiment:** A. W. Zobel et al., "Effects of the High-Affinity Corticotropin-Releasing Hormone Receptor 1 Antagonist R121919 in Major Depression: The First Twenty Patients Treated," *Journal of Psychiatric Research* 34 (2000): 171–81.

195 **Sapolsky . . . science to its limits:** For an overview, see the section on "gene therapy sparing hippocampal synaptic plasticity from stress," in R. M. Sapolsky, "Altering Behavior with Gene Transfer in the Limbic System," *Physiology and Behavior* 79 (2003): 479–86. Most source material on these topics is highly technical. See H. Wang et al., "Over-Expression of Antioxidant Enzymes Protects Cultured Hippocampal and Cortical Neurons from Necrotic Insults," *Journal of Neurochemistry* 87 (2003): 1527–34; H. Zhao et al., "Bcl-2 Overexpression Protects Against Neuron Loss Within the Ischemic Margin Following Experimental Stroke and Inhibits Cytochrome C Translocation and Caspase-3 Activity," *Journal of Neurochemistry* 85 (2003): 1026–36; M. A. Yenari et al., "Gene Therapy for Treatment of Cerebral Ischemia Using Defective Herpes Simplex Viral Vectors," *Annals of the New York Academy of Sciences* 939 (2001): 340–57; and many similar, detailed articles in this series. Also, Sapolsky, personal communications, 2001–2004.

195 **neuroprotectants:** There are many such substances. Some perform functions as simple as allowing the neuron to utilize more glucose, to produce energy. Others protect against particular stages of the cell injury process. As we shall see, in certain models, estrogen in the brain acts as a neuroprotectant.

SIXTEEN: HERE AND NOW

199 **fail with some . . . injure others:** I know from my contacts with the press that people who have not read *Listening to Prozac* often carry a misimpression about how I described the new antidepressants. In truth, I was lucky enough to have anticipated the concerns about Prozac that have arisen in the twelve years since the appearance of my book. I listed a variety of side effects, including sexual dysfunction, which I said occurred more frequently than had been reported in the official literature. I referred to concerns about late-appearing (tardive) neurological syndromes. I discussed "tolerance" to Prozac, in which the medication's effect wears off. I sided with researchers who believed Prozac could cause suicidality. The cataloguing of negative effects was extensive for a book intended to discuss theoretical and not practical issues. Regarding efficacy, see the note "early antidepressants . . . are as effective" on p. 322; for more on suicidality, see the note "suicidal thoughts and impulses" on p. 301.

199 **work by halves:** See Martin Keller's work, cited in the notes to chapters 4 and 13.

199 **when they succeed:** From my conversations with general audiences, I know that there is widespread doubt as to whether antidepressants work

at all. The skepticism arises in part from uncritical media coverage of what is, to my mind, a weak challenge, by psychologists who favor psychotherapy, to the body of research that has demonstrated the efficacy of these medications.

Like the challenge, the objections to it are technical. In the studies in which antidepressants appear ineffective, the patient sample seems to contain people who are not depressed and who therefore tend to improve spontaneously (or just to look healthy when retested); as a result, it is hard for the medication group to look different from the group given the placebo.

Antidepressants have proved effective in large-scale, multi-site trials whose results would have been published either way, pro or con. Antidepressants prevent interferon-induced depression and poststroke depression, they reverse pseudodementia, and they are effective in a range of hard-to-treat conditions, from postpartum mood disorders to chronic, recurrent depression. The medications work in depression-like syndromes in lower mammals. It would be cause for great scientific curiosity if these medications failed uniquely in run-of-the-mill depression in humans.

To my reading, Donald Klein is convincing in his detailed response to the efficacy challenge. See D. F. Klein, "Flawed Meta-Analyses Comparing Psychotherapy with Pharmacotherapy," *American Journal of Psychiatry* 157 (2000): 1204–11; D. F. Klein, "Listening to Meta-Analysis but Hearing Bias," *Prevention and Treatment* 1 (1998): article 0006c; and many others on this topic.

For a neutral overview of antidepressant efficacy, see J. W. Williams et al., "A Systematic Review of Newer Pharmacotherapies for Depression in Adults: Evidence Report Summary," *Annals of Internal Medicine* 132 (2000): 743–56. This assessment, conducted by a team headed by a primary care epidemiologist, uses the criteria of "evidence-based medicine." Antidepressants were $1\frac{1}{2}$ to 2 times as effective as placebos; a majority of patients on antidepressants experienced a greater than 50 percent improvement in symptoms. The studies summarized in the analysis are marred by high dropout rates; this problem seems to mask the efficacy of the antidepressants, so that clinical improvement rates may be higher. Efficacy in children is low, but see the TADS research cited on pp. 327–28.

200 **tianeptine:** A. C. Shakesby, R. Anwyl, and M. J. Rowan, "Overcoming the Effects of Stress on Synaptic Plasticity in the Intact Hippocampus: Rapid Actions of Serotonergic and Antidepressant Agents," *Journal of Neuroscience* 22 (2002): 3638–44; B. Czeh et al., "Stress-Induced Changes in Cerebral Metabolites, Hippocampal Volume, and Cell Proliferation Are

Prevented by Antidepressant Treatment with Tianeptine," *Proceedings of the National Academy of Sciences, USA* 98 (2001): 12796–801; B.S. McEwen et al., "Prevention of Stress-Induced Morphological and Cognitive Consequences," *European Neuropsychopharmacology* 7 (suppl. 3) (1997): S32–38; M. Frankfurt et al., "Tianeptine Treatment Induces Regionally Specific Changes in Monoamines," *Brain Research* 696 (1995): 1–6; A. Kamoun, B. Delalleau, and M. Ozun, "Un stimulant de la capture de serotonine peut il etre un authentique antidepresseur? Resultats d'un essai therapeutique multicentrique multinational," *L'Encephale* 20 (1994): 521–25; and Y. Watanabe et al., "Tianeptine Attenuates Stress-Induced Morphological Changes in the Hippocampus," *European Journal of Pharmacology* 222 (1992): 157–62.

200 **neuroplasticity and neurogenesis:** These changes do not take place immediately but play out over the course of four weeks. This pace of change in rodents parallels the time course of action of antidepressants in humans— the medication response generally takes weeks. These and other details of the research gave an initial suggestion that the antidepressant action might be linked to the effects on nerve cell growth.

200 **Ronald Duman:** See the note "brain-derived neurotrophic factor" on p. 305, especially the papers on neurogenesis and neuronal plasticity. Again, the neurogenesis (using "typical" antidepressants) is not apparent early in treatment but occurs after two or four weeks—with a 20 to 40 percent increase in new cell formation. Electroconvulsive seizure therapy, the most effective treatment for depression, increases neurogenesis by 50 percent. Psychoactive medications that do not act as antidepressants (for instance, the painkiller morphine and the antipsychotic medication Haldol) do not stimulate nerve cell production.

Research suggests a mechanism in the case of medications like Prozac. In rodent models, the release of serotonin causes an increase in new cell formation in the hippocampus, while blockage of serotonin pathways results in a loss of neurogenesis. As for new connections among existing neurons—sprouting or neuroplasticity—antidepressants both increase levels of neurotrophic factors, such as BDNF, and block the ability of stress to inhibit the production of these factors.

201 **René Hen:** R. Hen, personal communication, 2003; and L. Santarelli et al., "Requirements of Hippocampal Neurogenesis for the Behavioral Effects of Antidepressants," *Science* 301 (2003): 805–9.

201 **whether neurogenesis is critical:** Dean Hamer has called the serotonin transporter "genetic Prozac." It may be that when the transporter gene (5-HTT) protects people from the depressant effects of adversity, the

mechanisms of action include those attributed to the antidepressant, namely, the muting of stress hormone activity and the promotion of brain cell growth. See Hamer and Copeland, *Living with Our Genes*.

201 **reanalysis . . . Sheline's study:** Y. Sheline, M. Gado, and H. Kraemer, "Untreated Depression and Hippocampal Volume Loss," *American Journal of Psychiatry* 160 (2003): 1516–18.

202 **ineffective for adolescents:** Sharon Begley summarized interviews with researchers on these topics in "Why Depression Looks Different in a Kid's Brain," *Wall Street Journal*, October 15, 2004, A1, A4. Other researchers think that the difference in response has primarily to do with differences in impulsivity, which may themselves be related to the immaturity of the prefrontal cortex in adolescents. (In some studies, such as TADS [see the note "findings are not uniform," below], cognitive therapy appears ineffective in adolescents, perhaps for the same reason.) There may be wide variation, so that antidepressants are harmful for some adolescents and of immediate use for others. The critical issue of protection—whether these medications halt the progression of mood disorder in adolescents—has not been well researched.

202 ***Moments of Engagement:*** New York: Norton, 1989.

203 **psychotherapy research in the last decade:** The leading research has been from the University of Pittsburgh, under the leadership of Ellen Frank and Michael Thase. Two good starting points are E. Frank and M. E. Thase, "Natural History and Preventative Treatment of Recurrent Mood Disorders," *Annual Review of Medicine* 50 (1999): 453–68; and S. D. Hollon, M. E. Thase, and J. C. Markowitz, "Treatment and Prevention of Depression," *Psychological Science in the Public Interest* 3, no. 2 (2002): 39–77. One new emphasis is on briefer treatments: H. A. Swartz et al., "A Pilot Study of Brief Interpersonal Psychotherapy for Depression Among Women," *Psychiatric Services* 55 (2004): 448–50.

203 **traumatized in early childhood:** C. B. Nemeroff et al., "Differential Responses to Psychotherapy Versus Pharmacotherapy in Patients with Chronic Forms of Major Depression and Childhood Trauma," *Proceedings of the National Academy of Sciences, USA* 100 (2003): 14293–96.

203 **antidepressants and psychotherapy:** An influential paper is M. B. Keller et al., "A Comparison of Nefazodone, the Cognitive Behavioral-Analysis System of Psychotherapy, and Their Combination for the Treatment of Chronic Depression," *New England Journal of Medicine* 342 (2000): 1462–70.

203 **findings are not uniform:** Another large-scale effort, the Treatment for Adolescents with Depression Study (TADS), has been disappointing in its initial results. Looking at 439 teenagers, the study found that Prozac was effective

in the early phases of treatment of depression, while cognitive behavioral therapy was indistinguishable from or only slightly more helpful than placebo. In this trial, Prozac decreased suicidal thoughts but was associated with extra "harm-related events," including suicide attempts. There was a suggestion that when combined with medication treatment, the psychotherapy mitigated the tendency to self-harm and slightly enhanced the overall treatment effectiveness. TADS Team, "Fluoxetine, Cognitive-Behavioral Therapy, and Their Combination for Adolescents with Depression: Treatment for Adolescents with Depression Study (TADS) Randomized Controlled Trial," *Journal of the American Medical Association* 292 (2004): 807–20; R. M. Glass, "Treatment of Adolescents with Major Depression: Contributions of a Major Trial," *Journal of the American Medical Association* 292 (2004): 861–63. For an overview more favorable to the psychotherapy, see S. N. Compton et al., "Cognitive-Behavioral Psychotherapy for Anxiety and Depressive Disorders in Children and Adolescents: An Evidence-Based Medicine Review," *Journal of the American Academy of Child and Adolescent Psychiatry* 43 (2004): 930–59.

The seminal study of cognitive therapy for depression found few advantages over routine clinical management without psychotherapy: I. Elkin et al., "National Institute of Mental Health Treatment of Depression Collaborative Research Program: General Effectiveness of Treatments," *Archives of General Psychiatry* 46 (1989): 971–82. But see: M. E. Thase et al., "Is Cognitive Behavior Therapy Just a 'Nonspecific' Intervention for Depression? A Retrospective Comparison of Consecutive Cohorts Treated with Cognitive Behavior Therapy or Supportive Counseling and Pill Placebo," *Journal of Affective Disorders* 57 (2000): 63–71.

203 **The most important study:** K. Goldapple et al., "Modulation of Cortical-Limbic Pathways in Major Depression: Treatment-Specific Effects of Cognitive Behavior Therapy," *Archives of General Psychiatry* 61 (2004): 34–41; see also A. L. Brody et al., "Regional Brain Metabolic Changes in Patients with Major Depression Treated with Either Paroxetine or Interpersonal Therapy," *Archives of General Psychiatry* 58 (2001): 631–40. Comparable research into brief treatments for other mental illnesses has demonstrated similar outcomes: a redistribution of energy utilization in the brain.

204 **"enriched environments":** Gould, "Experience-Dependent Effects." For similar results in rodents, see G. Kemperman, H. G. Kuhn, and F. H. Gage, "More Hippocampal Neurons in Adult Mice Living in an Enriched Environment," *Nature* 386 (1997): 493–95. Interestingly, mild stress at a reasonably mature stage of development can "inoculate" against future

stressors: K. J. Parker et al., "Prospective Investigation of Stress Inoculation in Young Monkeys," *American Journal of Psychiatry* 61 (2004): 933–41.

204 **One thoughtful study:** K. L. Harkness et al., "Does Interpersonal Psychotherapy Protect Women from Depression in the Face of Stressful Life Events?," *Journal of Consulting and Clinical Psychology* 70 (2002): 908–15; for similar results with medication, see P. M. Furlan et al., "SSRIs Do Not Cause Affective Blunting in Healthy Elderly Volunteers," *American Journal of Geriatric Psychiatry* 12 (2004): 323–30.

205 **Theorists working on neurogenesis:** Duman, "Regulation of Adult Neurogenesis by Antidepressant Treatment" *Neuropsychopharmacology* 25 (2001): 836–844.

206 **bold theoretical paper:** B. L. Jacobs, H. van Praag, and F. H. Gage, "Depression and the Birth and Death of Brain Cells," *American Scientist* 88 (2000): 340–45. See also Jacobs, "Adult Brain Neurogenesis."

SEVENTEEN: THE END OF MELANCHOLY

211 **Hippocrates:** Throughout, I have relied largely on the work of my late, beloved psychotherapy instructor, Stanley W. Jackson, and his *Melancholia and Depression: From Hippocratic Times to Modern Times* (New Haven: Yale University Press, 1986). I refer extensively to Raymond Klibansky, Erwin Panofsky, and Fritz Saxl, *Saturn and Melancholy: Studies in the History of Natural Philosophy, Religion, and Art* (London: Nelson, 1964).

212 Aristotle, *Problemata/Problems*, trans. W. S. Hett, 2 vols. (Cambridge, Mass.: Harvard University Press, 1970–1983).

212 **melancholy was troublesome:** H. M. Northwood, "The Melancholic Mean: The Aristotelian *Problema XXX.1*," paper presented at the World Congress of Philosophy, Boston, Mass., August 12, 1998; the author explains how the extremes of melancholy might, after all, comport with the golden mean.

214 **German sociologist:** Wolf Lepenies, *Melancholy and Society*, trans. Jeremy Gaines and Doris Jones (Cambridge, Mass.: Harvard University Press, 1992).

216 **Saint Teresa considers melancholy:** The passage is extracted in Redden, ed., *The Nature of Melancholy*, pp. 111–112.

217 **melancholy enters England:** Lawrence Babb, *The Elizabethan Malady: A Study of Melancholia in English Literature from 1580 to 1642* (East Lansing: Michigan State College Press, 1951).

217 **literary sleuth:** J. L. Lowes, "The Loveres Maladye of Hereos," *Modern Philology* 11 (1914): 491–546. See also Babb, *The Elizabethan Malady*, 128–74.

217 **second classical tradition:** Martha C. Nussbaum, *The Therapy of Desire: Theory and Practice in Hellenistic Ethics* (Princeton, N.J.: Princeton University Press, 1994).

220 **Cervantes:** Jean Canavaggio, *Cervantes*, trans. J. R. Jones (New York: Norton 1986, 1990); my colleague at Brown, Antonio Carreño, kindly filled me in on subsequent progress in research on Cervantes's life.

220 **"[M]adness . . .":** Ibid., 217

221 **"made of Hamlet a Werther":** "Hamlet and His Problems," in T. S. Eliot, *The Sacred Wood: Essays on Poetry and Criticism* (London: Methuen, 1920); Eliot is one who thinks Hamlet, the character, lacks psychological coherence.

221 **Hamlet as a flowerpot:** Johann Wolfgang von Goethe, *Wilhelm Meister's Apprenticeship*, 1796; Carlyle was an early translator of the work into English.

222 **Carlyle's fictionalized spiritual autobiography:** *Sartor Resartus: The Life and Opinions of Herr Teufelsdröckh in Three Books*, 1833–1834.

222 **Goethe's later writing:** *Wilhelm Meister.*

222 **particular favorite:** W. Dilthey, "*Sartor Resartus*: Philosophical Conflict, Positive and Negative Eras, and Personal Resolution (1891)," trans. Murray Baumgarten and Evelyn Kanes, *Clio* 1, no. 3 (1972): 40–60.

223 **"What is a poet? . . . :"** Søren Kierkegaard, *Either/Or*, trans. D. F. Swenson and L. M. Swenson (Princeton, N.J.: Princeton University Press, 1944, 1959), vol. 1, 19.

223 **"No torture of body . . .":** *Anatomy of Melancholy*, first partition, section 3, member 1, "Prognostics of Melancholy."

224 **thoughtful review:** Harvie Ferguson, *Melancholy and the Critique of Modernity* (London: Routledge, 1994); I take the phrase "melancholy is the depth of modernity" from Ferguson.

225 **joint biography:** Diane Middlebrook, *Her Husband: Hughes and Plath—A Marriage* (New York: Viking, 2003).

225 **"in the West . . .":** Joseph Skibell, *The English Disease* (Chapel Hill, N.C.: Algonquin, 2003), 185.

226 **Hemorrhoids:** Oddly, hemorrhoids had a long run as a mood disorder. As late as the last decade of the twentieth century, a prominent specialist in psychosomatic medicine favored a theory in which the waxing and weeping of piles was an emotional marker. He kept a log of the behavior of his own dilated veins—they bled most on the anniversaries of significant life events—and he shared his history with colleagues in a keynote speech to the Society of Behavioral Medicine's annual meeting in 1994.

226 **Cultures sustain:** Harold Bloom, *The Anxiety of Influence: A Theory of Poetry* (New York: Oxford University Press, 1973).

227 **"You are depressed . . ."**: Walker Percy, *Lost in the Cosmos: The Last Self-Help Book* (New York: Farrar Straus Giroux, 1983).

230 **Schizophrenics are alienated:** Until recently, most arguments of this sort were, in fact, made about schizophrenia and related states. See, for instance, the discussion of detachment in Louis A. Sass, *Madness and Modernism: Insanity in the Light of Modern Art, Literature, and Thought* (New York: Basic Books, 1992).

EIGHTEEN: ART

232 **manic depression:** The classic study remains Frederick K. Goodwin and Kay Redfield Jamison, *Manic-Depressive Illness* (New York: Oxford University Press, 1990).

233 **a different type of neuron:** Stephan Heckers, personal communication, 2004, and S. Heckers et al., "Differential Hippocampal Expression of Glutamic Acid Decarboxylase 65 and 67 Messenger RNA in Bipolar Disorder and Schizophrenia," *Archives of General Psychiatry* 59 (2002): 521–29; C. Konradi et al., "Molecular Evidence for Mitochondrial Dysfunction in Bipolar Disorder," *Archives of General Psychiatry* 61 (2004): 300–308. See also D. Cutter, "Reduced Glial Cell Density."

233 **hypomania:** Hypomanics are prone to depressive episodes, and mixed states exist, of agitated depression. These conditions, along with frank mania, appear (biologically, genetically, and in terms of course of illness and clustering in families) to be related not to major depression but to bipolar affective disorder.

233 **best-designed modern study:** N. C. Andreasen, "Creativity and Mental Illness: Prevalence Rates in Writers and Their First-Degree Relatives," *American Journal of Psychiatry* 144 (1987): 1288–92.

234 **book-length consideration:** Kay Redfield Jamison, *Touched with Fire: Manic-Depressive Illness and the Artistic Temperament* (New York: Free Press, 1993).

234 **technical problems:** The concern my informants mentioned most often concerned (unintentional) researcher bias. If we were led to our hypothesis because Byron and his fellows so obviously look mood disordered, do we need then to exclude the romantic poets from our research? In statistical research, if a hypothesis is developed through observations in one sample, it generally needs to be tested in another, independent sample.

235 **hypomania . . . seems helpful:** Regarding hypomania, see the extensive work of Hagop Akiskal. Interestingly, Oliver Sacks has argued to the

contrary. In his estimation, it is the burst of creativity that confers energy, not the reverse. Oliver Sacks, *An Anthropologist on Mars: Seven Paradoxical Tales* (New York: Knopf, 1995), and O. Sacks, "Time and the Nervous System," Harriet W. Sheridan Lecture, Brown University, Providence, R.I., April 13, 2004.

235 **bipolarity and leadership:** Jamison, *Touched with Fire*, and "Manic-Depressive Illness, Creativity, and Leadership," in Goodwin and Jamison, *Manic-Depressive Illness*, 332–67.

235 **suggestive of bipolarity:** J. F. McDermott, "Emily Dickinson Revisited: A Study of Periodicity in Her Work," *American Journal of Psychiatry* 158 (2001): 686–90.

235 **"I write when . . .":** Jamison, personal communication, 1995.

236 **contrast in our perceptions:** See also the discussion of lithium in *Listening to Prozac.*

236 **study of bipolar artists:** M. Schou, "Artistic Productivity and Lithium Prophylaxis in Manic-Depressive Illness," *British Journal of Psychiatry* 135 (1979): 97–103.

236 **"lithium prevented . . .":** "Autobiography by Mogens Schou," April 2002, posted at http://www.laskerfoundation.org/awards/library/1987_bio_schou.shtml; the essay is from a work in progress on the history of lithium therapy, edited by Johan A. Schioldann.

238 **so Renaissance authors say:** "I write of melancholy, by being busy to avoid melancholy," Burton informs his reader in the Preface to the *Anatomy.* Michel de Montaigne makes similar comments.

239 **"The Alligators":** John Updike, *The Same Door* (New York: Knopf, 1959).

240 *The Centaur:* New York: Knopf, 1953.

240 **autobiographical essay:** John Updike, *Self-Consciousness: Memoirs* (New York: Knopf, 1989); for psoriasis and its connection to writing, see F. Meulenberg, "The Hidden Delight of Psoriasis," *BMJ* 315 (1997): 1709–11; Vladimir Nabokov was an adept.

241 **"The name of . . .":** "From the Journal of a Leper," in John Updike, *Problems and Other Stories* (New York: Knopf, 1976).

241 **"fictive world is poor . . .":** C. Ozick, review of John Updike, *The Early Stories,* in *The New York Times Book Review,* November 30, 2003.

241 **Herzog:** In the eponymous novel (New York: Viking, 1964).

242 **recent biography:** James Atlas, *Bellow* (New York: Random House, 2000).

242 **military hero:** Canavaggio, *Cervantes.*

243 **"the cripple who is sound . . .":** Ibid., 310.

NINETEEN: THE NATURAL

246 **popular writers and philosophers:** For example, Daniel Goleman, *Emotional Intelligence* (New York: Bantam Books, 1995), and Martha C. Nussbaum, *Upheavals of Thought: The Intelligence of Emotions* (New York: Cambridge University Press, 2001).

246 **evolutionary psychology:** Here, I rely heavily on the summary in R. M. Nesse, "Is Depression an Adaptation?," *Archives of General Psychiatry* 57 (2000): 14–20. My opposing argument bears a relationship to the theoretical formulations of Jerome C. Wakefield, in such essays as: J. C. Wakefield, "Spandrels, Vestigial Organs, and Such," *Philosophy, Psychiatry, and Psychology* 7 (2001): 253–69; J. C. Wakefield, "Evolutionary History Versus Current Causal Role in the Definition of Disorder," *Behaviour Research and Therapy* 39 (2001): 347–66; and others dating to 1992. Donald Klein applies this theory to mental illness, in D. Klein, "Harmful Dysfunction, Disorder, Disease, Illness, and Evolution," *Journal of Abnormal Psychology* 108 (1999): 421–39.

250 **In a famous essay:** S. J. Gould and R. C. Lewontin, "The Spandrels of San Marco and the Panglossian Paradigm: A Critique of the Adaptationist Programme," *Proceedings of the Royal Society of London,* 205 (1979): 581–98; see also S. J. Gould and E. S. Vrba, "Exaptation—A Missing Term in the Science of Form," *Paleobiology* 8 (1982): 4–15.

251 **The symptom clusters vary:** M. A. Oquendo et al., "Instability of Symptoms in Recurrent Major Depression: A Prospective Study," *American Journal of Psychiatry* 161 (2004): 255–61.

253 **line of research:** R. C. Kessler, J. D. McLeod, and E. Wethington, "The Costs of Caring: A Perspective on the Relationship Between Sex and Psychological Distress," in Irwin G. Sarason and Barbara R. Sarason, *Social Support: Theory, Research, and Applications* (Dordrecht: Martinus Nijhoff, 1985). See also R. C. Kessler and J. D. McLoed, "Social Support and Mental Health in Community Samples," in *Social Support and Health,* ed. Sheldon Cohen and S. Leonard Syme (New York: Academic Press, 1985); R. C. Kessler, "Gender and Mood Disorders," in *Women and Health,* ed. Marlene Goldman and Maureen Hatch (San Diego: Academic Press, 2000); and R. C. Kessler, "Gender Differences in Major Depression: Epidemiological Findings," in *Gender and Its Effect on Psychopathology,* ed. Ellen Frank (Washington, D.C.: American Psychiatric Press, 2000).

255 **"In Venice . . .":** Andre Codrescu, *Casanova in Bohemia* (New York: Free Press, 2002).

256 **90 percent of adolescents:** The result is from periodic polls at the start of this decade by the New York University Child Study Center. See Harold S. Koplewicz, *More than Moody* (New York: Putnam, 2002). See also B. Birmaher et al., "Childhood and Adolescent Depression: A Review of the Past Ten Years, Part I," *Journal of the American Academy of Child and Adolescent Psychiatry* 35 (1996): 1427–39; P. M. Lewinsohn et al., "Major Depression in Community Adolescents: Age at Onset, Episode Duration, and Time to Recurrence," *Journal of the American Academy of Child and Adolescent Psychiatry*, 33 (1994): 809–18; P. M. Lewinson et al., "Adolescent Psychopathology, I: Prevalence and Incidence of Depression and other DSM-III-R Disorders in High School Students," *Journal of Abnormal Psychology* 102 (1993): 133–44; H. Z. Reinherz et al., "Prevalence of Psychiatric Disorders in a Community Population of Older Adolescents," *Journal of the American Academy of Child and Adolescent Psychiatry* 32 (1993): 369–77; and J. E. Fleming and D. R. Offord, "Epidemiology of Childhood Depressive Disorders: A Critical Review," *Journal of the American Academy of Child and Adolescent Psychiatry* 29 (1990): 571–80. The consistent result in these studies is high rates of diagnosable depression. Other studies find high rates of recurrence into adulthood.

257 **a quarter of students:** This estimate is from the comments of Steven Hyman at a colloquium, "Ethical Issues in the Psychopharmacology of Mood," New York Academy of Sciences, New York, N.Y., July 13, 2004. For a broad overview of depression treatment on campus, see the May 2002 issue of *Blues Buster*, edited by Hara Estroff Marano.

TWENTY: ALIENATION

261 **"[S]uppose you are . . .":** C. Elliott, "The Tyranny of Happiness: Ethics and Cosmetic Psychopharmacology," in *Enhancing Human Traits: Ethical and Social Implications*, ed. Eric Parens (Washington, D.C: Georgetown University Press, 1998).

262 **ethics of enhancement:** Carl Elliott, *Better than Well: American Medicine Meets the American Dream* (New York: Norton, 2003).

263 **"sound strikingly . . .":** Elliott, "Tyranny of Happiness"; see also C. Elliott, "Prozac and the Existential Novel: Two Therapies," in *The Last Physician: Walker Percy and the Moral Life of Medicine*, ed. Carl Elliott and John Lantos (Durham, N.C.: Duke University Press, 1999). I originally answered certain of Elliott's arguments in P. D. Kramer, "The Valorization of Sadness:

Alienation and the Melancholic Temperament," *Hastings Center Report* 30 (March–April 2000): 13–18, collected in Elliott and Chambers, eds., *Prozac as a Way of Life*, 48–58.

265 **epilepsy and overt psychosis:** See, especially, Walker Percy, *The Second Coming* (New York: Farrar Straus Giroux, 1980).

265 **"I do not want to . . .":** Elliott, "Prozac and the Existential Novel." To clarify a condition of the philosophical discussion: We are not considering cases when antidepressants induce side effects, like apathy. Even in imagining "cosmetic" interventions, the presumption is that medication moves a person to a normal but more desired or better socially rewarded temperament or state of mind.

265 **Holy Communion as a dietary issue:** Ibid.

272 **Isn't the hypersensitivity *justified?*:** See also C. Freedman, "Aspirin for the Mind? Some Ethical Worries About Pharmacology," in Parens, ed., *Enhancing Human Traits*.

273 **"functional autonomy":** See *Listening to Prozac*, and D. F. Klein, "Cybernetics, Activation, and Drug Effects," *Acta Psychiatrica Scandinavica* 77 (suppl. 341) (1988): 126–37.

273 **influential critic:** Philip Fisher, *The Vehement Passions* (Princeton, N.J.: Princeton University Press, 2002).

274 **Walter Benjamin:** Max Pensky, *Melancholy Dialectics: Walter Benjamin and the Play of Mourning* (Amherst: University of Massachusetts Press, 1993).

274 **separates grief from depression:** Even if he or she otherwise meets the criteria, a patient cannot be diagnosed as depressed if he or she has just lost a loved one—unless "the symptoms persist for longer than two months or are characterized by marked functional impairment, morbid preoccupation with worthlessness, suicidal ideation, psychotic symptoms, or psychomotor retardation." The attempt here is to distinguish those among the bereaved who will go on to suffer depression. The DSM criteria rely heavily on research by Paula Clayton, especially P. J. Clayton, "Bereavement," in *Handbook of Affective Disorder* ed. Eugene S. Paykel (Edinburgh: Churchill Livingstone, 1982).

274 **elements of grief often differ:** P. J. Clayton, "Bereavement and Depression," *Journal of Clinical Psychiatry* 51 (7, suppl.) (1990): 34–38; S. Zisook and S. R. Shuchter, "Major Depression Associated with Widowhood," *American Journal of Geriatric Psychiatry* 1 (1993): 316–26; S. Zisook and S. R. Shuchter, "Uncomplicated Bereavement," *Journal of Clinical Psychiatry* 54 (1993): 365–72; S. Zisook and S. R. Shuchter, "Depression Through the First Year After the Death of a Spouse," *American Journal of Psychiatry*,

148 (1991): 1346–52. These studies look at widows and widowers. Less is known about the form of grief in parents who have lost a child. Of course, loss can trigger pathology. See H. G. Prigerson et al., "Traumatic Grief as a Risk Factor for Mental and Physical Morbidity," *American Journal of Psychiatry* 154 (1997): 616–23, and Selby C. Jacobs, *Traumatic Grief: Diagnosis, Treatment, and Prevention* (Philadelphia: Brunner/Mazel, 1999).

275 **symptoms of anxiety disorders:** S. Jacobs et al, "Anxiety Disorders During Acute Bereavement: Risk and Risk Factors," *Journal of Clinical Psychiatry* 5 (1990): 269–74.

275 **Freud . . . the ambivalent:** "Mourning and Melancholia" (1917).

275 **a different sort of grieving:** P. D. Kramer, "Hartstochtelijk Rouwen," *Nexus* 39 (2004): 137–45.

TWENTY-ONE: AFTER DEPRESSION

281 **dank joylessness:** the characterizations are William Styron's; see chapter 7, p. 77.

282 **"Happy Souls":** Published as Leon Kass, *Beyond Therapy: Biotechnology and the Pursuit of Happiness* (New York: ReganBooks HarperCollins, 2003).

282 **16 or 17 percent:** See notes to chapter 12 and Kessler et al., "The Epidemiology of Major Depressive Disorder."

283 **love more generously:** See my testimony before the President's Council on Bioethics (posted at www.bioethics.gov), "Happiness and Sadness: Depression and the Pharmacological Elevation of Mood," Washington, D.C., September 12, 2002, particularly the interchange with Gilbert Meilaender.

284 **"Terence, This Is Stupid Stuff":** A. E. Housman, *A Shropshire Lad* (1896).

285 **"Much as I love . . .":** Josipovici, *Moo Pak*.

285 **Kundera . . . reserves special praise:** Milan Kundera, *Testaments Betrayed: An Essay in Nine Parts*, trans. Linda Asher (New York: HarperCollins, 1995); Kundera gives a horrifying account of the political effects of the lyrical poetic temperament in his novel *Life Is Elsewhere*, trans. Aaron Asher. (New York: Perennial, 2000) or trans. P. Kussi, (New York: Penguin, 1986).

285 **Mikhail Bakhtin:** *Rabelais and His World*, trans. Hélène Iswolsky (Cambridge, Mass.: MIT Press, 1968), and M. M. Bakhtin, *The Dialogic Imagination: Four Essays*, ed. Michael Holquist, trans., Caryl Emerson and Michael Holquist (Austin: University of Texas Press, 1981).

286 **Shakespeare's Falstaff:** Harold Bloom, *Shakespeare: The Invention of the Human* (New York: Riverhead Books, 1998).

286 **Dante:** R. W. B. Lewis, *Dante* (New York: Lipper/Viking, 2001).

287 **the ideal life:** Karl Marx and Friedrich Engels, *The German Ideology*, written 1845–1846.

290 **to form new neural connections:** Of course, I mean new connections that work in the interest of resilience. Although in this book I have emphasized the loss of dendrites in the hippocampus as a possible cause and result of depression, research sometimes shows a contrasting set of events in the amygdala. There, in addition to causing neuronal pruning, stress may result in the formation of new connections, ones that reinforce fear responses.

Index